ISLANDS of FIRE, ISLANDS of SPICE

ISLANDS of FIRE, ISLANDS of SPICE

Exploring the Wild Places of Indonesia

RICHARD BANGS

CHRISTIAN KALLEN

SIERRA CLUB BOOKS · SAN FRANCISCO

The Sierra Club, founded in 1892 by John Muir, has devoted itself to the study and protection of the earth's scenic and ecological resources— mountains, wetlands, woodlands, wild shores and rivers, deserts and plains. The publishing program of the Sierra Club offers books to the public as a nonprofit educational service in the hope that they may enlarge the public's understanding of the Club's basic concerns. The point of view expressed in each book, however, does not necessarily represent that of the Club. The Sierra Club has some sixty chapters coast to coast, in Canada, Hawaii, and Alaska. For information about how you may participate in its programs to preserve wilderness and the quality of life, please address inquiries to Sierra Club, 730 Polk Street, San Francisco, CA 94109.

LIBRARY OF CONGRESS CATALOGING-IN-PUBLICATION DATA

Bangs, Richard, 1950–
Islands of fire, islands of spice.

Includes index.
1. Natural history—Indonesia. 2. Indonesia—
Description and travel. I. Kallen, Christian.
II. Title.
QH186.B29   1988   508.598   88-1996
ISBN 0-87156-798-9

Production by Eileen Max
Jacket and book design by Wilsted & Taylor
Map by Earth Surface Graphics
Printed by Dai Nippon Printing Company, Ltd., Tokyo, Japan

10 9 8 7 6 5 4 3 2 1

CONTENTS

ACKNOWLEDGMENTS

A book held at arm's length, it could be said, is a bit like an Indonesian rainforest when viewed from the air. With a sweep of the eye both appear orderly, orchestrated, elegant—perhaps the work of a single artist. There is little evidence of the chaos beneath the canopy, of the great tangle of organisms, their complex interrelationships, and the monumental amount of energy involved in creating the complicated but deceptively simple-looking whole. From 35,000 feet you can't see the trees for the forest; and at arm's length you can't know the contributors to a book for the large type that tells title and authors. Yet both are very much cooperative efforts, and it is here that we, unlike Mother Nature, can name some of the people, organizations, and companies who helped bring our idea from seed to sapling to tome.

First and foremost, Dr. Halim Indrakusuma, the visionary Indonesian dentist who quit his practice to become involved in adventure and the creative promotion of his country. He is the director of PACTO, the Indonesian tour agency that handled most of our in-country ground arrangements and acted as our guide and host. Without the extensive support of Halim and his organization this book could not have come into being. Invaluable support was also provided by Pamela Roberson and Dr. George Fuller, who traveled with us to several islands to lend their photographic talents; many of their images appear within these pages.

Thanks also to the following: Joop Ave, Director General of Tourism, who gave us guidance and blessings; Dra. Cri Murthi, Director of Marketing of Tourism for Indonesia; John Senduk, former director of the Indonesian Tourist Office in San Francisco, who introduced us to Indonesia and got us on the right track with the correct contacts; Garuda Indonesia airline, who saw us safely across the Pacific and between islands many times; within Garuda, Mr. Sunaryo, John Sahelangi, Karl Rosen, Laura Babcock, Harry Soeharman, Haryadi Rahardjo, and M. J. Wattimena; Daisy Hadmoko, tireless editor of *Travel Indonesia* and *Garuda* magazines; Mandala Airlines; Jodi Coleman of Malaysian Airlines, who helped us get to Borneo; Rick Laylin, formerly of Pan American Airlines, now of United Airlines, who helped our crew get to Sumatra; Merpati Nusantara Airlines, including Sancha Bachtiar of the main office, director of marketing Andreas Prayogo, and Drs. Ibrahim Hamid, head of international marketing; Singapore Airlines; Jakarta Mandarin Hotel and general manager A. Graeme P. Laird; Hotel Indonesia, including marketing manager Darma Setiawan and sales manager Suhartini; Hotel Borobudur Intercontinental and director of sales Toto Sudharto; Nusa Dua Beach Hotel and manager Paul Blake; Legian Beach Hotel and manager Peter Arya; and the Bali Oberoi and Tiara Medan hotels.

For the "Fire" chapters (Sumatra, Java, Kalimantan, and Bali): Bill Graves of *National Geographic*, who once again put his name on the line and helped sponsor the original Florence-Sobek Expedition on the Alas River in Sumatra; Peter Pilafian and Lisa Samford, filmmakers for the Alas; Patti Hecker, production assistant on the Alas; the Explorers Club, whose flag we carried on the Alas; Mobil Oil, who loaned us a helicopter; the heretofore unmentioned members of the original Florence-Sobek Expedition, including Stan Boor, George Goen, Michael Ghiglieri, Dave Shore, George Wendt, Mike Walker, Jim Slade, Bart Henderson, Jill Botway, Ken Jarkow, Carol Mason, Dr. Stuart Wilber, Jacopo Mazzei (who helped conceive the Alas project), Branca Niccolo, Mario Attardo, Riccardo Aichner, Francesco Mazzei, Alessandro Fonseca, Vieri Calamai, and Farid Badres of PACTO, Medan; Dr. Axel Ridder of the Carita Krakatau Beach Hotel; Dave Ferguson of Kalimantan; Extrasport

Lifejackets, who provided flotation on the Alas; The North Face, who provided much of the backpacking gear for Sumatra, Java, and Kalimantan; Minolta Cameras, who provided the tools that made many of the pictures herein; Pelican cases; Royal Robbins Wear; Carlisle paddles; Gott coolers; Thermarest; Sony Corporation; Motorola; Steiner Binoculars; Patagonia; Global Van Lines; Carlson Pumps; El Rancho Best Western; and Tevas, KangaROOS, Vasque, and Rockport shoes.

For the "Spice" chapters (Nusa Tenggara, Sulawesi, Maluku, and Irian Jaya): the Makassar Golden Hotel, Ujung Pandang; Hotel Missiliana, Rantepao; Hotel Nirwana, Ternate; Hotel Baliem Cottages, Wamena; Boet Nanlohy and Sumber Budi Tours, Ambon; Jan A. Westplat, Ternate; Rudolph William, Insatra Tours, Irian Jaya; Jack Daniels of Spice Islands Cruises and the crew of the *Island Explorer*, especially Brenda Unseld; Chris Drew of R. J. Reynolds International, Inc., and Kaypro Computers, upon whose machines this entire book was written.

We are also indebted to John Yost, dedicated vice president of Sobek; Erin Broglio, who spent endless hours typing and retyping manuscripts; Shaun Manuel, the Sobek Indonesian expert; Paul Henry, Sobek controller, who desperately tried to keep finances under control; John Kramer, Sobek equipment manager for the Indonesian expeditions; Peter Buchanan, our attorney; Karen Bridges, Sobek slide librarian, who helped round up several thousand images; John Leedom, who did much of the library research; Leslie Jarvie, who assisted in tying up the final package; Ann Cassidy, who provided her Lake Tahoe retreat as a writing den; Michael K. Nichols, whose photos and enthusiasm for Indonesia helped spark this book; Eric Oey, who loaned us books from his extensive personal library on Indonesia; Ma and Pa Bangs, who gave half this team the eyes to see the wonders of Indonesia; Barbara Timmons, who passed on to her son Christian an insatiable curiosity; and, last, but far from least, the staff at Sierra Club Books, including Jon Beckmann, our publisher; Linda Gunnarson, our editor; Carey Charlesworth, freelance copyeditor; Sam Petersen, publicist; Eileen Max, production director; and Peter Beren, marketing director.

This is a brief and inconclusive list of the myriad talents that went into creating this book, and to those not here mentioned, please know that we thank you, for such a book, again like the rainforest, is a creation whose whole is not greater than the sum of its parts.

INTRODUCTION

The paeans of praise for the islands known throughout history as the East Indies, Spice Islands, the Malay Archipelago, and Nusantara—which now sail under the red and white flag of Indonesia—have often soared to dizzying heights. There is no refuting that these 13,677 islands compose a special span, a dazzling equatorial island necklace that evokes powerful, even passionate imagery. Yet despite its romantic role in history and the resonant charge its toponyms carry (Borneo, Java, Bali—names more conducive of myth than guidebook reality), Indonesia as a nation remains even to this day largely undiscovered by the West.

Indonesia is surrounded by the better-known countries of Australia, the Philippines, China, and Vietnam, so its location alone makes its strategic importance enormous. It is also greater in both size and population than most of the world's countries, ranking fifth in both categories. While it is a member of OPEC, only readers of the fine print in almanacs know it is also the world's largest Moslem nation. Some of its islands are immensely overcrowded—Java is burdened with nearly a thousand people for every square kilometer—but Indonesia is home to the greatest concentration and variety of wildlife in Asia and to a full ten percent of all the plants and trees in the world. In the forty years since achieving full independence from the Dutch in 1949, Indonesia has wrestled with communism and democracy in search of its own distinct identity among modern nations, an identity rendered elusive by the nation's diversity.

These, then, are the facts. The reality encountered by the authors through much of the past year shows a far different and far more seductive face. For here, Nature was lavish with her paint: the jade green of the rice fields is hallucinatory, a mask of innocence, geometries worthy of the parklands of a prince. Teak-colored girls swing crescent knives, their bright sarongs swaying like the wings of butterflies. Beyond the wet rice pad-

dies and the tea estates, the deep-green slopes of terraced hills rise, dotted with distant settlement, and beyond them are glimpsed the silk-blue cones of the great volcanic chain that is Indonesia's spine.

In these islands of diversity, the extremes are stupefying, from miasmic lowlands swamps, where even the gnarled wood is the color of rust, to glaciated ranges, where pyramid peaks pierce the obscuring clouds and allow the sun's rays to reveal dark, steamily oppressive, and luxuriant forests that seem to pant for release. Wooded folds of mountains twine for miles, silent, motionless, a green tapestry stretching into the next world, slightly blurred by the heat. Coffee-colored rivers tear through the jungles, wild to get to the sea. Helmeted hornbills swoop like pterodactyls over waterfalls that make a tremendous fuss of the descent. There is little subtlety here, but a world painted in bold, unrepentant strokes.

It is a sweet-and-sour mixture of sensations: scents of frangipani and jasmine, of copra and moist earth. It is a medley of wildlife both plentiful and scarce, from carpet-covered, chocolate-red orangutans to elephants startlingly elusive, who can disappear into the jungle in the twinkle of a wrinkled eye. It is a melange of contrast, a living oxymoron. It is the summerland of the world, the garden of the East, the cabinet of the Seven Seas, and the ark of Asia, sailing through a whirlpool that threatens to tip the boat and spill its precious cargo. It may be the finest celebration of nature ever known on this planet, and it is balancing precariously on the precipice of disaster.

In less time than it takes to read a chapter in this book, enough trees in Indonesia will fall to the axe, sickle, chain saw, and bulldozer to reforest New York's Central Park. More importantly, in the same span of time, several species of plants and animals may vanish from the earth forever. The focus of this game of ecological roulette is the tropical rainforest, a life zone that faces elimination worldwide. One of the planet's most significant arenas of creative evolution—the richest, most complex, and oldest ecosystem we know—the rainforest around the globe is dwindling toward extinction.

During 1987, the year the human species welcomed its five billionth baby, no fewer than 17,500 other plant and animal species became extinct. Most of these life forms were denizens of the tropical rainforest, which in the last thirty years has lost no less than 40 percent of its dominion—lost it to a lumber-hungry world, which presses into the sanctuaries of the rainforest with a writ of false promises. Nations claim they are only relocating their crowded citizens, offering them the right to farm their own land; but the thin soils of the rainforest are infertile without the humus and shelter that trees provide.

More, the issue is greater than a supply of trees; if it were only cabinetry at stake, we could all become accustomed to knotty pine. But remember for a moment the bane of malaria, which afflicted nearly every tropical traveler for centuries. It was only held at bay by quinine—an extract from the bark of the quinoa tree, a rainforest native. Some scientists warn that among the tens of thousands of species being wiped out this year, a cure may have been lurking for next year's catastrophic plague. If the rainforests are on the edge of extinction, perhaps we are not so far from that final threshold ourselves.

Although such apocalyptic concerns are not limited to Indonesia, Indonesia is at the center of them nonetheless. Much of the modern age's momentum has been directed toward the bounty of the tropics in general and the East Indies in particular. The spices of the Indies were not the least of the plunder of the crusades, raising the expectations of backward Europeans. Marco Polo was the first European known to visit this aromatic Oz, as a way station on his Oriental wanderings, writing of his 1232 visit to Sumatra that "the quantity of treasures on the islands is beyond all compare." Centuries later, Columbus responded to the lure of the East—and its power to cloud the minds of sober men—and imagined that he had arrived in these Indies when it was a new cluster he found, peopled with new "Indians." The culmination of the pull of clove, nutmeg,

and cinnamon was no less than the Age of Discovery and the colonial era that followed.

In 1519, Magellan set out in explicit search of the western route to the Spice Islands when he embarked on his circumnavigatory voyage. Spain, Great Britain, and the Netherlands followed the Portuguese lead and competed with the Chinese, the Japanese, and with native sultans for a foothold in the Indies. Other foreign powers, including the United States, have not been without interest in the region, up to and including the present time. The unstated common objective: to siphon off the wealth of Indonesia for profit—first from the spice trade, and then from the mines, plantations, and oil wells. The present-day rape of the rainforest is merely the latest chapter in the serial crime of the centuries; the myth of the unlimited wealth of the Indies is so deeply imbedded in Western consciousness, and entwined with our notions of progress, that it is virtually impossible to eradicate.

Perhaps it goes even deeper than that. Consider the government tourist officials of the Dutch East Indies during the period between World Wars I and II, whose brochures and magazine advertisements attempted to lure world-cruise travelers to the "Tropical Garden of Eden." This Edenic myth is deeply implanted in Western tradition, with roots in both classical and biblical soil. It was kept alive in the Middle Ages by cartographers, who customarily showed the authentic location of this antediluvian promised land as in the Orient, between the Tropics of Cancer and Capricorn. The romancers of the Age of Discovery had little difficulty in placing Elysium in the exotic lands that curl through the equator, which they would people variously with noble savage, lost tribe, or superior human being. The early explorers, both globe-trotters and narrators—Columbus among them—gave open support to this kind of thinking. And it is this mind set that persists today in the expectations of tourists who flock to Bali and other Indonesian isles, searching blatantly for Paradise.

The tourists' impact, as should be expected, is quite the opposite. Resort tourists too often see what cannot naturally occur, an idyllic insulated retreat with all the amenities of a Beverly Hill hotel. It is for these deep pockets that the resort are built—trees felled, swamps drained, rivers dammed, and villages shoved aside to preserve the "natural feel" of this contrived Paradise. Even more sadly, the villagers themselves may find their traditional livelihoods as fishers, farmers, and artisans supplanted by a resort economy built around touro-dollars; they can find work only in the white-smocked service and support industries, learning new words for new skills and new vices. The end result of this type of tourism is all too often pollution, both environmental and cultural, and the damage is too frequently irrevocable.

There is, we are pleased to note, another breed of tourist. We prefer to call the people in this category travelers, or visitors—those who immerse themselves in a foreign experience and come back wiser and concerned, educated and motivated. These travelers are the ones who accept what they find, learn to appreciate it on its own terms, and become passionate enough about their adventures to join in the effort to preserve these life forms, cultures, and ecological systems. It is to be hoped that many people make the trip to Indonesia, then come home with a commitment, forged by their own experiences, supporting efforts to save as much of it as they can.

Ours is not a scholarly work; we're not academicians who spend decades preparing dissertations dissecting a subject. Rather, view this book as the harvest of two curious adventurers who, perhaps selfishly, wanted to see something special before it vanishes. We wanted to explore, to turn stones, to determine the acreage of Paradise. And then we wanted to invite others to share what we found because a bountiful garden can offer a feast for all. The gravest scenario would be if the readers of this book longed to see what we did but could not because it was no longer there, and so find herein a reliquary, a reminiscence, a testimony to the way it was. Our greatest hope is that the reader who finds this book in a dusty trunk a hundred years from now will be aroused to seek the riches we found in Indonesia—and that he or she will find them still.

In any shared creative endeavor, the task of dividing the pie is problematic. Ironically, considering the enormous wealth of material proffered by this tropical island nation, the division of labor was easy, for in a sense it had already been done for us more than a century ago. Alfred Russel Wallace, whose book *The Malay Archipelago*, the chronicle of his eight years in that region, still ranks among the great travel books of all time, was a naturalist, zoologist, and theorist of broad reach, but his single most famous stroke is the line he drew between Bali and Lombok, Borneo and Sulawesi, a line that neatly divides Indonesia in two. The Wallace Line, as it is known even today, divides the islands with life forms of strictly Asian affinities from the islands with organisms of Australian associations.

The invisible line is actually the meeting place of continental plates, carrying their isolated cargoes on a collision course. On the western side, the Asian land barge has carried wildlife from India and Africa, such as apes, tigers, elephants, and rhinos; on the eastern side, just a few kilometers across the waters, no such animals have ever roamed. Instead there are marsupials, such as those found in Australia, and the colorful birds that inhabit the tropical canopies of New Guinea.

The differences in geography are less absolute but too poetic to overlook. The islands to the west are dominated by hundreds of volcanoes, the result of the caroming of the plates that caused massive underground pressures, released through fiery vents in the earth's crust. But the islands to the east, though some are volcanic, are chiefly the product of uplift and coral accretion, the result being soil conducive to nutmeg, cloves, and the other spices whose scent drove the explorers to their greatest achievements and excesses.

Thus, like the colonial powers of old, we divvied up the booty: Richard took the territory to the west of the Wallace Line, and Christian wandered the isles to the east. The "islands of fire" would be Sumatra, Java, Borneo, and Bali; the "islands of spice," Sulawesi, Nusa Tenggara, Maluku, and Irian Jaya. And with that, we each set out to survey our domain. We hoped to fathom the allure of this emerald chain, to excavate the treasures that define the archipelago, to snatch away the veils of myth, and to reveal the gleaming gemstones of the wild places of Indonesia.

THAILAND

LAOS

CAMBODIA

VIETNAM

SOUTH CHINA
SEA

Bohorok
Rehabilitation
Center

Kutacane

*Gunung
Leseur*

Alas River

Medan

WEST
MALAYSIA

BRUNEI

EAST
MALAYSIA

B o r n e o

Long Uro
Long Lebusan

*Boh
River*

Mahakam R.

Samarinda

Strait

SULA

SUMATRA

KALIMANTAN

Makasar

SULAWES

Rantepao

Sunda Strait
Krakatau

Jakarta

JAVA SEA

Ujung
Pandang

INDIAN

*Mount
Merapi*

Yogyakarta

JAVA

*Mount
Bromo*

Probolinggo

BALI SEA

BALI

Lombok Strait

Lombok

FL

NUSA T

Komodo

OCEAN

Denpasar

*Gunung
Agung*

*Bukit
Badung*

Sumbawa

Flores

Sumba

SAVU

Savu

0   600 miles

0   1000 kilometers

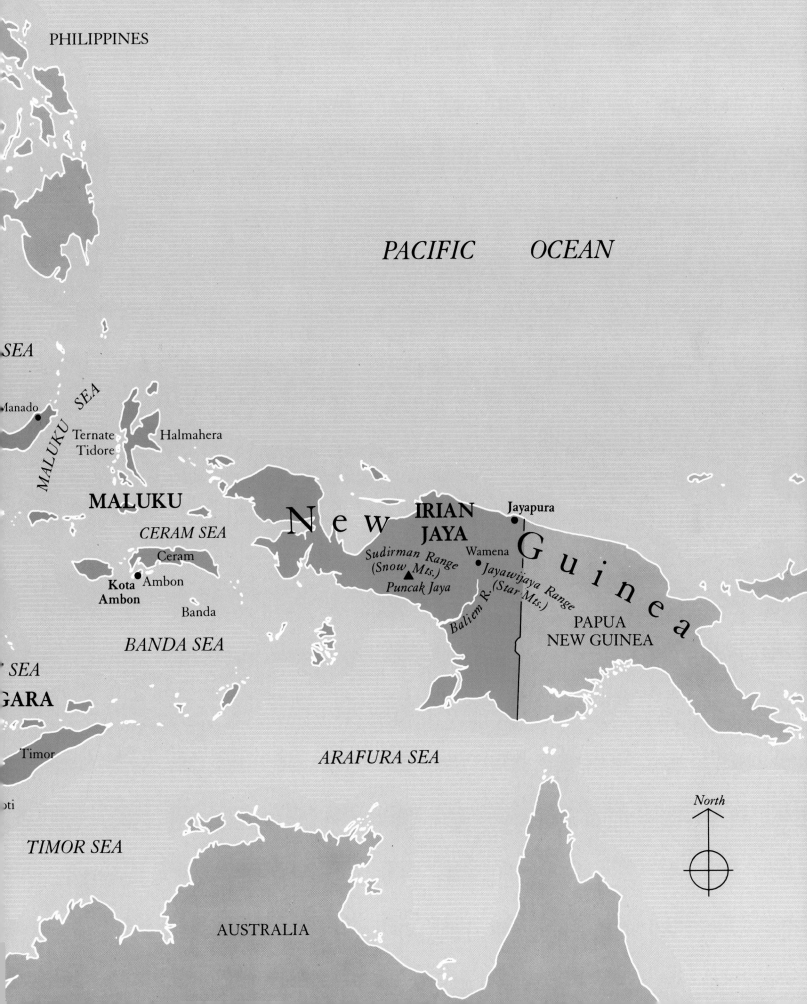

INDONESIA

PHILIPPINES

PACIFIC   OCEAN

SEA

Manado

MALUKU SEA

Ternate   Halmahera
Tidore

MALUKU

CERAM SEA

Ceram

Kota Ambon
Ambon

Banda

BANDA SEA

New **IRIAN
JAYA** Jayapura

Sudirman Range
(Snow Mts.) Wamena

Puncak Jaya Jayawijaya Range
(Star Mts.)

Baliem R. PAPUA
NEW GUINEA

New Guinea

SEA

GARA

Timor

ARAFURA SEA

TIMOR SEA

oti

AUSTRALIA

North

SUMATRA

Rafting the River of the Red Ape

BENNY was seven years old and frightened to death. When she was barely an infant, her father abandoned the family. Her mother was shot and killed. Adopted by a policeman, she grew up confined to a small house, with no playmates, no peers.

Five months ago Benny was brought to this special place and for the first time fed well and showered with consistent kindness. Johanne Ranger, a twenty-four-year-old Canadian, took up the task of caring for Benny, regularly hugging her, talking to her and tending to her cuts and bruises. Johanne became Benny's surrogate mother.

Today, however, would be Benny's last day with Johanne, her final day with a roof over her head. For today Johanne would take Benny for a walk up a muddy path deep into the forest and then, with a brief hug and goodbye, turn and leave her alone, crying among the vines and tall trees. Today Benny would be officially rehabilitated. And our expedition crew would witness the plaintive event.

Benny, of sloe eyes and carpet red hair, was a Sumatran orangutan, one of the great apes, and she was participating in a bold and controversial program designed to help a threatened species take a few steps back from the precipice of ex-

tinction. Twelve of us would be watching Benny's reluctant release into the jungle at the Bohorok Orangutan Rehabilitation Center on the eastern edge of the Gunung Leseur National Park—the largest in Southeast Asia. The park is also just over the montains from the Alas River, which on this trip was our target.

Never before nagivated from source to sea, the Alas River twists through the richest wildlife region outside of Africa, lapping one of the last great primary forests on the planet. Our hope was to combine adventure with a geographical, biological and anthropological survey of this little known but globally significant region.

Sumatra is the westernmost—and next to Borneo, the largest—of the Greater Sunda Islands in the Malay Archipelago. If we do not consider Greenland an island, Sumatra is, as ranked by area, the fourth largest island in the world. Neatly sliced in two by the equator, it is Indonesia's treasure chest: it provides 80 percent of this OPEC nation's crude, and nearly as much of Indonesia's second greatest source of income, timber. Its timber income was more than a billion dollars in 1983 (according to the *Indonesian Times*). Indonesia, in fact, fells its tropical forests at the highest rate of any nation on earth. And considering that there has been near-continuous exploitation of Sumatra's natural riches since the Portuguese arrived in 1509, it is surprising so much pristine, primary rainforest still exists.

The Alas River springs from the denuded northern face of Gunung Leseur, at 3380 meters Sumatra's second highest mountain and the namesake for the national park that surrounds most of the river's course. *Gunung* means "mountain" in Bahasa Indonesia, the official language of the archipelago, but *Leseur* is of uncertain origin. Gusnar Effendy, a seventy-year-old native guide who led perhaps the first expedition to the top of the mountain in 1939 for American millionaire George Vanderbilt, told me that a German who wandered the area prior to World War II with a Mauser strapped to his belt became known locally as "Mr. Mauser." Somehow, Mr. Effendy believes, that evolved to *Leseur*, and hence the name that graces almost a million hectares of protected parklands.

Our project was organized under three flags: those of the United States, Italy and Indonesia. From the first came a team from Sobek Expeditions, which has pioneered a number of first descents of rivers; from Florence, Italy, came a team led by Jacopo Mazzei, the man who made the first raft descent of the Blue Nile in 1973; and the Indonesian contingent was led by Dr. Halim Indrakusuma, a former dentist who one day "just got tired of looking at cavities" and turned in his drill for a backpack, becoming Indonesia's premier adventure-travel organizer.

The official title for our undertaking was the "Florence-Sobek Expedition," and on October 4, 1984, the twenty-six members convened for the first time in Medan, the busy capital of northern Sumatra.

The first stop on our way to the river's source was Bohorok, where we met Benny and Johanne. On the ninety-minute drive into the interior from Medan we crossed a vast patchwork of lawn-green and gold rice fields, like the parklands of a prince. Sleepy water buffalo lifted their heads to gaze, sunken eyed, at our passing vehicle. Girls clothed like butterflies swung crescent-shaped knives, harvesting. Bullock carts often blocked the skinny road; and men in *pitji* caps, the badge of Indonesian Islam, waved from their doorways and windows.

Once we reached the village of Bohorok, it was a half-mile walk through the rainforest, through a limestone cave, to the edge of the Bohorok River, the boundary of the national park. The river serves to keep tourists at bay and to prevent the orangutans from straying into the wrong hands. A single dugout canoe ferries visitors to the center, where twice a day they can watch the released orangutans gather on a wooden platform to be fed powdered milk and bananas by the park rangers. The platform is a sort of halfway house between forest and civilization, and part of a weaning program: the meal quantities are gradually reduced, and the platform is moved every six months, so the orangutans will, in theory, eventually learn to survive on their own in the forest. More than ninety-five orangutans have been rehabilitated since the center opened in 1973.

During their three-hundred-year occupation of Indonesia, the Dutch started the practice of capturing baby orangutans, after killing their mothers, and raising the babies as household pets. Illegal since 1931, the practice continues as some wealthy Indonesians emulate the colonialists. Orangutans confiscated by conservation officials, or donated by owners, are brought to the rehabilitation center, where they are taught how to live in the forest and then released.

The rehabilitation concept is an outgrowth of an inaccurate estimate in 1964 that only 800 to 1500 orangutans remained in Sumatra. Because 140 were being smuggled illegally each year for high-status pets and the zoo trade, and because this resulted in an annual loss of 200 due to the practice of killing the mother to capture the infant, if the estimate had been true orangutans could have been eradicated from the island by 1970. The report prompted several conservation projects in Borneo and Sumatra. Now the guess is that the original estimate was off by a few thousand, and there are currently about 5000 red

PAGE XIV: *An inflatable raft purls through a quiet section of the gorge on the Alas River in Gunung Leseur National Park. The Alas passes through one of the last great primary forests on the planet. (Dave Heckman)*

An orangutan at the Bohorok Rehabilitation Center swings down for a hug from Richard Bangs. When orangutans kept illegally as pets are confiscated by conservation officials, they are brought to Bohorok to be reintroduced into the wild.
(George Fuller)

apes within Gunung Leseur, but the numbers are still alarmingly small and, with accelerating loss of the rainforest habitat and continued poaching, they are still decreasing.

The first such rehabilitation center was at Ketambe, on the banks of the Alas. Established in 1971 by Dutch scientist Herman Rijksen, Ketambe was at the heart of Sumatra's most popular orangutan hangout. And this caused problems. Some rehabilitants had acquired human diseases, which spread to the wild orangs. Also, the wild

apes were reluctant to accept strangers into their territory, so the process was retarded—sometimes arrested. The wild apes would not mate with the rehabilitants. Rijksen was foster mother to nearly three dozen orphaned orangutans at Ketambe, and about half died (some by clouded leopard and tiger; others by diseases). So, in 1973, Rijksen moved the center over the mountains to Bohorok, to a spot where fruit trees were in abundance but wild orangs were not. Thus, the reintroduced apes would not have to compete with feral apes. Instead, they would have to contend with tourists.

The orangutan, or "man of the forest," as the Malay word translates, has for centuries been a source of fascination for humans. The creatures were once thought to be strange-looking wild people rather than animals, and native legends had it that the apes could speak but refused to, for fear they would be put to work. They are in the family of great apes—gorillas and chimpanzees make up the other members—and some scientists believe they are the closest relatives to humans. First discovered in Sumatra, they exist in the wilds only here and in Borneo, in rapidly depleting numbers. Tailless, similar to people in teeth, blood composition, reasoning strategies, tool use, much social behavior and in walking upright, the orangutans even look like us.

While illegal trade and poaching threaten the apes of Sumatra, the more serious danger is the destruction of their habitat. Since social and economic development of the Western type has become a major objective of Indonesia, the orangutan is facing the imminent, almost total destruction of its environment. Orangutans can live only where fruit trees bud, so the upper elevations of Sumatra's mountainous outback are inhospitable. And the lowlands are being cleared by timber concessions and devastating, shifting slash-and-burn agricultural methods. The last stand for the orangutans—and for many other endangered species—may be the protected Gunung Leseur National Park, and only then through continued education. That's where tourists come in.

Bohorok is a station caught between two purposes, existing in tenuous balance. On the one hand, the directive of the center is to get orangutans to readopt independent forest living as soon as possible, to help perpetuate their species. Any contact with humans retards that process. On the other hand, the tourists who flock to Bohorok learn much about the value of rainforest conservation, and about the plight of the apes, through firsthand observation, and there is no better way to imbue a lesson. Also, though the original rehabilitation centers were funded by the World Wildlife Fund and the Frankfurt Zoo, those monies have dried up, and now the pro-

gram must exist from the comparative pittance allocated by the Indonesian government plus the fees brought in by the visiting tourists: the equivalent of ten cents each for Indonesians and two dollars for foreigners. On the Sunday we visited the center, 212 tourists (99 percent Indonesian) attended the afternoon feeding. The solution is likely to be the opening of a new rehabilitation center—one far from the tourist path and dedicated to pure rehabilitation—and development of Bohorok into an outdoor zoo and teaching center with a few orangutans around to entertain and educate.

Johanne Ranger is a wildlife biologist from Dalkeith, Canada. She had applied for a job as a nature interpreter in Malaysia but had been offered the volunteer position at Bohorok, where she has lived as the only Westerner for nine months of her two-year stint. The job was arranged through CUSO (Canadian University Services Overseas), the equivalent of the U.S. Peace Corps. Pale and soft-spoken, Johanne has come to feel at home in the forest and treats her simian guests like family. When relaxing, Johanne squats on her haunches, arms on knees, as do people around the world who live in places with no furniture. On the wall of her simple wood hut was a poster of Sumatran wildlife running from a poacher with the tag line "Am puuun!! Kemana lagi kami harus men cari tempat hidup," which translates to "Give us grace!! Where else do we have to look for a place to live?" And it's a cry that pours from the lips not just of orangutans. The Sumatran rhino, hunted for his matted-hair horn, is among the rarest of creatures; not far behind are the sun-bear and the clouded leopard; and the once-plentiful population of elephants and tigers in northern Sumatra is now pitifully small.

But the orangutans are the celebrities of Sumatra, and Johanne, for a select few, has been their stage mother. Benny, who has mastered the art of human mimicry, has been a favorite, and it was easy to see the mutual affection as Johanne coaxed the cabbage-patch ape from her cage for the long walk to freedom. Benny wrapped her long arms tightly around Johanne as they moved to the platform. They arrived at feeding time, and a dozen other apes were swinging from the forest to indulge. Benny didn't eat; instead she clutched Johanne, like a child at her first day of preschool. The other apes tweeked and pinched and teased Benny. When Johanne tried to escape down the ladder, Benny squealed and plunged after her, knocking them both to the ground. Finally, Johanne walked Benny to a clearing in the forest, gave her a final hug and fled, leaving the little ape alone, confused, somewhere between the two disparate worlds of human and simian and hopefully on the trail to rehabilitation into the forest, where she will grow and mate and help perpetuate a species in jeopardy.

From Bohorok, we trundled into the mountains toward the Alas in our truck. The jade green of Sumatra was like a hallucination. As we drove, the road wound higher; the blazing air became more tepid. On our left we passed Gunung Sibayak, a 2440-meter peak where two Americans disappeared on an overnight hike last year. But the land looked innocent. The slow breeze of the beginnings of the northeast monsoon moved in the coconut palms beside the road, and a sweet-sour mixture of smells reached us: scents of frangipani and jasmine, copra and moist earth. The humid land was like a huge creature stirring to life. Beyond the wet rice paddies and the tea estates rose the deep-green cones of terraced hills and finally the silk-blue cones of the great volcano chain that is Sumatra's spine. Above us, fat stone-gray clouds were strung like glass beads; the landscape appeared to wait for some vast event.

As we crossed the divide to the western watershed of the Barisan Mountains, we could see, for the first time, the Alas Valley. The river itself wound a lazy, crawling course through a tableau luminous and arresting. The horizon—of rice paddies and hills and fields again—picked out in a medley of green, loomed up in such unremitting similarity I felt it must stretch into the next world. As we dropped into the Alas Valley we passed beneath a crude arch that marked our exit from Christian Batak North Sumatra to the radically Islamic province of Aceh, which literally means "the verandah of Mecca." Appropriately, the arch was marked on either side with a church and a mosque.

The day died in flaming splendor. In these hours, it seemed Nature was lavish with her paint. Brilliant birds wended their noisy way home. Soon it was dark with the sudden, velvet blackness of the tropics. Reaching the village of Agusan, we made camp in a schoolyard on the edge of the Alas escarpment and dropped into the deep sleep that follows a long day.

With the dawn, we arose, as all life does in the tropics. It is an exquisite experience, dawn uprising, cool as a mountain stream before heat becomes the order of each blazing day. The two-hundred-inhabitant village of Agusan is a cluster of mud-walled structures poised over the Alas Valley. Marco Polo first visited here in 1292, and things haven't changed much since then. As we prepared our gear, we met Mr. Nasori S. Djajalaksana, chief of Gunung Leseur National Park, who had come to check on our safety. He told us, grinning wickedly, that nineteen people had been killed by tigers in the area in the preceding five years. He added that a week earlier a tiger had killed a dog and a small buffalo just beyond the perimeter of our camp. But wildlife was not the worst of our worries. With daybreak we had gotten the first real look at our target river, and it was a disappointment. Jacopo and I had scouted the river months before and recognized then that the flow this far up was too little to float a boat. But, studying the volume charts, we judged that with the start of the rainy season in October the river would rise sufficiently to allow passage without having reached the flood-stage madness that comes midmonsoon. Thus we had timed our expedition with the start of the rains. The problem was, the rains were late—they had yet to commence at the end of the month's first week—and the river appeared lower than during our dry-season scout. Two dozen of us had traveled halfway around the world for this event, and now it might not happen. Most of the group wanted to drive downstream to a point where added tributaries would swell the river proper to navigable volume. But a few purists were reluctant. After all, we had planned to run the river from its highest possible put-in point to the sea.

Dave Shore, a former Sobek international guide who had retired to sell insurance after a near-fatal accident with a client on the Bio-Bio

River in Chile three years previous, was here as the leader of our whitewater effort, enticed out of retirement. He wanted to give this upper Alas a try with a crack team of rafting veterans and a couple of light boats with no gear. So did Michael Ghiglieri, a primate biologist and river guide here to interpret orangutan behavior for the rest of us. I threw in my hat, as did several others. Suddenly we had seven Americans and a full complement of Italians eager to give this trout stream a try. A hasty plan was crafted. The rest of the crew would move overland downstream about eighteen miles to a point where the river swept by another village, Rambung, and set up camp. The river teams would take nothing except paddles, some matches, a couple of tents in case of emergency and a lunch and would attempt to reach this village camp. If our timing was off, or something went wrong, the boat crew would have to bivouac in the jungle with little gear.

Before we embarked, we were able to get an unusual overview. Prior to our leaving Medan, Mobil Oil had volunteered to loan the company's leased fourteen-seat Puma helicopter for a short aerial scout. Arrival of the chopper had been prescheduled, though at the appointed time nothing stirred in the brazen sunlight—not even a cloud flecked the hard blue sky. But soon, with a faint whop-whopping, the machine appeared over the green horizon, spotted us and arrived like a meteor, landing just beyond our camp, sending tents and unanchored clothing flying. With straws, we selected the lucky fourteen, then filled up the giant helicopter cabin and lifted off for a rare sight.

From the helicopter, I could see wooded folds of mountains that twined for mile upon mile; a silent, motionless green tapestry stretching to the horizon, slightly blurred by heat. Below the helicopter's right portal the silver snake of the Alas uncurled itself in the sunlight, only to be lost as it pitched over the edge of my vision. Cutting through the cumulus, we flew up the ever-shrinking course of the upper Alas to its very source, some fifty kilometers upstream of Agusan, where a thin waterfall spills its sparkling beginnings off the rocky crown of Gunung Leseur. Now, I thought, if we make it to the ocean, this will be a true summit-to-sea expedition.

Back on earth, we began the long carry down a 150-meter embankment from Agusan to the river's edge. Though we were just two degrees north of the equator, pine trees mixed with the tropical vegetation and a chilling breeze forced us to our sweaters, giving testimony to the effects of elevation. Curious villagers eyed our operation from a distance, puffing their clove-spiced *kretek* cigarettes, their teak-colored bodies contrasting with our rice-white complexions.

After two hours of assembling the two inflatable rafts, we were ready to launch, and with little fanfare we pushed off into the clear, shallow waters of the Alas. We bumped and scraped over the first riffles, but within a hundred meters the first tributary added needed water, and the going was suddenly easier. The river was boulder strewn, and we bounced between and off them like pinballs. Despite the strong spirit of international cooperation that had infused the project from its inception, the American team, by far the more experienced in the ways of white water, couldn't help but feel a bit smug as we worked our way through the first of the rapids and looked back to witness the Italians floundering and crashing into rocks at every bend.

Then, as though the Alas disapproved of our mild but palpable arrogance, it wrested our raft from our control and stuck it like a postage stamp against a rock. Shipwrecked, stranded midriver with no recourse, we looked upstream to see the Italian team ferrying across the currents to a vantage just above our accident. In minutes, lines had been tossed to us and secured to the raft, and the Italian team was playing tug-o-war with the river. Thousands of gallons of water press the fabric of a "wrapped" boat against an offending rock, and it can sometimes take hours to wrench such a raft free; sometimes days. Sometimes it never comes loose. The wrap can have dire consequences—in our case, a bivouac, possibly a forced march out the river canyon through the jungle. It would be unsafe, and impossible with our numbers, to attempt to continue toward the day's goal with the one remaining raft.

With the Italians pulling from shore, we tried every angle and trick to liberate the raft, then tried again. It was no easy contest. After ninety minutes of attempts the Alas hadn't yielded an inch.

The Italian team from the Florence-Sobek Expedition punches through rapids in the main gorge of the Alas River. More than two hundred major rapids trouble the course of the Alas from source to sea, and none had been rafted before this expedition. (Riccardo Aichner)

Then, as the first hints of twilight pulled at the sky, and it seemed our expedition might indeed be doomed after a single day of rafting, the Alas, perhaps tired of its teasing, perhaps content its lessons had been conveyed, released the raft to a final Herculean tug by the Italian team. Humbled, and unwilling to barrack at either the river or our Florentine friends again, we drifted into a sandy cove where we pitched a makeshift camp just before sunset, exhausted and pleased though many kilometers from our scheduled rendezvous.

We had scarcely set up camp when the heavens began to mutter and a huge cloud rose out of the south. It reared up, menacing and majestic, with the black and purple coloring of a bruise, and it stooped over the river as an overhanging cliff stoops over the sea. One by one the stars went out,

snuffed by the climbing black pall. Soon we were enclosed as in a lightless room. A deadly silence settled over us. We talked instinctively in lowered voices. Suddenly, out of a quiet that was almost a vacuum, a roaring, mighty wind swept past us, swaying the trees. In a moment every one of us had retreated from the red circle of the fire and into the tents. Through the mosquito netting of our tents, as far as we could see, rain was falling—falling small-dropped and steady, so that the air itself was watery and came into the lungs wet and weak.

The next day the rains had ceased, but the age-old Alas, released from the leanness of the dry season, was enjoying itself. The river was still sucking up water from the wet earth and was still rising. Large, coffee-tinted waves jostled past our camp, ridged in furrows like a potato field, and hurled toward the horizon. The Alas was boiling, clucking among the overhanging rattan vines. It gouged at the bluffs, undercutting the shore. Out in the channel the current rose like the back of a snake. There was a crackling from the fast water like the sound of torn air and, in the distance, the ululating call of a treetop gibbon.

As we prepared for a second day of Gonzo rafting, the astounding heat of Aceh closed over us like a sack. We moved slowly, as though old men. Finally, rigged and ready, we pushed the two rafts into the current. Though the overland crew was still waiting for us somewhere downstream, one member, Gerrit Schilperoot, had hiked up to our bivouac that morning and handed me a note just as we separated. As we swirled into the current, I took a look: "Love many, / Trust few. / Always paddle / Your own canoe."

The Alas here was a devil of a river, a rolling wall that reared against its banks, crooked as a street in San Francisco. It was no river at all, but a great loose water that leaped from the mountains and tore through the jungle, wild to get to the sea. In sync with it, we made our rafting tighter, coordinating our strokes and strategies, slipping between boulders and down tongues. We were, at times, pinball wizards.

At one point we rounded a dark bend to find a river otter plying the currents. Helmeted hornbills swooped over us like pterodactyls. Waterfalls, sliding quite easily over the canyon walls, made a tremendous fuss of their descent, which they accomplished in a series of flashing leaps so white that the clouds seemed as soiled as last week's linen.

We continued to carom and crunch, plunging over small shelves, bending through boulder-strewn slots, bucking over waves, sliding down chutes and portaging every mile or so—once when a fallen tree completely blocked passage and other times when the rock configurations created impossible cascades or too-tight passages.

Then, late in the afternoon, we confronted another impasse, one greater than all before. A jumble of boulders barricaded passage and sent the currents scurrying underground, then over a thin waterfall at the far end of the dam. Here the water flexed smooth muscled at first and then

broken, flying in foam, filling the eyes with its gushing spray. To plot our strategy, we gingerly inched one raft to the edge of this precipice while the water boiled against its nose, and then held it on the edge, where it bucked like a scared horse before a fence. No way we could run this falls. We had to portage. We wrestled the raft to shore as water beat against its side, then beached it for the chore.

In the midst of the portage, an old man wearing a fez appeared from the forest and promptly leaned into the task of wrestling our inflatable downstream. He worked with us, silently, intensely, as though his fate depended on the safe movement of our craft downstream. Sweat poured down his rich, dark skin, a skin that glowed with the color of pure tobacco. For an hour he strained beside us, and then when we finally pushed the raft back into the current, at the base of the boulder garden, the man disappeared back into the jungle, without a word or gesture. It is one of the misfortunes of travel that personalities flash across one's path and, like shooting stars, vanish forever in the darkness.

Once again, we pulled into camp just as the crimson, bulbous sun sank into the green horizon. We prepared dinner under a darkening landscape that had transformed itself into a Chinese painting: high, indigo peaks suspended in cloud; gigantic white masks of mist coming down into the river valley, swirling and changing with eerie speed. Fireflies sparked in frantic motion.

We were camped at the edge of Uning Puni, a government-created village carved from the jungle consisting of ninety-seven seven-meter-square wooden huts with corrugated tin roofs. The park boundaries were gerrymandered so as to skirt Uning Puni and other projects like it. The reasons for the village are multiple: to entice the Gayo peoples, who traditionally lived within the park boundaries, to move from the rainforest, where they practice destructive slash-and-burn agriculture methods and illegally hunt the park's endangered species; to place a rebellious sect under government scrutiny (Aceh Province has for years threatened to secede from Indonesia, as it is one of the richest regions in the country and the most independent) and to secure national sovereignty by establishing a presence in this frontier region; to teach the young Gayo the national language and instill common national goals and values; and to produce cash crops that will boost the national economy. The Gayo were enticed to the village with free housing, education and seeds for planting: corn, tobacco, coffee, cabbage and so on. But though the village was once filled, the Gayo felt uncomfortable in their new surroundings, and after a few months most retreated to the forest. At our arrival there were but a handful of families occupying what appeared to be a ghost town, and most were refugees from a landslide at a village just a few miles up the government road. One man, with a saturnine air and a soulless smirk that passed like a wind eddy in a pool, told us that two days ago he had lost ten goats to a tiger; the previous week he had lost three dogs. He complained that with the protection tigers have newly been granted within the park they are multiplying as never before and causing more damage. At camp that night the darkness came crashing in, full of scents and queer smells and the conjured cries of tigers. Sleep, for most, was fitful at best, and the rain came again, teeming, destructive.

Dawn broke bell clear, and we hastened to launch. This time our target would be the village of Serikil, twenty-five kilometers downstream. Again an overland crew would establish a point of rendezvous and, there, not only set up camp but work on hewing new paddles out of native wood, as we had lost two to the currents the previous day.

As we floated in the early light, all the colors of the landscape—the violet of marching volcanoes, jade of paddy fields, orange of flame trees—seemed more vividly unlikely than usual. At one point we passed a wide field of *Cannabis sativa*, marijuana, a cash crop that fuels an enormous underground economy in Aceh. In fact, because foreigners were always suspect when discovered traveling through this remote province, we were required to carry documents with twenty-two different government signatures and seals, from the governor's to those of the head of national security, to prove our legitimacy to local authorities.

After an hour, the banks began to tighten, the river quickened, and the crude map we carried showed a series of contour lines practically touching—all signs of a steep gradient up ahead. We pulled over to a small village before entering what appeared to be a gorge, and a local man told us "*Tirjung*"—"waterfall"—and indicated with his hand that a sizable one was impending. This sent pulse rates flying. A waterfall on any river is bad news to a rafting party, but on an exploratory trip—with so many factors unknown—and on a fast river, the possibility of not being able to stop the boat in time is a serious specter. With extreme caution, we proceeded.

The gorge was dark, with the treetops on either bank touching, covering us with what seemed like a rotted tarpaulin. We floated past a dead and bloated *sambar* deer, washed against a logjam. Around a bend the river went berserk, breaking through a jumble of boulders in spectacular flashes of white. With little trouble we pulled over to scout and realized this was the dreaded falls—only it was not really a falls but a five-mile staircase of treacherous cataracts. After a long scout, and long minutes of argument between senior raft guide Jim Slade and Michael Ghiglieri as to how to tackle this gauntlet, we began the tedious task of lining—working the rafts down the edge of the river with tethered ropes held from shore. In places we could actually board the rafts and paddle for a few yards, but then the chaos returned, and we resorted to the ropes.

Progress was slow. Hours passed, and the day discolored like a contusion. It was twilight when we completed the last line. The river had dropped almost fifty meters per mile throughout the day; the Colorado River through the Grand Canyon drops less than four per mile. As the light raced away, we sped through a series of Class IV rapids, hoping to make Serikil. The equatorial light shows no mercy; it snuffs itself every day between 6 and 6:30 P.M. At 6:15 we pulled into a cobbled excuse for a beach that sloped like a freeway ramp. Nobody wanted to bivouac here, so we pressed on, into the near-night. Jim Slade pulled out a walkie-talkie from its plastic waterproof sheath and pushed the talk button, as he had done a dozen times in the last hour, but with static the only response. "Don't waste time, Slade.

We need to paddle," Dave Shore barked. But the walkie-talkie barked back. John Kramer, the expedition equipment manager, was on the other end, saying he could see our rafts. We looked ahead along the fifty-meter bank and saw a flashlight waving. "You're a mile away from camp. Go for it," the radio cackled with the spirit of a cheerleader. It was 6:30, almost completely dark, but we paddled on, crashing through warm waves, bumping into rocks and logs, fumbling like blind men downstream. In a photo finish, we pulled into camp just as the curtain of total darkness dropped, and the sky above groaned. It was 6:37. As we slapped backs and shared the hugs of survival, the rain came like pewter sheets of water and was so loud normal speech was impossible.

The next morning the scene was like some misty and mildewed Arthur Rackham drawing come to life. The rhythmic calls of two siamangs washed through camp like gentle rain. At last the river was large enough to launch all six rafts and put all expedition members on the water. The valley had broadened, attenuated, though the jungle was impenetrably thick, a true primary forest.

As we drifted, purple orchids studded the tapestry of green, poking their parasitic heads through the rotting forks of trees; lianas hung in slender loops and festoons; underbrush cluttered the ground in luxuriant profusion. And over all hung a brooding, watching silence like that of a crouching tiger. We were rowing straight into the sun's eye.

A reverie was broken when suddenly our raft passed beneath a curtain of rattan tendrils with thorns like iron claws. One grabbed Dave Shore's life jacket and jerked him from his perch, tossing him into the drink like trash; another raked Michael Ghiglieri's face, imbedding itself just a fraction of an inch from his eye; a third stabbed the fabric of the raft. After retrieving Dave we pulled over to pluck the sliver from Michael's face, patch the raft, and assess the damage. The lesson stuck: a moment's lapse could spell disaster, and we had come perilously close.

In an hour we were back on the horse, galloping through spirited rapids and passing monitor lizards a meter long, now-ubiquitous fish-drying platforms and the giant leaves of the tapioca; passing beneath the periodic bamboo and wire bridges. Though the forest was dark, from the rafts we watched as the sun leaned out of the heavens to touch the surface of the water, and we narrowed our eyes at the bright flash of retort.

At three we drifted into a small eddy that marked our arrival at Ketambe, the famous primate research center founded by Herman Rijksen. We beached on the eastern bank of the Alas, where a few crude bunkhouses were in various stages of construction in anticipation of the upcoming tourist trade. A pair of identical preteen orangutans, clutching one another as though attached like Siamese twins, greeted our party. Sinfully cute, with delicious red-chocolate coloration and pink rings around their close-set button eyes and shiny bald heads, they were products of the rehabilitation program gone wrong. Though they had been brought to Ketambe with the idea of reintroducing them to the forest, the local rangers instead adopted them as pets and encouraged their presence as curiosity pieces for the occasional tourist.

After we unloaded the rafts for a stay at Ketambe, a group of local boys from the nearby village of Blangkajeren showed up and began to perform a dance in our honor. It was the "Dance of a Thousand Hands" or Saman dance, after the Moslem chief who introduced Islam to Indonesia here in Aceh in the twelfth century. The dance is performed by teenagers, who work themselves into a feverish trance, not unlike the whirling dervishes, and enact an intricate body and hand hoedown on their knees. From the side it does seem as though hundreds of hands are clapping and spinning the tale of the dance. Pure Islam condemns dancing as decadent, but the exception was made in Indonesia hundreds of years ago to attract to an ascetic religion a culture that prized body expression. The first exposure to Islam came from Arab traders seeking spices, and as the two cultures mixed an odd synthesis evolved, the Saman dance being living attestation.

The following morning Michael Ghiglieri led a mission to cross the Alas in a local dugout canoe to visit the only two Anglo-Saxons living along the length of the Alas: Dr. Jan de Ruiter and his wife, Margo. Sixth in a succession of Dutch sci-

The Saman dance, or "Dance of a Thousand Hands," is named after the Moslem chief who introduced Islam into Indonesia in Aceh in the twelfth century. (John Kramer)

entists doing doctoral research at Ketambe, Jan, thirty, was six months into a continuing study focusing on individual behavioral differences in long-tailed macaques (little gray monkeys), such as migration patterns, mating tactics (courting, monogamy, polygamy), rank acquisition and maintenance. His is a neo-Darwinian theory—that the ultimate goal of individuals is to produce a maximum number of surviving offspring. Jan's work consists of endless hours of patient observation, learning to recognize the individual monkeys from behavior characteristics, then tracing their life histories. From a biological point of view, it is meaningful to relate the differences in behaviors to differences in the numbers of offspring produced. It is hoped that the final results of Jan's study will add to the body of information on the population dynamics of the species, and that this in turn can be applied to the conservation planning of many species, including humans' population planning. Jan complained that no matter how carefully he explains his work to the local people they still can't accept that he is spending his time looking at monkeys. They think he's really looking for gold.

Being on-site, in the middle of the whirlpool of issues spinning in this region of Sumatra, Jan has been a keen witness, and he talked about life in Gunung Leseur National Park, faunistically the richest reserve in Southeast Asia.

"There are a lot of problems here," Jan told us. "Destructive logging, population pressures, devastating agricultural methods, tourist impact. Timber is a most important part of Indonesia's economy, and the short-term profit picture has often prevailed. Even here, the boundaries of the national park have been gerrymandered to accommodate timber concerns. As for tourism, I'm against it here. This is a research station. People coming here contaminate the primates with human diseases. Even the dropping of trash, soda bottles, candy wrappers, can do harm. And it's difficult to do research when tourists are milling around, trying to feed the animals.

"This used to be a very primitive wilderness area. But when they paved the tract that runs through the center of the park in 1980 people from overcrowded provinces moved in, commerce came, poachers found life easier and the range of certain animals was cut, furthering their road to extinction. It also changed the value system of the local people. Where once the greatest goal was to create a family, now everyone wants a motorbike. And they'll gladly kill wildlife to raise the money to buy one. Fish can bring a pretty penny—one that's sixty centimeters will bring in ten dollars, almost a third the average monthly wage, and so locals sometimes put DDT in a coconut, drop it in the Alas a few miles upstream of their village and then pick up the dead fish as they float by their homes. The social system here has been screwed up by the Western world's supermaterialism, trucked in on the new road. For example, my assistant here has a television set, which he may have purchased with money he earned illegally cutting trees. Yet his family is inadequately fed. He would let his family starve before he would sell his status-raising television. Now, things are in a state of uncertainty. There is no baseline information. Nobody knows if things are getting better, if animal populations are increasing. On paper, there are severe penalities for infractions in the park, but in practice they aren't enforced. The rangers are friends or relatives of practically everyone in the park, and blood runs thicker than the law. Shifting cultivation is another problem. Locals cut trees recklessly for a plot of land, which they exhaust with a couple of years of planting; then they move on.

"The core of the park is, I believe, fairly safe for another five years or so. But the lowlands near the buffer zones are vulnerable, and they are also the richest wildlife regions."

After we'd sipped cold beer in Jan and Margo's jungle bungalow—perhaps the only source of alcohol in the dry province of Aceh—our hosts offered to take us on a forest walk to see the famous Rafflesia—the world's largest flower, with a blossom that can stretch a yard across and weigh up to eleven kilos. The flower blooms just once a year, for up to a week, and we had just missed the full spectacle but could still witness its waning glory. It was a three-kilometer hike through the heart of the rainforest, which shimmered in the heat with a perpetual glassy haze dancing through the topmost branches. It was swampy, miasmic; the jungle breathed a musty odor on us that was peculiarly its own. Tropical parasites stretched toward us from the trees on which they were battened, while orchids and lianas fingered us as we passed. The heavy, drenched languor of the tropical midday hung breathlessly. An owl flew over like gunshot; then a flying lizard followed. We heard queer little noises we could not explain. At last, after a twist in the path, we came upon the Rafflesia, named for Sir Thomas Raffles, the founder of the modern city of Singapore. "It's a pretty ugly flower," was Ghiglieri's first response.

And indeed, it is not something to send on Mother's Day. Among the melange of green, it squatted like a giant rusted sunflower with a black hole in its eye. It exuded a stench that attracted carrion-feeding flies by the score, who in turn would help it pollinate. It also attracted leeches. As I looked to Dave Shore, I saw dried runnels of blood tracing his leg, the legacy of a leech orgy. I chuckled at Dave's predicament, as he plucked the tiny bloodsuckers from his skin; then I looked down and saw a skein of leeches working my own lower body. Expedition cook Bart Henderson remarked, as he, too, plucked, "When you hike here, more than a quart of water you need a pint of blood."

That night, about eleven, a branch cracked and fell just a few feet from Bart's tent. Then a deep growl echoed through camp. Unmistakably, it was a tiger. I pulled back the flaps of my tent and revealed only a crawling grub, with the row of glowing spots on its side giving it the appearance of a miniature train chugging through the night. Within minutes, the twenty or so locals

The world's largest flower, the meter-wide Rafflesia is found only in Sumatra. Its cabbagelike buds swell and once a year, usually in October, burst open in enormous blooms. (Riccardo Aichner)

who manned the Ketambe camp area were huddled together on an elevated platform, and they broke into a nervous two-hour hootenanny, strumming guitars and hoisting voice to keep the man-eater appreciating their music from a distance. It worked. The tiger didn't make another appearance.

With morning, we once again loaded the rafts, leaving behind a cache of canned goodies for Jan and Margo, and pushed into the clear currents of the Alas. Now we were in the quick of the Alas Valley, a wide, fertile rift in the mountain chain, and the character of the river bore no resemblance to the spunky stream we had fought earlier. Here it was fast and swift—about eight meters per hour—but also flat and its banks populated. We drifted past durian plants and nut trees, fez-topped old men, children inner-tubing, dogs barking. The call "Gila" sailed to us from the villages we passed, and Sophian Tengku, our thirty-four-year-old Indonesian guide, translated it to mean "Crazy!" "They have never seen such a sight," he added. At one settlement, Sobek guide George Wendt decided to demonstrate the art of rafting to a few curious children—and suddenly the six-man raft was crammed with forty squealing, laughing kids, who splashed it through a couple of hundred yards of riffles in sheer delight, the Aceh equivalent of the Space Mountain ride at Disneyland.

We pulled in for an early camp at 4:30, yet already a slight heaviness in the corners of the sky and a flushed richness where the sun smote the clouds hinted at the approach of darkness. As we landed the rain began, whirling and hissing, lashing at the surface of the rafts. We camped on a gravel-bar island, and except for the temperature the scene was one out of southeast Alaska: the mantle of clouds, the deep-blue cast, the distant emerald mountains, the braiding river, the herons, the rain. But unlike in Alaska the rain here seemed to be quite forgiving, letting loose only late in the day or after dark. We set up a camp canopy and put the pots on the stoves, pulled out the cards and talked about life in the rainforest and how, if every man in authority were forced to spend a fortnight in it, alone, and live with the humbleness that nature teaches in its classrooms, there would likely be less arrogance and misery in life.

We arrived at Kutacane, the market center of Aceh, the next morning and resupplied with fried bananas and fresh fruit. It was just south of here, at the village of Kuto Reh, that one of colonialism's more ignominious moments occurred. In 1904, in what the Dutch called a "pacification program," they sent the zealous Lt. Gen. G. C. E. Van Daalen on a blitzkrieg campaign down the Alas Valley, where a knot of independent tribespeople were resisting Dutch hegemony. In a My Lai–type sweep, Van Daalen massacred 561 of the people of Kuto Reh, including 241 women and children. In all, Van Daalen claimed 2549 Acehnese lives in his 163-day march through the Alas Valley from the north coast to beyond Lake Toba. Despite this and other atrocities, Aceh was never really "pacified," and even today a strong contingent of freedom fighters, known as "Aceh

Merdekas" for "Aceh Freedom," keeps up the age-old struggle for independence. Now, however, the independence they want is from the central government in Java rather than a European power more than twelve thousand kilometers away. The Acehnese, like all peoples of the planet, are concerned first with their own survival. Foreigners, white or brown, along with the forest and its wildlife, have been the greatest traditional threats. To outsiders the Acehnese methods of survival may seem nonsensical, shortsighted and irrecoverably harmful to the environment. But to those eking out an existence along the Alas, reaping enough food to last the dry season and protecting their babies from soldiers and tigers are all-consuming efforts. They are neither noble nor savages—just people trapped in poverty in a hostile landscape, trying to make the best life possible for their families, friends and themselves.

Days passed. Below Kutacane the river veered from civilization, and wilderness crept back. The river was now too wide for bridges, flowing at about six hundred cubic meters per second, about the average volume of the Colorado through the Grand Canyon. By late afternoon Dave Shore complained of a hankering for a coconut, so we pulled over and tramped up a path toward a coconut grove. It turned out to be a small village, Salim Pinem, and its residents claimed we were the first Westerners to ever visit there. Most of the elder women in Salim Pinem chewed betel nut, a mild narcotic that is the drug of choice throughout the Pacific. In Sumatra, ingestion is a ritualistic process. First a piece of the green nut is dabbed with a little lime and wrapped in pepper leaves. Then the mixture is chewed together with a wad of tobacco; all of this is stuffed into the lower lip, where it might sit for hours. The "high" is a comparatively tame one, but the physical aftereffects are not—black and dark-red stains that permanently discolor teeth and gums. But, for some with a traditional bent, it is a mark of beauty.

Camp that evening was just north of the North Sumatra border at Simpany Enpat (Four Crossings), where four tribes mix: Gayo, Alas, Dairi

OPPOSITE: *The open market at Kutacane, the commerce center of Aceh Province and the largest trading post along the Alas. (George Fuller)*

A fisherman along the Alas smokes a filtered kretek *cigarette, the clove-laced Indonesian favorite. (Bart Henderson)*
OPPOSITE: *Acehnese boys along the Alas River climb a favorite tree and mug for the camera. (George Fuller)*

and the Christian Karo Batak. The last, once notorious cannibals, emigrated first from the mountains of Thailand and Burma over fifteen hundred years ago to the Toba Lake district in the highlands of Sumatra. They were converted to Christianity by missionaries in the nineteenth century, in the process giving up their cannibalism. Then, with mounting population pressures, they spread their clans to the fecund banks of the Alas.

One Karo Batak fisherman spotted our motley camp and, with his clothes piled atop his head, swam over to join us. He greeted us, opened his crude fishing net to show off his catch—a half pound of river crayfish caught on the down side of a rock—and, with some coconut oil, sat down and fried up a batch to share with us. We returned the favor with a dollop of canned tuna, which he found distasteful.

Next stop was Lingga Alas, the last village before the lower gorge. Here we were overwhelmed by the numbers of children, gaggles of them, clutches of them, everywhere, and all seemingly the same age. The women were even more of a curiosity to us; they appeared with pasted faces, as though in the midst of a bizarre beauty treatment—which they were. Their makeup consisted of rice powder, ginger, palm oil and water. And unabashedly they passed their days in this thick makeup so as to preserve their skin and keep themselves beautiful as they winnowed rice or swung their *ani-anis* (small-bladed scythes) in the paddies, often in bright cotton sarongs and lace *kebayas* (bodices).

As we approached the final gorge, the temperature seemed to rise with the banks. A haze of red-hot air from shore reduced our movements to the merely automatic and our mentation to

dream states. The forest was as dank and torpid as an unsqueezed sponge. We floated past a salt seep and were reminded that elephants frequent the lower Alas seeking such salt mines. As we paddled, a hornbill rode the afternoon breeze, broad winged, silent, patient.

We moved into increasingly rugged terrain, as sheer beetling gray granite and shale walls, three hundred meters high, replaced the rubber and banana trees. Now there was a sharp contrast between the cool, wet movement of the river and the harsh, hot immobility of the cliffs, topped with mahogany and ironwood trees twisted in oblique angles.

As we approached the first rapid in the gorge, we were stunned by its ceaseless, full-throated roar, and its appearance: it was so full it bulged in the middle and there were a dozen different currents, each fighting the others in a test of strength. At first, the rapid looked frightening, perhaps impossible. But then, as we surveyed its muscle, we sighted two thin canoes being merrily poled up the shoulder of the rapid. As one reached our scouting rock we greeted its occupants: an Old Man of the River with his teenage son, small daughter and a chicken in a bird cage. He told us he had purchased his leaky dugout for twenty dollars in Singkil, a village near the Indian Ocean, and had spent three days poling to this point. Somehow his presence defused the danger of the rapid, and, as the canoe continued upstream, we boarded the rafts and shot down into the white water.

Wet and woolly, the rapid spun and torqued the rafts, then spit them out right side up at its other end, as three leaf monkeys gamboled along shore. We next slipped through a blizzard of saffron butterflies, and soon we were searching desperately for a camp, in a gorge so tight the walls cut into the river like knife blades. At dusk we spied a spit of level ground on the western bank where a tributary spills into the Alas, and we barely made the pull-over. It turned out to be a vacant game-warden camp, with a primitive shelter, a fish-drying platform and mortar-and-pestle rocks. After settling in, we decided to explore the tributary, and while foraging upstream Michael Ghiglieri almost collided with a bamboo pit viper, a lime-green venomous serpent. Just beyond the snake Michael made another find—a

series of snares, cleverly engineered with nylon fishing line and green saplings, designed to catch argus pheasants wandering down to the river.

The next day the gorge got narrower still, sparkling in spots from its rhyolite walls, and the forest canopy from either side almost touched above. Waterfalls traced stunning white ribbons down the limestone canyon walls. Midday we came upon a father and his two sons busily stringing a gill net at the base of a cave. In the cave, which they called Segembual, meaning "boiling water," where they had been living for ten days on straw mats, there were thirty fish being smoked over a bamboo grill. The father gave us the short tour, then warned us that just a few hundred meters downstream was the last and worst rapid in the gorge—"Bumbun Alas" or "Batuingin," meaning "elephant rock," after a boulder in the heart of the rapid.

Silently, with bald anticipation, we floated toward Batuingin. The quieter we got, the louder the sawing of the cicadas from shore. A pied hornbill landed on a tree above us, his pinions whistling in the wind. He raised his heavy, helmeted beak to give a series of single sad calls. His hoots continued for about three minutes, becoming gradually faster and finally racing to a staccato climax that broke into a hideous, chuckling cackle. Then the leaves rustled below the bird, and our eyes swept to a large, wild, wide-cheeked male orangutan moving slowly through the branches like a red ghost. For twenty minutes we exchanged glances with the animal perhaps the closest runner-up in the race of hominid evolution; then he turned, perhaps bored, and disappeared in the foliage.

When we arrived the elephant rock was covered with the high water, and so this dreaded rapid, though large, did not appear formidable. Feisty, straightforward, it sent the rafts bounding through the waves like porpoises. The breakers at the close of the rapid were merely waved, like the hair of an Italian dandy. We pitched and tossed through the turbulence, and then the river spread itself into a placid sheet. And we drifted quietly along.

The drone of motorized canoes coming upstream interrupted the daydream. We were leaving the wilderness. We stopped and asked the canoe pilots how far to the timber-mill town of

The venomous bamboo pit viper feeds on small mammals. A heat-sensitive pit midway between each nostril and eye helps it locate warm-blooded prey. An injection of venom into the human bloodstream can kill a person within hours. (George Fuller)

Gelombang, the first major outpost of civilization marked on the map. "Two hours," they agreed. We were about to learn our first lesson in *jam karat*, or "rubber time." Two hours later, with no sign of Gelombang, we asked another fisherman. "Four hours more," he offered with a nod of experience. But then we stopped an upstream canoe, crammed with people and umbrellas so that it had less than an inch of draft, and canvased the riders. "If you hurry, six hours," said the captain. But almost nobody agreed. More elastic than *mañana*, rubber time is a way of life in Sumatra, and slowly we succumbed. It took us hours, maybe days.

The gorge opened out, and we paused at a tributary to refill our water jugs and came upon a piece of white linen the size of a pillow case hanging from a branch. Sophian Tengku explained it is called Parbegu, an animistic offering to the spirits and gods, a Karo Batak custom. White is a holy color, and the gesture was meant to extract a blessing for good fishing. It seemed to work, for every fisherman we passed was loaded down with his day's catch.

At the confluence with the Bengkong River we officially exited Gunung Leseur Park, and it didn't take long to encounter rude affidavit—a grunting bulldozer on the left bank mowing down trees like weeds to complete a 32-kilometer road that would open the region to easier timber extraction. For thousands of years the Alas people cleared the forest for crops and homes, but with hand tools and small fires. When the soil went barren they would move to a new plot and the forest would slowly reclaim the former tract. Today, bulldozers imported from Singapore destroy more in a day than a forest family did in a

lifetime. For the next 140 kilometers to the Indian Ocean we would be witness to the complete transformation of Sumatran rainforest to a continuous riverside tropical "desert," pocked with clear-cutting, stained with slash-and-burn residue, supporting great sweeps of useless *alang* grass. Here was dramatic demonstration of how quickly the richest, oldest, most complex ecosystems on earth—tropical rainforests—can be destroyed. In fact they are being destroyed faster than any other natural community. A few thousand years ago, the equatorial rainforest belt covered two billion hectares—12 percent of the earth's land surface. Man has already destroyed more than three quarters of that.

Between 40 percent and 50 percent of all the varieties of living things—as many as five million species of plants, animals and insects—live in tropical rainforests, though these forests now cover less than 2 percent of the globe. And it is easy to see how much we depend upon the goods and services these forests provide: medicines, rubber, a cornucopia of fruit, coffee and millions of other products. It is doubly sad that the rape of rainforests is being carried out not to improve the lot of the poor and landless but for the benefit of a wealthy few. The permanent, wide-reaching benefits of the intact forest—the protection of wildlife, water catchments and soil, and the provision of food, medicines and building materials—are sacrificed for short-term profits for a small group of investors and consumers.

At midafternoon on our next-to-last day on the river we docked at the Gelombang ferry crossing and pulled the rafts up for storage. From this point on, the river had passed to old age, slow and bent, its urchin energy left behind, and our whitewater-design rafts would not be needed. Instead, for two hundred dollars we chartered a leaky, ten-meter-long diesel-powered riverboat named *Happy* and strapped our gear on top for the twenty-one-hour chug to the sea. Mr. Tajul, our fifty-six-year-old captain, stern and laconic as Bogart, steered us among the sandbars, into the stormy night, toward the brine, in his rickety *Asian Queen*.

Below Gelombang the river was opaque with the loam it had scraped from the raw banks in its scurry toward the sea. All of us were dirty, clothes had been trademarked by the river and, in the three weeks since our meeting in Medan, beards had long ago made the passage from down to stubble to shabby riots of hair. Endless games of hearts were played to pass the time on the narrow, cramped boat, interrupted only at the river teahouses, where we would fill our bellies with IndoMie (hot, spicy, instant Indonesian noodles), bananas and biscuits.

Then, with seeming suddenness, in midafternoon on October 25, after the long, tedious welter of the motor trip, the low banks tapered back, the horizon dipped and there was the sea, rolling into the river. Gone was the stuffy, enclosed atmosphere of the forest, teeming with constriction and decay; gone the solid, inexorable walls enclosing the Alas and its villages and ravaged plots.

We beached at the breakers, stripped and raced into the rolling surf, ⅜ kilometers downstream from Agusan, and celebrated with a pounding bath the wildness that we had just traversed and hoped would survive for eyes not yet born to see. We had negotiated a region that has been called the finest celebration of nature ever known on the planet, one of the last remaining strongholds of primary forest on earth. Once part of the millions upon millions of hectares of rainforest that girdled the equator, Sumatra's primary forest is now one of the mere pockets that survive—in New Guinea, Borneo, Central and South America, the Congo Basin and here. Every minute of every day almost twelve hectares are destroyed forever. Each year an area the size of Nevada is razed. Gunung Leseur National Park, more than most, is set apart from civilization, and so perhaps the park's natural luxuriance, its special wildlife, its remaining undisturbed rainforests have a chance. Maybe not. Yet the park, the region and the Alas River must be preserved—not just for the ecosystem wrapped around them but for the planet they support, and all life on earth.

OPPOSITE: *A buffalo enjoys a rare moment of peace on the lower Alas. These beasts of burden are used for plowing, hauling and transportation while they live and are butchered and eaten in* sate, *the Indonesian shish kebab, when they die.* (Bart Henderson)

JAVA

Climbing the Cracks of Doom

"THE truth is, you've got a 20 percent chance of making it out and back in a small boat; 80 percent in a large boat."

Dr. Ridder's warning echoed in my sleep-resistant mind as the boat shuddered with another wave. At least, I tried to reassure myself, we had exercised the wiser option in an unwise exercise; we'd hired a "large boat," a ten-meter traditional *pinisi*, a diesel-powered fishing trawler, to navigate the forty kilometers across the Sunda Strait from western Java. But the fact that twice I had put my hand through the dry-rotted sideboards of our hired *Ernarosa* while being bounced about below deck didn't inspire any extra cheer. Nor did the bold truth that we were attempting this jaunt in January, the stormiest month of the monsoon. Still, it was late, and the boat's pitching was generally rhythmic, keeping time via the slap of an untethered hatch door, and I could feel myself drifting into the sleep I much needed.

But the dusty moment of unconsciousness was swept clear by a wild list of the boat that tossed me off the bench I was calling a bed and onto the keel floor. Trying to take it in stride, I rolled over, still on the keelson (baseboard), pulled the sheet over my head and tried to force sleep. But it wouldn't come. Instead, the *Ernarosa* took another lurch, and with a crack like a cannon report a wave burst into our compartment and washed over me.

"George, I think we're sinking," I yelled to my companion, who was still hanging onto his narrow bench.

We could hear the pandemonium above deck as our Indonesian crew scrambled and screamed at one another. Then another wave crashed into the hold, and we grabbed for our possessions. Robert, the one crew member who spoke a bit of English, poked his head into the darkness. "We must go island," Robert volunteered with a hint of panic. The boat pitched again and this time seemed to stay at its cant, a forty-five-degree angle. Through another rolling wave George and I worked our way up the ladder to a tilted platform middeck. The only stable exit was on the island side of the boat through the privy, but a plywood wall blocked passage. Robert kicked it down like some clumsy martial arts instructor and pointed the way. I jumped first, into inky water that flashed blue with phosphorescence, and was surprised to find it just waist deep. George threw me our packs, then leapt in as well, and the rest of the crew followed. We waded to shore and turned our flashlights back to the *Ernarosa*, which, slapped by another breaker, had collapsed on its side, where it seemed to move in small breaths with the waves like a dying sea mammal.

As a means of conveyance, the *Ernarosa* looked washed up. It was 4:00 A.M. We were marooned. It dawned on me then that this small island was not an insignificant one; we were shipwrecked on Krakatau, one of the most destructive volcanoes of all time.

At 9:58 A.M. on Monday, August 27, 1883, the cone of Krakatau (also known as Krakatoa) ripped itself apart with the biggest bang ever recorded on our planet. The noise was heard over one-thirteenth of the earth's surface, from Sri Lanka (then Ceylon) east to the Philippines and south to southern Australia, almost four thousand kilometers away, where sheep were startled into a stampede. If Krakatau had been in New York, the noise could have been heard in both London and San Francisco.

With the cataclysmic explosion, Krakatau spewed into the air nearly 20 cubic kilometers of airborne ash, rock and pumice, the record column reaching a height of eighty kilometers. By contrast, Mount Saint Helens in 1980 disgorged a mere 1 cubic kilometer of ejecta. The energy released from Krakatau's blast was equivalent to one million times that of a hydrogen bomb. The airborne pressure waves spread out in all directions, meeting on the opposite side of the world (near Bogota, Colombia) and bouncing back to their origin, where they rebounded outward again so that some barographs recorded the same wave seven times as it bounced back and forth between Krakatau and its antipode. Dust clouds traveling at 120 kilometers an hour plunged the earth within a five-hundred-kilometer radius into darkness for three days. In Poughkeepsie and New Haven, fire departments were called out when the intense reds of the sunsets created by volcanic aerosol in the atmosphere looked like conflagrations in the distance. For three years dust circled the earth, creating strange and spectacular sunsets. The fine particles filtered out enough sunshine to lower global temperature by nearly a degree Fahrenheit for several years.

At the hour of the paroxysmal blast hundreds, perhaps thousands, of people were burned to death by the rain of red-hot ash and rock that had been molten until it exploded upward and solidified on contact with the air. Far more destructive, however, were the tidal waves that were triggered, many scientists believe, by the collapse of Krakatau's cones into its empty belly. Giant tsunamis, more than forty meters high, swept over the nearby shores of Java and Sumatra, hurling one steamship three kilometers inland. The resulting waves were recorded as far as Hawaii, the Bay of Biscay and Cape Horn, and even the level of the River Thames was affected. Coastal Java and southern Sumatra were devastated: 170 villages and settlements were destroyed and more than thirty-six thousand people killed, another record in Krakatau's long list. No one within the shadow of the volcano survived.

My friend George Fuller and I had come to this unusual roost as part of a self-invented scheme to survey the volcanoes of Java, the most populous and the most volcanically active island in the world, smack in the middle of the Ring of Fire. Though 121 volcanoes (about 35 of which are classified as "active") dot the California-sized island, our plan was to climb just three from among the infamous cinder cones for first-hand looks at the forces responsible for shaping a landscape and a culture: Krakatau, west of Java; Mount Merapi, the youngest and most volatile mountain, in Central Java; and Mount Bromo, in East Java.

To get to Krakatau, we had first traveled four hours and 175 kilometers southwest of Jakarta, Indonesia's steaming, teeming capital, to the Carita Krakatau Beach Hotel, an unpretentious ramble of bungalows set amidst tangled pandanus and coconut palms. In this set piece Joseph Conrad might have written into being we found proprietor Dr. Axel Ridder, a forty-eight-year-old, Berlin-born refugee from civilization who has become something of a student of the volcano he can see from his breakfast table. Ridder, who holds master's degrees in economics and languages and a doctorate in philosophy from the University of Cologne, arrived in Indonesia in

PAGE 22: *A recent eruption of Anak Krakatau ("Child of Krakatau"), the 200-meter-high volcano that has emerged from the sea off the coast of West Java, where the 800-meter-plus cone of Krakatau once stood. (Travel Indonesia)*

Children playing on Carita Beach in West Java, across the straits from Krakatau. This beach was hit with forty-meter-high tidal waves and completely covered with ash during the 1883 eruption of Krakatau. (Richard Bangs)

1970, at the age of thirty-two, to teach economic management in Jakarta. When his contract expired in 1973 he decided to "drop out" and fashion his own little piece of paradise. Now he rules over Carita Beach like an Indonesian *dalang* (puppet master) of his own Wayang shadow show, the only Westerner for kilometers, a post-colonialist creating a private kaiserdom on the edge of the jungle.

"It's far more dangerous to live in San Francisco with its earthquakes or Germany with its Pershing missiles than here, forty kilometers from Krakatau," Ridder told us before our fateful voyage. "It would be near impossible for the volcano to erupt with enough force for effluviant to hit us. And it's more likely Manhattan will be leveled by a tsunami than Carita Beach." The lo-

cals don't necessarily agree. For weeks after the August 1883 explosion, bodies washed up on the beach where Ridder now has a seventy-five-year lease to operate his hotel. Hawaiians believe that volcanic activity is the work of Pele, an orgastic goddess. The Romans acknowledged the existence of a god of fire, Vulcan (from whom we get the term *volcano*), and the Sundanese of West Java know that the smoke and fire of the Sunda Strait flares from the nostrils of Orang Alijeh. Tales of the terrible destruction caused by the awesome anger of Orang Alijeh, the volcano spirit, circulated the region after the big blow. And the bay facing Krakatau became known as the "Beach of Stories," (Pantai Carita). Survivors of the eruption and succeeding generations feared the area, and even today only small, iso-

lated settlements and one town of any size, La-
buan, exist in this fertile and scenically stunning
stretch of shoreline on the planet's most crowded
island. For many Indonesians, Krakatau and its
environs are still danger zones, and Orang Alijeh
could vent his anger at any time.

For George and myself, however, Krakatau
was a refuge, a life-saver, solid ground. We toted
our gear above the high-tide mark and crawled
under a plastic tarp to await dawn. Since we were
just six degrees south of the equator, first light
came at six, as it does every morning throughout
the year. The first order was to inspect the *Ernarosa*, which had been left high and dry on its side
by the receding tide. The hull was damaged, perhaps beyond repair, and, even if it weren't, negotiating it back to deep water looked as though
it would take a lot more muscle than the nine of
us possessed. Our only guess about how the accident had occurred was that the captain had not
secured a strong anchorage when we arrived,
early the evening before, after a choppy four-
hour trip from Carita. We had dropped anchor a
hundred meters off the island and decided to
sleep on board where it would be cooler, with
fewer insects. The storm that came up in the early
morning must have pulled the anchor loose.
There was nothing we could do to get off the island, except receive a rescue party, so we decided
to explore while we waited.

Technically we were not on Krakatau but
Anak Krakatau, which means "Child of Krakatau" in the official Bahasa Indonesia. Thousands
of years ago the cone-shaped mountain of Krakatau, some two kilometers in height, was destroyed in an unrecorded but no doubt devastating eruption. Legends have it that the islands of
Sumatra and Java used to be connected by an
isthmus. The wrath of Orang Alijeh changed all
that. A mention in the Javanese royal annals, *Par-
araton* ("Book of Kings") says that in the year 338
Saka (or 416 A.D.), "The world was shaken with
violent thunderings that were accompanied by
heavy rains of stone. . . . Kapi [probably an ancient name for Krakatau] burst into pieces and
sank into the depths of the earth. The sea rose
. . . inhabitants . . . were drowned and swept
away with all their property . . . and Java and Sumatra were divided into two parts."

In the summer of 1883 Krakatau was a group
of islands, the tips of a huge underwater caldera,
the main one of which was also called Krakatau.
For the previous couple of hundred years it had
been considered a "dead" volcano. It was 9 kilometers long, 5 kilometers wide and had three
volcanic cones: Rakata ("crab," in old Javanese), Danan and Perbuatan. Rakata was the tall-
est, at more than 800 meters. When this collection of cones blew itself out in 1883 the earth's
crust collapsed, forming a monstrous 41-square-
kilometer submarine caldera, 290 meters deep,
with a bubbling sea where once a luxuriant rainforest had covered the islands.

In 1927 fishermen saw reddish glows at night
where the mountain had once loomed. Deep beneath the surface, volcanic vents were vomiting
magma, and by late January 1928 a small island
had emerged, to submerge again after several
weeks. It emerged again, submerged again,
emerged on and off—until August 12, 1930,
when a stable cinder cone was established: Anak
Krakatau, or Krakatau Junior, a baby volcano
that these days is almost 200 meters high and is
more than a square kilometer in area. It's growing still, several meters a year, rising like a phoe-
nix from the ashes of its own destruction. Or,
rather, it is rising like a Garuda, the mythical Indonesian sunbird that reincarnated from the cin-
ders of its own pyre. This current incarnation
was our sanctuary and our prison—our own little Devil's Island.

George and I decided to hike to junior's rim.
We first had to whack through a wall of vegetation about twenty meters thick. Then we
emerged on the base of the basaltic cone. We
stepped along fine pumice sand, then obsidian
gravel, pitchstone and pieces of glass-rich augite
andesite as we began the steep ascent. Above we
could see little puffs of white smoke—a good
sign, as gray is supposedly a portent of trouble.
We puffed, ourselves, as we scrambled up the de-
tritus slope, and after twenty minutes we stood
on the rim—of the wrong caldera. This was a
false summit, a newer, currently inactive vent. A
few hundred meters to the west and a few meters
above was the true caldera, the bowllike depression that characteristically caps a volcano. We
trudged along the ridges, at last reached the thin

The caldera of Anak Krakatau, where fumaroles spit steam and sulfur dioxide, venting the gases escaping from the mantle of the earth. (Andreas Bender)

lip and looked down into the fire and brimstone of Hell itself, nature's crucible of death. It was incredibly exciting—and frightening—to be on the edge of one of the most powerful and destructive of all of earth's forces, knowing that it could, and would, explode again and that we were tempting that fate. The air was thick with the smell of sulfur dioxide, and fumaroles by the score—smaller, scattered holes to the depths—were spitting steam. Deep in the ash-gray guts of the volcano a pool of boiling mud plopped, hissed and sputtered in a scalding dance. Beyond, we could see a shimmering, pearl-colored, calm sea and the holms of Sertung, Rakata and Panjang (also called Rakata-kecil or Lang Island), pieces of the prehistoric caldera rim that survived the 1883 blast and have grown, by layers of pumice and ashfall. Now completely cloaked in veg-

etation, the three remnants surround Anak Krakatau like giant sentries. To the east we could barely make out the hazy shore of Java; to the north, Sumatra was tracery on the skyline. It was a spectacular and scary vista. We drank it all in for a couple of hours and tiptoed around the knife-edge ridge for different perspectives. At one point I stepped on a yellow-brown layer of crust that crumbled like old cake, sending my leg into a fumarole, microwaving the bottom of my foot amidst belching sulfur fumes that caught the back of my nose and throat. The burn was minor, but it seemed a good excuse to head back down to base camp and reevaluate our situation.

In our absence the crew had constructed a series of shelters out of our tarps and rain gear, and now they were busy examining the damage to the *Ernarosa*. I checked our food and water supply: a jar of peanut butter, a loaf of moldy bread, a bag of hard candy, two packages of raw peanuts and seven liter bottles of water. No need for worry. It's said that if you're twenty kilograms overweight, which is about a hundred forty thousand calories, you can last seventy days without food. George and I didn't have quite that reserve, but we had indulged over the recent holidays and had enough saved up to see us through some long days. Besides, we reassured ourselves, our stay would never equal the ordeal of Rickey Berkowitz and Judy Schwartz sixteen months earlier.

In late August of 1985, the two twenty-seven-year-old Southern Californians took the same boat trip to Krakatau that we had, though it was the dry season, the seas were calm and the journey was made out and back in a day without incident. But then they decided to visit Ujung Kulon, a national park and wildlife refuge on the remote southwestern tip of Java, cut off from the rest of the island by a narrow, marshy isthmus and a wall of mountains, the Honje massif. It was once a populated peninsula, until the ashfall and tsunamis of the 1883 Krakatau eruption wiped out all life. The people never returned, though the vegetation and wildlife did, and now, on an island packed with more than a hundred ten million people (the average rural population density is two thousand people per square kilometer, by far the world's highest), the 510 square kilometers of Ujung Kulon stands as a port of wilderness in a sea of humanity. Lushly enveloped in a thick mantle of jungle, it is the last refuge for the once-plentiful one-horned Javan rhinoceros, and it hosts good numbers of wild oxen, leopards, panthers, pythons, tigers, mouse deer, boar and bats. If it hadn't been for Krakatau's devastation and a century of regeneration without the presence of man, Ujung Kulon would long ago have been overrun by "civilization" and the Javan rhino would likely be extinct.

The only way to get to Ujung Kulon is by boat, usually hired at the same bay from which Krakatau trips are launched. Though Rickey Berkowitz and Judy Schwartz had requested a "big" boat for the nine-hour trip, they ended up with a four-meter fiberglass runabout, piloted by two non-English-speaking Indonesians. Just sixteen kilometers from their destination, the boat's engine quit. There were no oars or paddles, no sail or rudder, no emergency equipment. They were adrift in the shark-infested waters of the Sunda Strait, the channel between Java and Sumatra that links the Indian Ocean and the Java sea.

After their first night at sea the boat had drifted past Ujung Kulon; by the third day they had lost sight of land altogether. The women had brought food and water for several days, and both were blessed with some excess body weight, so they weren't too worried. They had registered their trip with the Park Service before departing, Dr. Ridder knew of their journey and a friend had stayed behind, so they figured a rescue would be launched by week's end. But when the seventh day came and went without a ship on the horizon or a plane in the sky they began to wonder.

And they began to act. With a tent fly, a rain poncho and two sarongs they fashioned a crude sail, and they pointed their tiny vessel toward Sumatra.

While it must have seemed to the four souls lost at sea as though they were sailing through a vacuum, there was a typhoon of activity on shore. By the beginning of the second week the girls' parents had flown to Indonesia, and a full-scale aerial and water search was being coordinated by the U.S. Embassy. The village of the two Indonesian boatmen went into mourning, assuming the worst for their sons. According to local belief, every year Nyai Loro Kidul, goddess of the South Sea, demands a human sacrifice. One of the American women had worn a green Bay-to-Breakers Race T-shirt that was the same fatal green favored by the goddess, and some villagers speculated that the Americans weren't ordinary women at all but agents for Nyai Loro Kidul, out to claim her due. To appease the sea goddess, one of the wives killed two white chickens and threw their blood into the ocean. Witch doctors were hired to work their black magic. All to no avail.

In the second week of drifting, a rift, more than cultural, grew between the Indonesian men and the American women. The Americans had tried to ration what little food and water they possessed by dividing it equally between the four of them. But the Indonesians, who had been brought up with a "live for today" philosophy in the primitive affluence of a fertile, tropical coastline, couldn't grasp the concept and wolfed down their share as they got hungry. Then at night they stole from their female companions. The only sustenance the women could keep from their boatmates was a small tube of Colgate toothpaste, to which they treated themselves a finger smear each evening in what they called their "happy hour."

On day ten, one of the Indonesians went berserk and with a rusty machete started chopping at the boat with Bruce Lee–like moves and grunts. He smashed the front window, destroyed the bunk benches and finally stopped when Schwartz offered him her last three peanuts, the last food on the boat. From that point on all they had was the infrequent rainwater.

It would be another ten days before they sighted land, the southwestern shore of Sumatra. If they missed this landfall, the next one likely in the path of the currents would be the African island of Madagascar, some eight thousand kilometers farther west. Yet for days they drifted no closer. Finally, in the middle of their twenty-first night at sea, a wave picked up their beaten boat, flipped it over, and smashed it against a Sumatran coral reef. All four were safely washed to shore, where the next morning some lobster fishermen escorted them to the closest village for a feast of shellfish and hot rice. Within a week the two Americans, now trim and tan as they had never been before, were back home appearing on talk shows and negotiating with publishers and movie producers, while the two Indonesians, practically cadaverous with their weight loss, were confined to a Sumatran hospital where the police kept grilling them in the belief they were drug smugglers. Three weeks adrift in an open boat with two American women just seemed too preposterous. And it still does.

After stashing my one tube of Crest toothpaste to carry along, I thought I would get out and try to enjoy this castaway stuff. I stripped down to my shorts and started some barefooted beachcombing. The tide was low, so I could wander along a black-sand beach that curved around a short horizon. The shoreline was piled high with debris of all sorts: rubber balls, shampoo bottles, Japanese light bulbs, American aerosol cans, a brassiere, bottles without messages and flip-flops—hundreds and hundreds of those cheap rubber sandals and even a dozen or so sheets of rubber from which the soles had been punched out. It looked as though a flip-flop barge had done just that off the coast of Krakatau.

I continued my tramp and surprised two meter-long monitor lizards, both of whom scampered into the sea. Their flight disturbed a dozen ghost crabs, which burst pale green and rectangular out of burrows in the sand and, bodies raised high on absolute tiptoe, skittered around from one piece of jetsam to the next. Their eyes were on stalks and hinged, so they could be either laid back into protective sockets in the carapace while the crabs were burrowing or raised to peer from above when the crabs were foraging. Evolving on unprotected shores where they had to rush down to feed between one huge wave and the next, they could outrun and outmaneuver most terrestrial predators. The only way to get a close look at them was to sit absolutely still and to flick small objects out onto the sand in a way that attracted their attention and brought the closest ones in *en bourrée* to investigate. All this activity reminded me of a passage I had read, written nine months after the 1883 eruption, declaring that only one microscopic spider could be found on the remaining ancient caldera rim wall of Krakatau. Today there are more than six hundred species of animals and some two hundred plants covering the island in an almost impenetrable tangle. Though Anak Krakatau is not nearly as fecund and thriving as its neighbor, due largely to its younger age and its repeated minieruptions that scrape the landscape clean, it is by no means barren. There are bats and birds, molluscs and six different reptiles, not to mention a forest of fig trees (not in season, unfortunately) and bamboo.

After about a kilometer, the beach ended where a paw of basalt clawed its way into the sea, a remnant of a 1981 eruption. The flow didn't appear to be too wide, so I thought I could scramble over it, then continue my walk along the beach. But the hardened lava was much too sharp for my feet; a single step and my foot was bleeding, pieces of glasslike basalt embedded in my sole. Not to be defeated, I simply stepped back down the beach until I found a couple of flotsom flip-flops that were my size and favorite color and then headed up onto the basalt. Two hours later I was still picking my way across this sharp, hot jumble of black razor rocks, and there was no end in sight. I realized the beach was the exception for Anak Krakatau's shoreline; lava was the rule, and, in fact, about 70 percent of the island has basalt cutting its way down the cone and spilling directly into the water.

Then it happened. My right flip-flop blew out. The front strap that pokes between the toes popped from its hole through the sole. Now, on the beach or in the backyard this is no big thing. But here, several kilometers deep into a pile of rock razor blades, this was disaster. I forced the strap back into its socket, but after a step it ripped out again. I repeated the exercise with the same sad results a half-dozen times. The landscape was so jagged I could barely balance myself on one foot as I kept trying to repair the blowout, and I tested the surface again with my bare foot, but it was no use. I couldn't even put it down for fear the rocks would cauterize my toes. I couldn't even sit down to think about it. I was in a vast garden of branding-iron-hot, burnished broken glass. Now I was truly marooned.

With a bit of panic welling I tried to think creatively. Then it came to me. I took off my expedition shorts and fed the sandal strap through the broken sole hole, then through the buttonhole of my shorts. The reinforced cotton canvas shorts, now a buffer between the metal-filing-like basalt and the flip-flop, held the strap in the busted sole socket. Hallelujah! I could walk again! Naked from the ankles up, I flopped my way across the jumbled lunarscape, finally reaching the black sand two hours later. I limped into camp completing perhaps the first shoreline circumnavigation of Anak Krakatau, a dubious achievement I can't imagine anyone ever wanting to repeat.

That night a storm ripped through our makeshift camp, knocking down our tarp tent but filling our water bottles—like Krakatau itself, a mixed blessing.

After a breakfast of peanut butter on wet bread, I rousted our Indonesian crew for an impromptu game of stickball, using a driftwood bat and a plastic jetsam ball. Afterward, while George retreated into a book, I decided to go back up on the flank of the volcano for a longer look.

Halfway up the cone I passed an uneven row of lenticular, locomotive-sized chunks of basalt, somber as tombs, looking as though they'd been planted in black cement eons ago. They weren't, of course. They were recent ejecta bombs, spewed like spitballs as the volcano cleared its throat. As I looked over the horizon I couldn't imagine a scene more serene: a mirror-smooth, pellucid sea, a brilliantly clear day, a hint of a cool breeze. And as I trekked up the mountain I couldn't help but feel I was on terra firma. But of course I wasn't.

A volcano is little more than a hole in the ground through which hot gas, molten material and rocks erupt like the sudden opening of a shaken bottle of soda pop, with superheated steam in place of carbonation bubbles. If only it were so simple. Volcanology is a new science, one that first found legitimacy in the wake of Krakatau's eruption, and the chemistry and plumbing of volcanoes is still hotly debated.

Though there is no scientific unanimity, it is generally theorized that the surface, or upper crust, of the planet is really a mosaic of huge, rigid "plates" floating on an inner sea of hot, plastic rock. Indonesia straddles a collision zone between two such jigsaw puzzle pieces (called tectonic plates): the Alpine-Himalayan (or Indian) continental and Pacific oceanic plates. As the thinner, denser oceanic plate has been ground against its thicker, lighter neighbor, it has been bent and folded underneath the continental plate into the hot mantle, the three-thousand-kilometer-deep layer beneath the thirty-kilometer-thick crust. Moving northeastward at speeds of about six centimeters per year, the Pacific Plate is in the midst of a million-year dive into the earth's core (a process called subduction). In the collision zone, part of its mass melts from friction and chemical processes and metamorphoses into volcanic magma, superheated

The remains of Rakata, the largest of Krakatau's three cones before it erupted in 1883. Rakata was reduced to a barren caldera wall after the explosion, but today hundreds of plant and animal species cover the island. (Vikki Stea)

material that is under great pressure. That pressure continues to build until it finds relief through cracks and rips in the earth's crust. Escaping gas and magma can shoot up these infernal chimneys, and the venting creates the bulges on the earth's surface that become volcanoes, sometimes chains of mountains, sometimes entire archipelagoes. Indonesia, in the strike zone of two of the earth's most restless and relentless plates, is the most volcanic region in the world, the Andesite Line, a rattling string of giant worry beads. In Holocene time—the past ten thousand years—at least 132 volcanoes in Indonesia have been active and 76 have had historic eruptions. The high number of eruptions, combined with the high population density, claims 33 percent of the world's total of volcanic-related fatalities. Despite this toll, population density re-

mains strongly correlated with volcanic activity, because, in regions where the nutrients in new ash are swiftly leached by heavy rainfall, the enriched soil can support more people. The Javanese volcanoes are instruments of destruction and, as well, vessels of replenishment.

The original elements of matter in ancient Javanese cosmology were water, air, earth and fire. As in the case of Krakatau, all four would periodically collaborate to impress their awesome powers of life and death upon the Javanese by rousing from slumber one of the majestic edifices of the Javanese landscape, the volcanoes of the great Sunda mountain system. It extends some seven thousand kilometers from Burma to Bali (about the same length as the Cordilleras de los Andes of South America).

Myths and legends have always surrounded

the Javanese volcanoes. Their summits, rising thousands of meters toward the heavens, have been the seats of the divine, the gods and ancestral spirits. Beneath their ash-swept bases resided wicked spirits, who, if not propitiated by proper sacrifices, made the earth tremble and spit fire. In the ancient cosmology, long before the arrival of Mohammed or Shiva or Buddha or Christ, the center of the Javanese universe was a now-unknown volcano. In prehistoric Java, stepped altars were built on the slopes of many volcanoes, as were temples to the glory of the gods and kings with the advent of Hinduism. Today, though Islam has emerged as the state religion, Indonesians in fact embrace a syncretic tangle of Hinduism, Buddhism, Taoism and Christianity, all overlaid on a web of mystical animistic beliefs that draw sustenance from the fiery bosom of the mountains. As with the benevolent kings and deities of the Indonesian landscape, volcanoes themselves would dole out a great deal of favors, such as the rich volcanic soil that made the land so eminently capable of supporting life; and they would occasionally punish. The holocaust of Krakatau was one such punishment.

The volcano of Krakatau was not treated kindly nor with respect before it raised its true voice. It was an island of evil reputation, once inhabited by pirates who carried off women from the mainland. In 1809 a small penal colony was established there. Villagers from coastal Java, who would canoe out to take its wild fruit, didn't bother to leave behind offerings. It was marked on regional charts as a peril of intricate navigation. It was considered extinct, like a volcano on the moon. Few people knew of its existence; fewer knew its name, which, one legend tells, came from a none-too-bright Indian prince who asked his ship's captain its name while passing through the strait. "I don't know," the vessel master replied, employing the word *kaga-tau*, and the prince recorded a bastardization as the island's name.

On August 26, the day before the big blow, Krakatau began its castigation. At 1:00 P.M. the volcano roared and ominously belched a pillar of steam that took the shape of a gigantic pine tree and that reached upward to a height more than double that of Mount Everest.

To one witness, a Dutch telegraph master on the Java coast, it appeared as if thousands of white balloons had been suddenly released, rolling, twisting, turning, expanding and bursting—a lyrical image, in the poetry of grand concussion. Captain Sampson, of a British ship anchored off the Sumatran shore, was more reverent when he wrote in his log, "So violent are the explosions that the ear drums of over half my crew have been shattered . . . I am convinced that the Day of Judgment has come."

For the next twenty-one hours Krakatau continued to peal and spit, until the grand finale, the "Crack of Doom," at 9:58 A.M. on August 27, which in seconds obliterated a landmass almost the size of Manhattan. But it was the killer wave kicked off by the cataclysm that took lives most widely—and spared them most sensationally.

One survivor was lifted up by the wave and deposited on a hill while still lying on his bed. Still another found himself being swept inland next to a crocodile. He couldn't swim, so he climbed on the reptile's back, hanging on by pressing his fingers deep into its eye sockets. Another man found his saving angel in the corpse of a cow. He climbed on and floated to safety. Others were able to run to high ground, and one woman reportedly gave birth to her child while racing up the hill. Tens of thousands of other souls weren't so fortunate. A mosque filled with people was dragged into the sea, as were offices, homes, lighthouses, forts, and, in fact, the whole of the townships of Anjer, Tjeringin and Teluk Betung and some 165 other villages. If ever there had been punishment from the gods, this was it. But then, once it had been meted, the world was quiet.

No great sounds came from the Sunda Strait for forty-four years, until the birth of Anak Krakatau, which blows fits and tantrums periodically, little hot-blooded shows of muscle and voice that are like firecrackers compared to its father's final outburst of rage, fury and pyrotechnics. In fact the loudest noise in the passage since may have been punishment of a more predictable sort. The shores reverberated once again to the roars of explosion on February 28, 1942, when six allied warships encountered a Japanese fleet in the Strait. The U.S. cruiser *Houston*, the Australian cruiser *Perth* and the British destroyer *Evertsen* sank within sight of Krakatau.

Stumbling back down to camp, I passed carbonized tree trunks from a recent eruption and also a freshwater spring percolating from a lava spit that I thought might be useful if a rescue boat did not soon appear. The crew of the British naval ship the *Discovery* landed on Krakatau in February 1780 on their voyage home after Cook's death in Hawaii and reported finding a freshwater spring. It was a different mountain back then; every step I took was on ground sparked from nature's forge in the last thirty-five years.

Our makeshift camp was animated as its rock backdrop. It was steamy hot, and there were few diversions, so we all took to lounging. At noon, after a feast of peanut butter smeared over sourballs, I drifted off to sleep under a fig tree, but thirty minutes later I was brought back by the buzz of activity beachside: a rescue boat had appeared. At first the rescue crew surveyed the *Ernarosa* to see if there might be some way to pull it back to deep water and make repairs. But that salvation was quickly dismissed, and within an hour we were hoisting a lanteen sail over the new boat and heading back to Carita. The boat was a poor man's version of the *Ernarosa*, only narrower, shorter, older and nameless, but it was headed in the right direction. The captain sat high on a box at the stern and used his bare feet to work an ironwood rudder hanging in a plaited sisal sling, while a couple of prepubescent boys stoked a fire on the bow for tea and fish. I looked back over my shoulder, across a sea the color of a slug's tail, and watched as the pyramid of Rakata faded.

Back at the Carita Krakatau Beach Hotel, Dr. Ridder served up cold Bintangs (the Indonesian brew of choice), rubbed his Coke-bottle-bottom spectacles and fired questions about our brief maroon. I responded with a question about how he had figured the odds of our getting into trouble at the outset. It turned out he too had sacrificed a boat to the Krakatau trip, in his case a sleek inboard speedboat full of VIP travel agents that also broke down and that eventually washed up on a beach, making him no friends among the passengers. He had thus done, as he described it, empirical field research.

Voltaire said that while men argue, nature acts. And so it is with Krakatau, a spokesman for nature who speaks now in whispers and moves in mild ways, indulging the foibles of many, but who will someday rear back again and roar.

Climbing volcanoes is never a matter of conquest, as Krakatau keenly demonstrated. The success of a climb, the maintenance of health and of one's very existence is at the mountain's caprice. There is no way to humble nature's dissilient brat. You may visit its domain at your own invitation, but you leave only if it so wills.

As an exercise, Krakatau took the wind out of our sails, but it was a classroom quiz compared to the too-nearly-final exam we encountered as our next emprise: traversing Merapi, the 2511-meter-high "Fire Mountain," perhaps the world's most active killer volcano, in Central Java.

To get to Merapi George Fuller and I first took the first-class Parahiyangan train to the cool highlands city of Bandung, the capital of West Java and headquarters for the Volcanological Survey of Indonesia. Though the third largest city in Indonesia, it's known for its gardens and its decaying Art Deco architecture, as well as for its quinine factory, the world's largest. At the station, we could see a tangle of volcanic peaks to the north and south, a reminder that wherever one scans a horizon in Java one is likely to see a volcano.

We then boarded the "People's Train," the all-third-class Cepat, for the ten-hour trundle to the city of Yogyakarta, the site of the first great empire in mid Java, an empire that may have been obliterated by nearby Merapi. Along the way we witnessed from our open window all the fecundity that has made Java at once so agriculturally rich and so overcrowded. While volcanic ejecta in many parts of the world is acidic, in Java it is chemically basic, rich in soluble plant nutrients such as calcium, magnesium, nitrogen and phosphorus. For millennia this rich ash deposit has blanketed the island and turned it into a rioting garden. At the turn of the last century, Java was known as "the granary of the East." Ironically, the numbers of people packing the island in recent times have led to food shortages, and in 1983 the island was the largest importer of rice in the world.

It wasn't readily apparent as the old train clacked along that Java was a ten-man life raft carrying a load of a hundred. Most of what we saw was bucolic, gorgeously scenic, and was added evidence to the cases made for calling the place paradise. In fact, I could forgive the lurid descriptions and sensational superlatives used to portray the island. Indeed, I could second them. It was the monsoon, and the landscape seemed drunk with color, in a fertile, festive mood as though adorned for a gala. We passed lines of tall tamarind and *waringen* trees, areca palms fluttering as softly as ostrich plumes and blazing Madagascar flame trees in glorious blossom. Nude little apricot-colored boys astride smooth gray water buffalo wallowed in the ooze of the sawah (wet rice) paddies; the slim, bent figures of working women in conical hats made them look like ambulating toadstools. Veronese greens shot through with diffused sunlight hung over topaz-colored streams. The truncated pyramids of powder-blue volcanoes scratched the cerulean sky, looking like fine line engravings.

Our late-afternoon arrival in the sultanate of Yogyakarta (Yogya for short) left no time for cultural acclimatization. We were whisked by our Indonesian associates to the downtown offices of PACTO, the tour organizers, and as we entered we caught a glimpse of the cloud-diademed peak of Merapi, just twenty-five kilometers away.

Perhaps a quarter of a million people have died in volcanic eruptions and the aftermaths in Java in the past century. Devastation, death, ruined crops and subsequent famine are common on the island, which has more volcanoes than any other. Merapi holds the grim world record for fatal eruptions.

Every year Merapi stirs in some fashion. Sometimes it spews fiery clouds of gases into the air and overflows with streams of bubbling molten rock, driving wild pigs into the lower jungles, turning rivers miles away into cocoa-colored torrents and devastating lush tropical terrain. Other years, Merapi only shudders and settles down. Currently, the Volcanological Survey of Indonesia estimates, Merapi threatens two million

people. And it is overdue for a major eruption.

In 1006, Merapi delivered a paroxysm that decimated the Hindu kingdom of Mataram and buried the grand Buddhist temple of Borobudur, an edifice carved from the lava of previous Merapi eruptions. One of the world's greatest ancient monuments, Borobudur was the largest in Southeast Asia in its time. It was built sometime between 778 and 842 A.D., during the Sailendra Dynasty—three hundred years before Cambodia's Angkor Wat and four hundred years before work had begun on the great European cathedrals.

A major eruption in 1672 caused an estimated three thousand deaths. In more recent times, a 1954 explosion killed several hundred villagers, and in late 1973 another blast sent streams of hot water, mud and ash through villages and killed a score more. In 1979, without warning, Merapi let loose another load of magma in a spectacular show of pyroclastic fireworks and killed 149 people in the mountain village of Dieng, two thousand meters up the volcano's side. And in 1984 another eruption killed 200 people with a *nuee ardente* (glowing cloud), a three-hundred-kilometer-an-hour cloud of incandescent fragments and gas that roared down the mountain. Just days later there were ominous stirrings from the Balinese volcano Gunung Agung. To appease the gods, Indonesia's president Soeharto and his ministers took part in a ceremony at Bali in which eighty animals were sacrificed. Agung did not erupt.

On Java, where volcanology is an ancient art, there is a lore that helps deal with the brooding power of volcanoes, and there are as many rituals as eruptions. Near the "Prince of Volcanoes," Merapi, some peasants have the curious custom when they feel the first tremors of a quickening of running around shouting "We are alive! We are alive!" in a state of great agitation. This is because, according to local legend, the island of Java emerged from the ocean on the back of a turtle, which is eager to return to the water but may not do so while it continues to be inhabited by men. From time to time the terrapin tries to find out whether his time has come by shaking himself and causing an eruption; it is then most urgent to convince him that the islanders are still

Woman drying bamboo on the road to Merapi in Central Java. Although the killer volcano erupts almost every year, villagers still live along its middle flanks, where the volcanic soil is extremely fertile and there is room to farm on the most densely populated island on earth. (Richard Bangs)

very much alive, otherwise he will take the fatal plunge and drown them all. Other villagers believe that with the first fiery exhalations they must go toward the volcano rather than away. And they never point at a fire cloud, lest it come toward them. Many pray and offer sacrifices.

President Soeharto, a Moslem, has encouraged the acceptance of Javanese mystical beliefs as part of the nation's unique identity. And after his last reelection in 1987 he sought to restore *kerukunan*—a sense of harmony—to his divinely mandated rule, after it appeared to have been shaken by bad omens such as eruptions and earthquakes.

Against such odds, science can make little headway. The villagers at Kaliurang, at the base of Merapi, believe that by watching how the corn grows or the birds fly they can predict the volcano's temperament. Such beliefs are troublesome to volcanologists, whose scientific findings they challenge. On the other hand, the volcanologist cannot prove that the ceremonies do not work. "I even believe some of it myself," says a volcanologist at the Plawangan seismological station. "I talk to the mountain and I think he hears me."

With the support of the government, volcanologists have encouraged the people who live within the 200-square-kilometer designated "forbidden zone" around Merapi to leave. But people continue to live there, in spite of the high risk, because the volcanic soil is so rich and the climate so cool. When the mountain's utterances crack foundations of houses and topple trees, the villagers simply rebuild and replant. "The gods are happy now," says one young mother, who studies the petulant mountain every day because she believes the longevity of her young son depends on the blessings of Merapi.

Most of the mountains of Java are what volcanologists call "composite volcanoes": cone-shaped peaks of explosive material, as distinct from the broader, less geometrically shaped "effusive" volcanoes, such as those in Hawaii, that emit mainly lava, relatively slowly. Indonesia has seventy volcanologists monitoring Java's active volcanic tribe. Because of its frequent eruptions, Merapi is the most closely watched. There are six observation posts high on its slopes, and periodically volcanologists wearing asbestos suits lower themselves into the crater to take the temperature of water and gases inside. The rest of the time, they sit in tiny shacks equipped with seismographs and hand-cranked hotlines to headquarters in Yogyakarta, twenty-five kilometers down the slope. But, unless the needles swing wildly, no call goes out. Merapi is always rumbling.

Generally, the volcanologists have little to do with the villagers, who know quite well that when snakes come out of their holes and slither down the mountain Merapi will soon erupt. To propitiate it, villagers make rice offerings and toss tonics of herbs and spices into the crater to ease the spirit's stomach. They hold an annual feast around the crater, with shadow puppetry, trance dancing and drum beating. And, for extra measure, the hereditary sultan of the old city of Yogyakarta—God incarnate to his subjects—offers snippets of his fingernails and hair along with a ceremonial silk robe for his faithful to deposit each year on his birthday at a sacred stone near the mountain's summit.

Since its worst known explosion, the one in 1006, Merapi has been tamer, and some volcanologists believe that the mountain's continuous venting prevents it from blowing its top. But then most scientists thought Krakatau and Mount Saint Helens, too, were tame beasts. Recent research suggests that over the centuries every Javanese volcano attaining a height of more than thirty-five hundred meters has exploded in a massive, paroxysmal blast. At just a bit over twenty-five-hundred meters in height, Merapi has a ways to go, but it is growing.

"Merapi currently does not have the potential," says Johannes Matahelumual, who headed the Indonesian volcanologist corps for a decade. "Merapi is just temperamental."

This time of year—January, when the rains are heavy and frequent—volcanologists cannot see Merapi's peak through the gray skeins of mist that envelope its upper reaches. "You can only feel him," said one Indonesian scientist. "I have to trust my instruments and my instincts. You have to know the mountain. It is a living thing."

One man who breathes the same air as Merapi but who doesn't feel he ever really will know it is Daddy Gondosuwandanash, the PACTO branch manager who was organizing our little off-season expedition to Merapi's summit. Fearing for our safety, Daddy (as he literally was named) had recruited four Indonesians to accompany us: Taufik, the son of PACTO's head-office director and an avid outdoorsman; Gareng, a mountaineer from Jakarta; Susilo, a respected local climber; and Sandra, a twenty-three-year-old music major at the Yogya Art Institute who boasted, when I asked about experience, that he had been up Merapi "countless times." Of our Indonesian partners only Taufik spoke fluent English, and George and I were sorry students of Bahasa.

Our plan was to hike up Merapi from Selo, a village on its northern flank, and then traverse the summit caldera and descend to the southern-side village of Kinahrejo, where Daddy would shuttle around and meet us with his van. With a midnight start, we hoped to arrive at the summit for a dawn view and then head down for an early-afternoon arrival in Kinahrejo. If all went as planned, after a long day we would be back at the hotel in Yogyakarta for cocktails and a scheduled hotel-lobby gamelan performance.

We bumped to the end of the road in Selo around nine at night, and as there were no commercial lodgings we arranged to catch a few hours' sleep on the floor of the home of the Kepala Desa, the head of the village. Around eleven the Indonesians started to stir, but it was pouring rain, and I was tired and shivering with the cold, so I made the excuse that we couldn't leave in such conditions as it would ruin my camera. That stole another hour's sleep, until the rain let up some, at midnight. The Indonesians insisted we get going, or we would miss the crowning dawn. I loaded a roll of film in my camera, checked my flashlight, pulled on my poncho and stepped outside into a chilling drizzle. Before we headed up the trail Daddy called together the six hikers for a moment of silent prayer, a special supplication to the gods of Merapi, and then handed a walkie-talkie to Taufik, our only bilingual, and told me to be sure we called the van every hour on the hour. He handed a first-aid kit to Gareng and a map and some extra food supplies to Susilo.

The trail was wet and slippery, switchbacking upward through a tangle of ferns, lianas, epiphytes and cassias. It seemed for every ten steps I'd slide back two. Sandra had quickly taken the lead, hiking with an elastic gait and the free carriage of the head that seems to be peculiar to people who spend much of their time in the mountains. I struggled to stay close behind Sandra's steps, and George trailed me by a few meters. Behind George—nobody. When we had been on the trail just thirty minutes we looked back to see no flashlights, and we heard no noise from the other three Indonesians. We stopped and called down the hill: no answer. Sandra indicated that we should stay put, and he bounded back down the trail in search of our missing party. George and I waited long minutes in the mizzly darkness, and finally Sandra reappeared,

alone, slogging back up the hill. He gestured that Taufik had fallen sick and that the others had taken him back to Selo.

That left three: one Indonesian, who spoke little English, and two *orang blandas*, white foreigners, who spoke less Indonesian. We now had no radio, no first aid, no map and only a snack's worth of food. We decided to go for it.

After a couple of hours we had lost the thin, overgrown, serpentine trail, and Sandra had us traversing the slope at a low angle that seemed to be taking us into a quagmire of rainforest. Looking up, I could see the silhouette of a ridge just a couple of hundred meters directly above us. "Sandra, let's go straight up," I pointed, but he didn't respond. George and I dutifully followed Sandra for another 20 minutes, but when we bogged down in the foliage I again beseeched a more direct route. Sandra shrugged, so I set out on a beeline for the ridge top, with George right behind. It wasn't easy; I had to bushwhack, using my arms as though they were machetes. But the progress was real, and after a quarter hour I pulled myself onto the ridge—and was hit by a convoy of winds that tried to knock me back down. I walked, above the tree line, balancing on a narrow ridge that dropped into unknown depths on two sides. George joined me a few minutes later, and not far behind was Sandra, who again took the lead. It was 3:30 A.M., and we negotiated the ridge with our bodies bent low to the ground to avoid being blown off. The wind was gothic, brutal, and got worse as we got higher. Finally, Sandra called time out and had us seek shelter a few meters down off the ridge behind a protective boulder, where we would wait until daybreak.

Using their ponchos as one-man tents, somehow George and Sandra managed to catch some sleep behind the boulder. I could hear their snores. But I was too cold for sleep. I spent forty-five minutes doing jumping jacks, waiting for that first blush of daylight.

It came, around 4:30, but it wasn't the day we had hoped for. There was no effulgent light and overpowering magnificence of color. Instead, first light produced a thick, cold fog that wrapped around me like a wet sarong. Visibility

was about one meter. For all I could tell, I was swimming underwater in a colossal cup of chilled cream soup, the most distinct sight being the blurred fingers of my extended hand.

I rousted Sandra and George from their naps and insisted we get moving. Sandra packed away his flashlight and again took the lead, as we continued to zigzag up the meager ridge and then onto the upper cone for Merapi's final pitch.

The scree slope was steep, a more than 35 percent grade, and the lava rocks loose and sharp, so we had to crawl on the final assault. We forged a chevron route, winding between hissing vents of steam, sulfur pots and car-sized rocks poised to roll. The higher we got, the deeper into Hell we seemed to descend. Then, after a diagonal detour around an overhanging cliff, I stepped onto a basaltic bench and reached up to nothingness. There was no place higher to go. We were astride the caldera rim, 2911 meters above the sea, 200 meters above a Dantean crater we couldn't see. We were on the edge of the world's most dangerous volcano, and, even though enshrouded by a mother-of-pearl haze, it was a heady moment. It felt like those juvenile moments when, on a dare, we'd run across a long, high railroad bridge with the distant rumblings of an approaching train at our backs. To mix some appropriate metaphors, we were standing on a barrel of gunpower, playing with fire and marching up the cannon's mouth. We were defying Merapi and gambling on being allowed to get away with it, even though Merapi held all the cards.

It was about 7:30, and we took a few minutes to pose for our version of classic Himalayan summit shots, arms raised in victory, eight-thousand-meter peaks shimmering in the background. Except our version replaced the peaks with London pea soup and the ice axe with a flashlight.

The wind was still whipping, however, and sulfur fumes were now stinging our nostrils, so it was time to continue our trek. The intended route was to cross the lip of the caldera north to south, through a field of fumaroles, to a point where we would descend to Kinahrejo. But as we tried to navigate through the smoke and steam we found ourselves engulfed by a miasmic gas and had to retreat, retching. Sandra tried several times to pierce this veil, but each time he fell back because of the noxious fumes. Frustrated, he led us back down the brow of the mountain about two hundred meters, and we tried a traverse that dead-ended at a sheer ravine created by a recent eruption. Sandra had us scramble back to the top for another try through the fumarole passage, but again, when we got into the thick of it, we were practically overcome. With throats seizing, eyes blinded, we stumbled back from the brink of asphyxiation. We had been told that last year a couple of young Frenchmen had tried this caldera-lip crossing, without a guide. They apparently passed out from the poison gases, fell into the crater oven, where the temperature is often more than two thousand degrees Fahrenheit, and were instantly cremated.

Not thrilled with the prospect of such an end, George and I pulled Sandra back from yet another try at the poison path. Sandra was becoming anxious, and next he led us down into the actual caldera as a route to the opposite side, but it too proved unfeasible when it simply became too steep. For an hour Sandra led us on a wild goose chase, up and down and all over the precipitous, muttering rim of Merapi. Finally, George lost his temper and yelled to Sandra that we had to give up and head back to Selo, even if Daddy would be waiting on the other side of the mountain. George's outburst only fueled Sandra's determination to find the passage, and he had taken off again into the sulfur haze when suddenly he broke through a layer of burnt-yellow crust and fell into a solfatara, a cauldron of bubbling mud. With a scream that could be understood in any language Sandra jumped back from his crucible, waving his arms as though in some danse macabre, and fell into my arms. He had second-degree burns on both his hands and above his shoe on his right foot.

I pulled out my spare pair of socks from my pocket and wrapped his hands. Even though

OPPOSITE: *Because of its frequent eruptions, the 2511-meter-high Merapi, or "Fire Mountain," is the most closely watched of Java's active volcanoes. (George Fuller)*

George was a medical doctor, we were helpless to do more without any first-aid supplies. We were woefully short of all supplies, but in fact the style of our little climbing adventure was inadvertently in keeping with climber Reinhold Messner's "fair means," the 1980s style of scaling peaks with no support—carrying just what can be carried on one's back. Our effort contrasted dramatically such earlier ascents as an 1836 collecting expedition by the Dutch naturalist Franz Wilhelm Junghuhn, who had on his equipment list a paper supply to dry collected plants, cases of writing and drafting materials, containers to store the plants, glass sheets to press them, hammers, a gun, tents, a barometer, thermometer, measuring tape, ten sacks of rice and other food supplies, fifteen flasks of *arak* (coconut-palm brandy, the local liquor of choice) and a supply of opium ample for the thirty porters. The lead guide, an old hermit with a long gray beard, refused to move unless fed the remedial opium.

Now Sandra seemed frozen in shock, and we had no supplies for reviving him. George used some bedside manner, talking cheerfully to Sandra in a tongue he couldn't understand but a tone he could. After a few minutes he came around and seemed ready to backtrack to the north side, back to Selo. George took the lead, and we stumbled along the caldera rim but then dropped off its side to the neck of the volcano, where the going seemed easier. We traced a line that dropped diagonally, calculating it would at some point intersect the path that descended to Selo, but the going was slow over the dreary lunar landscape. After a while we were crossing a steep gully created by a lava flow, tripping on the blue, metal-like shards of basalt and creating little avalanches. Midway we stopped for a respite and a draw of water.

As we sat down, for a fleeting moment the clouds cleared and a spectacular view spilled before our eyes. We could see down the gully, which soon turned to a full-bodied canyon, all the way down to the alluvial plains, where the glass of flooded rice fields reflected like a hundred black and silver mirrors, looking as warm and shining as tears of joy scattered upon the pristine earth. On the north wall of the canyon a palisade of towering, columnar basalt cliffs hung over an in-

viting passageway to what appeared to be a Garden of Eden compared to our immediate primeval setting. In fact, the original Garden of Eden may have been down this path, as the remains of Java man, the celebrated *pithecanthropus erectus* (no longer an ape yet not quite a man), were discovered in the lowlands on this side of Merapi in 1891. Probably a million years old, and one of the earliest known hominid fossils, Java man died out when today's Java was still an integral part of the Asian mainland.

As quickly as the clouds parted they shut their overcoat and locked us in gray. But now we had the impetus for a decision: to cross the gnarled gully and continue our traverse along this sawtoothed cowl back to the northern path we'd originally ascended or to head directly down this southeastern canyon to the Elysian fields below, from where we could walk or hitch to Kinahrejo, and perhaps even meet our schedule. If we elected the original Selo route we would end up on the wrong side of the mountain, in a village with no phone or transportation. At best, we would get ourselves to Daddy's waiting van several hours late. So we decided to try the untried route and headed down toward the canyon.

We didn't get far before our first incident. Sandra, still recovering from shock, was following us in a sort of *Night of the Living Dead* stiff trance, and he suddenly stopped and started to bellow and point. We scrambled back up to him, and he kept babbling something about a man on the other side of the gully we had to speak with. But there was nobody there. Sandra was hallucinating.

Again, George went to work with his talking cure. Within minutes Sandra was ambulatory and we were glissading down the lava-rubble slope into the canyon.

As we descended through the canyon it narrowed, and its walls vaulted into a mackerel sky. It was as though we were negotiating some spectacular, sinuous arroyo in Utah's canyonlands, replete with dry waterfalls every couple of hundred meters down which we had to climb, jamming hands into cracks and levering weight on small footholds in free-climbing maneuvers.

The sloping floor of the canyon was coated with a sheet of lava gravel, and at one point

George slipped and fell on his side, dislocating his shoulder. He shrieked and writhed in pain as I ran to help, but before I reached him he was able to pop it back. George and I exchanged glances. This was no place for an emergency. We'd been lucky.

As we proceeded, we found ourselves climbing down steeper and higher dry waterfalls, most of which provided a fissure, a runnel, a pleat of rock or an overhanging crag that allowed a relatively easy descent. But one ten-meter cascade had too much exposure for my taste, and I demurred as Sandra took the challenge. Sandra was an excellent climber, and he rallied whenever a rock gauntlet was tossed in our path. On this occasion, he bargained his way down a hair crack with ease. George followed and almost fell. I was unwilling to take the chance, so I went upstairs, into the jungle that had emerged on the rim. This may not have been the better route, as the rainforest was so thick I had to do a desperate breaststroke through a curtain of creepers for half a kilometer before I found an entry back to the canyon. Joining the others, I checked my pocket and found my flashlight had been pulled out by some jungle claw or vine. Not to worry, I thought. We'd be back to electric lights by nightfall.

We didn't travel far, however, before we came to another impasse, this one a fifteen-meter cliff broken by a two-tiered flume of polished rock that ended at the brink of another ten-meter fall. The flume looked like a kiddy slide at an amusement park, only with radical consequences if you didn't stop in time. Sandra again volunteered to go first, and he careened down as smoothly as though the slide were in his own backyard. I positioned myself to go next but insisted Sandra brace himself at the slide's end to arrest my fall, as my body weight was almost twice Sandra's, and I was afraid with the added mass the extra momentum would pitch me over the second cliff. Sure enough, I careened down the slide out of control and smacked into Sandra at the bottom, almost knocking him off the edge. With a sigh of relief, I moved out of the way as George lined up next, then barreled down like a runaway truck. Halfway, George stuck out his arm to slow his descent and twisted his upper body, which

again dislocated his shoulder. His face contorted in pain, George crashed into Sandra and teetered on the brink of the vertical drop. George screamed a scream that echoed up and down the canyon, then convulsed, trying to reach across his chest and reset his shoulder. He and Sandra squirmed on the very edge of the drop, George out of control, Sandra trying to find a handhold. I reached into the welter to help George but couldn't get a purchase on his palsied shoulder. His eyes flitted to the top of his head, and it seemed he was about to pass out. I looked back up the slide, but there was no way back; we had committed ourselves to the canyon by sliding down the flume. The walls were sheer, and we could only continue down the canyon to the exit, if indeed there was an exit.

We were ill prepared—without backup or the correct equipment. It reminded me how obvious had seemed the error in an account I had read a few months before of the descent of another volcano, Oregon's Mount Hood. Seven students and two adults had died while on a day trip when they were hit with an unseasonal snow storm and were without the proper gear. Now we were in a situation hauntingly similar. And as if to mock my thoughts it started to rain. I could see we were in a flash-flood canyon; if Merapi so willed, it could wipe us out, without a trace, within minutes.

As Sandra and I struggled with George on the edge of the cliff, there was a pistol-type "pop," and George collapsed in release. The shoulder was reset.

With George back in action, we started working our way down this soulless chasm again, now torn between the merits of a slow, cautious descent and a quick attempt at escape to outrun a possible flash flood.

But the rain let up, and the clouds pulled back again to let us view the valley; only this time it was a disappointment, as the jade-green paddies looked no closer than at our first glimpse, and it was now 3:30 in the afternoon. We had no choice but to continue.

The gorge pinched, got narrower and narrower, this rabbit hole curiouser and curiouser. Then around 4:00 we hit the hiker's nightmare: a twenty-meter pitch into darkness, a plunge

simple and sheer that cut across the canyon floor. There were no nubbins, no toe holds, no cracks or crannies. The walls on either side stretched five hundred meters up into the sides of green peaks, minivolcanoes growing like pimples on Merapi's chin, and we were trapped in a deep scar on the pocked face. Here we were smack in the middle of the most overpopulated piece of the planet, and we were utterly lost—not a soul in sight, not a trace of a human or his works in any direction.

As an expert mountaineer, Sandra refused to believe the finality of a dead end and scrambled back and forth at the lip, examining the rock, searching for some secret passageway. But after a thorough inspection, even he gave up.

The last possibility appeared, to the south, with another cloud diffusion. One side of the canyon tapered from our level upward for about a thousand meters to a tree-lined rim that looked like a saddle between two minor mountains. If we could whack up the side through the jungle to the rim, we might find a passage out of the canyon completely.

By now it was getting late. We were several hours behind schedule already and were certain Daddy was worried, perhaps even organizing a search party. George suggested we quit for the day—we'd been hiking for seventeen hours straight and were exhausted. But I was afraid of bivouacking; we were soaking wet, had no sleeping bags, nothing dry or warm to change into and we were still at the high elevation. I was afraid that if we stopped we'd freeze to death.

So we continued, bulldozing through the vines, slowly working our way up the cliff face. It was getting dark, and in fact we were working our way up to a higher elevation, where conditions would be worse if we had to crash for the night. And the going was painfully slow—only a few meters in a good minute. At this rate, it would take days to cross over the ridge and make it down to the rice paddies.

By default I was the trailblazer in this absurd exercise, trying to thrash a semblance of a path through the snarled, daedal jungle. It was exhausting work for an already fatigued body, and I felt I was about to drop, when I stepped onto a piece of packed earth and stopped. Wait a minute, I thought, this doesn't belong here. It was a path—a faint but very real trail. Not an animal trail, either. Looking closer I could see fresh machete marks, tiny swaths of white skin under the broken bark of overhanging twigs and branches. I even found the indentations of fresh footprints. At that moment, this hint of a trail looked to me like a turnpike, a superhighway headed off Merapi.

It turned out we had stumbled across a wood-collecting trail for a middle-elevation village. As we traced it up to the ridge we had no idea of its purpose, or destination, but we felt it could only lead us out of our predicament. The dark came with equatorial suddenness, and we were slogging along with just two flashlights between us. I now regretted not having gone back to find mine earlier in the day. At times we tripped off the path and slid down muddy slopes to canyon edges, only to have to crawl back up, Sisyphus-like, and search for the telltale machete marks.

We decided to break for a dinner of soggy bread and peach jam, with a few slugs of water. Sandra refused the food. His eyes glazed—he looked on the verge of collapse. I asked him if he wanted to call it a day, but he shook his head no; he wanted to keep going. I took the pack off his back to lighten his load, and we continued.

We kept trekking until ten, when, in the failing light of the flashlights, we lost the trail once again. We were mashing around a muddy slope looking for machete marks when a wave of exhaustion washed over me. "We gotta stop," I called out, and George didn't protest. We'd been been on the road nonstop for twenty-two hours. We had to rest.

I gestured to Sandra that, even though we were on a mean slope, we were going to stop and sleep. I thought he would be thankful, but he

PAGES 42–43: *The village of Probolinggo on the slopes of Tengger in East Java. The Tenggerese are an ethnic group of highland farmers. (Pamela Roberson)*

Tenggerese guide and his pony—upon which he takes tourists across the Sand Sea to the base of Mount Bromo—rest on the rim of the ancient Tengger caldera from which tourists begin their trek. (Andreas Bender)

launched into a tirade. His English improved 100 percent—he started screaming in full sentences that we couldn't stop. That his friend was waiting for him. That it was our fault we had led him down this canyon. That if he fell asleep we would abandon him. He seemed to be running amok. He rambled about how many times he had climbed Merapi, and nothing like this had ever happened. At first I tried to assure him things would be okay if we just caught some sleep, and that we would not abandon him, but as he continued his rantings I became too tired to argue and lay down in the mud at his feet and slept.

At first light I jumped up and slapped myself for warmth. I climbed back up the hill to look for the trail we'd lost last night, found a trail, fetched George and Sandra, and we followed my new trail to the edge of another cliff. Apologizing, I turned and headed back up the hill. Legendary for their emotional reserve, the Javanese are said to have a smile for every emotion. Sandra's long, smooth face was, at that moment, frowning. He clearly had lost trust in us, but he had few options.

An hour later George found the lost trail, which mysteriously headed back up the volcano but was a clear trail, and it seemed the only course to take. It was the correct course. The trail snaked up a series of interstitial canyons to points on the volcano where they could be crossed, then wound back down the other side, always moving in a southerly direction. We traversed a half-dozen small canyons in this fashion, sometimes intersecting with washes that invitingly headed straight downhill, and which enticed Sandra. When we said no to his appeals, Sandra would sneer and shake his head in disgust, then fall into line behind us.

Then, at around 8:00 A.M., we rounded a bend and met a family of four, including a man with a machete and his wife carrying a wood-collecting basket. We were almost home free. As we continued, the jungle gave way to *wils* grass and planted groves of sibilant pines and acacias, part of a government-sponsored program to reforest the devastated sections of the mountain's flanks with sturdy trees that would better resist the liquid fire of a lava flow.

Two and a half hours later I tripped over a rise and looked down on the characteristic *nipah*-thatched huts and red and brown terra-cotta roofs of Javanese village homes. We were on the road to Kinahrejo. At 3:00 P.M. we staggered up to a van that contained a shocked and relieved Daddy and the rest of our original climbing party, including a recovered Taufik. A corps of twenty search-and-rescuers Daddy had recruited swarmed around us, pumping our hands. They had spent the past twenty hours combing the mountain and had just returned with the conclusion that we were dead, poison-gas victims who fell into Merapi's maw.

There was cheer all around as we thanked all the rescuers for their efforts, around wedges of white bread and pasteurized cheese that we stuffed into our mouths in a burlesque of a Pan-

Looking into the steaming caldera of Bromo from its 2300-meter-high rim. During the annual Kesada festival, ritual sacrifices are made here in an attempt to appease the volcano's spirit. (Richard Bangs)

tagruelian feast. Sandra was smiling for the first time in a day and a half, and he even stole a few seconds from the celebration to give me a hug.

Then Taufik took me into a dark hut and introduced me to Marijan, the sixty-eight-year-old ambassador to the volcano spirit who is the latest in a lineage of guardians that dates back to the eighth century. According to legend, the king of Mataram, which was the region at Merapi's base, would ascend the volcano to meditate, and he hired a servant, Ki Jurumertani, to stay on the mountain and look after it in his absence. One day the servant ate a special egg left by the gods, and it turned him into a giant spirit that only the king could see. The king then gave the servant-spirit a special place on Merapi and appointed him the guardian of the volcano. The king hired a new servant to serve both him and the new spirit of Merapi, and for centuries the descendants of the second servant lived in this high village and oversaw all activity on Merapi, making sure the giant spirit was not unhappy with man's doings. Now, during every Javanese New Year, the believers who live in Yogya and in other towns and villages around Merapi come to Marijan and, with his blessings and supervision, make tributes to the Merapi spirit, with offerings of traditional dresses, yellow rice and vegetables. And they ask that in the next year the mountain be kind.

When Daddy had concluded we were lost he had gone to Marijan, who in turn asked the Merapi spirit to let us return safely. For this, I thanked Marijan profusely and left him a few thousand rupiah and the only extra clothing I had with me—the pair of socks.

As we boarded Daddy's van to head down to Yogya for a long rest, we turned and looked up to Merapi's summit. It was still wrapped in a shroud of shifting gray silklike clouds, looking as vaporous as a Japanese watercolor. I offered a nod of gratitude directly to the top.

Mount Bromo, located in East Java, is a major tourist attraction largely because of the volcano's accessibility. Just a two-hour drive southeast from Surabaya, Indonesia's second largest city, Bromo is a must-see for all residents and tourists in the area, like the Surabaya Zoo. It doesn't take a treacherous boat ride or a Herculean hike to get there. Every travel agency has coaches ready, and every day of the year scores of rubberneckers climb the 246 cement steps to Bromo's rim to stare into a bubbling gray pit, the entrails of the earth. However, one has to book months in advance to be one of the tens of thousands who attend the annual Kesada festival, which features a procession to Bromo's summit complete with candles and incense, chanted prayers, gamelan music and a ritual sacrifice of chickens and pigs. We had missed Kesada by three months, but the Bromo tour bus was packed full nonetheless. This was the party—and it was, relative to Krakatau and Merapi—that George Fuller and I joined.

Like untold millions before us, we left Surabaya after midnight and drove to the Tenggerese village of Probolinggo, arriving about 2:00 A.M. The Tenggerese are an ethnic group of highlands farmers with a history that traces back to the rule of the Hindu Majapahit Empire, when followers of Brahma worshiped on Bromo. From Probolinggo, visitors can either walk a paved path up to the rim or ride a pony. Feeling no shame—in more than a little pain, from shinsplints and broken toenails incurred in the Merapi ordeal—I chose the horse, and clop-clopped up the hill in the darkness.

At the rim we checked into the Bromo Permai Hotel, where a couple of dozen other tourists from half as many different countries were sitting around the restaurant sipping hot chocolate, tea and beer, babbling a polyglot and waiting for the magic sunrise. Over the loudspeakers Phil Collins, Stevie Wonder, Paul McCartney and a top-forty roster rocked us like no volcano had ever done. George checked out the bathroom and came back saying the tiny toilet closet was "too hard to squat in, and I didn't dare sit." After our last two volcanic experiences, this one seemed a sad parody.

But we went through the motions. At 4:45 we followed the crowd out into half-light and a filigree-fine drizzle and positioned ourselves on the rim of the huge ancient caldera, Tengger. As the dawn poured cups of milky light into the caldera, the twelve-kilometer-long "Sand Sea," a

Dawn on Mount Batok, the cone adjacent to Bromo. The classically shaped Batok rises in the middle of the Tengger caldera in East Java. (Pamela Roberson)

misty-olive and sere-gray surf of tussock and the shifting sands of a dried-out watercourse, shimmered and reflected light onto the glowering adjacent cones of Batok and Bromo. Though Bromo is the more famous, because it is active and continually venting thick plumes of steam, from a distance it is the less impressive of the two craters within Tengger's crater. Just a tad over 2300 meters above sea level, Bromo looks like a creature with its head cut off, a stunted dragon next to the full-figured, neatly seamed, classically shaped, towering Batok.

The story of the creation of Bromo, Batok and the Sand Sea is similar to other mountain-origin tales in Java, involving a princess, a prince and thwarted love memorialized. The princess in Bromo's case decreed that a great inland sea should be dug around the volcano's mouth. The

tool used was the hard half-shell of a coconut, which, flung away at the dawning hour, became Gunung Batok. (*Guning* means "mountain" universally in Indonesia; *Batok* means "coconut shell.") The broad, curved, iron-gray trench became the Sand Sea.

There is also the legend of the filial sacrifice. Kyai Dadaputih, ancestor of all the Tengger people, lived with his barren wife in abject poverty on a huge plain leading down to the sea, barely eking out a livelihood from the soil. The gods, from their seat on Gunung Mahameru, a huge volcano on the southern slopes of the Tengger massif, promised him children and an everlasting abundance of food, in the form of red and white onions, if he would sacrifice the youngest of his promised children in a crater in the sand field. Years passed, twenty-five children were born, and the new vegetables flourished, but Dadaputih and his spouse (sometimes identified as the princess of the Batok tale) were naturally reluctant to meet their side of the bargain; so the gods created a pestilence, killing many local villagers and threatening total catastrophe. Dadaputih had a vision reminding him of his debt, and he summoned all his children to ask who should be sacrificed. Only the youngest child, whose name was Kusuma, offered himself. His father took him down to the edge of the sand and left him there, on the fourteenth day of the tenth month, for the gods to claim. Immediately, a volcano erupted and Bromo was born. (One version of the story says that this son was plucked from the cauldron and taken to live with the gods.) Now, every year on the same day the Tenggerese, alongside thousands of spectators, climb Bromo and throw animal offerings into the crater to appease the spirit of the volcano and to honor the memory of the child Kusuma. And, like popular holidays the world over, it has become an event milked for its commercial potential.

There was no denying, despite the crowds, that the almond-blossom-pink sunrise over Bromo was special, and after breakfast we made the trek across the blistered wilderness of the Sand Sea to the mountain itself. I limped the whole way, still in convalescence, but was overwhelmed with the stark beauty of the tortured landscape, of this Salvador Dali–esque canvas of petrified minerals and the leftovers of titanic cataclysms.

From the railing at the rim top of Bromo I had two vastly different views. On one side I looked down into the wide, steaming funnel of Bromo's crater, where once the sacrifices regularly offered were human. White pillars of swiftly rising smoke cast a trembling purple shadow on both sides of the crater. Perhaps two hundred meters below, amber-colored, treacly bubbles angrily rose and fell, sizzling and hissing like reptiles in a snake pit. It was a sober, otherworldly sight, until I noticed the black scrawls of graffiti on the yellow rocks. Daring visitors had actually climbed into the crater and impiously painted their names in the middle of the cauldron, which was to some as sacred as any temple.

Turning the other way, I looked out to the outer rims of the greater volcano of which we were a small part—a blister, really—and saw a procession remarkably similar to that seen from the middle of Ngorongoro Crater in Tanzania, but with other than wildebeests and zebras. Instead it was a file of tourists, some on ponies rented for five dollars a ride, that streamed back and forth in seeming migration. From Krakatau, whose holocaust snuffed thousands of lives and to this day keeps the people away; to Merapi, a mountain in the middle, destined to destroy, which repels some but pulls others to its flanks; and finally to Bromo, which draws endless trails of thousands of tourists to its blistered lips, I felt we'd seen the energy spectrum of the volcanoes in Java. There is about them an awesome power of destruction, the virility of their soil contributions, the mana of their spirits, the moxie of their influence over a culture, and their beauty, a dangerous sublimity that at once attracts and repels.

Bromo, like Merapi and Krakatau and a hundred others throughout the island, imbues a sense of mortality on those who visit or live nearby, a correct feeling that the flame of terrestrial existence could be snuffed at any instant. And knowing this, being reminded incessantly by a volcano that looms behind one's back, allows a certain heightened appreciation of the specialness of the moment, of the beauty of life and of the potential destroyer itself. And it permits a peace of mind and an accord with Nature unavailable to those insulated from the forces of our fragile world. As the brazier pit of Bromo reverberated below me and I watched the cord of tourists crossing the Sand Sea, I felt a freedom from fear, a liberty in the untranquility of the volcano. There was an inexpressible vitality and exhilaration in all things—in the air, cool as well water; in the sparkle of the Sand Desert below; in the pungent smell of sulfur. I felt the blood tingling in my fingertips, my lungs filling with quickening air and my face awash in sunshine. I felt the keenness of life at that moment and loved it.

KALIMANTAN

Dancing with the Dayaks

WHILE war raged in Europe—the first war that reached global proportions and that would slaughter ten million people—a tribe of rainforest people on the equatorial island of Borneo was engaged in a contest of a similar nature. This contest was of a different caliber, however, and it had reached its apogee. Instead of howitzers and mustard gas they used blowpipes and machetes. Instead of taking dogtags and wedding rings from battle victims they took heads. This was the era when the headhunters—the Dayaks—were discovered by the civilized world, which was captivated by their grisly practice, featured them in headlines and dubbed them the "Wild Men of Borneo."

The third largest island in the world, Borneo has more land mass than California and Nevada fused, but in a steaming landscape—some seven hundred fifty thousand square kilometers of tangled trees, vines and creepers. And despite the twin juggernauts of bulldozer and chainsaw, the interior holds one of the last great stands of primary forest on the planet. With some twenty-five thousand species of flowering plants (all of Europe has fewer than six thousand; Africa about thirteen thousand), it is floristically the richest rainforest in the world. A remote and forbidding land whose impenetrability has preserved many of its mysteries from the leveling scrutiny of the outside world, Borneo even today conjures up vi-

sions of bloodthirsty savages, malarial and leech-infested swamps and explorers being swallowed up by the land or by the poison-dart-toting natives. The island is not-so-neatly divided among three nations, the results of the crude cuts of the colonialist penknife. The lower two-thirds of the island is Kalimantan ("Isle of Mangoes"), claimed by the Dutch in the seventeenth century and now part of Indonesia. The northern third, delineated by a watershed that slices through family and tribal groups, is further cut into the Malaysian states of Sarawak and Sabah, and a Liechtenstein of a country on the north coast is the independent but wildly oil rich sultanate of Brunei. To the north, the Philippines. To the south, Java, Bali and Lombok. While Sulawesi (formerly the Celebes) guards Borneo's eastern shore, Sumatra and the Malay Peninsula float off its western flank. It is the heart, if not the dark soul, of the Indonesian archipelago.

Viewed from the air, Borneo appears as a heaving sea of frozen dark-green billows, with feather-white streams tracing the faces of ridges and folds. Once the sparkling streams reach the flatlands they turn ocherous and meander like fat lines between the pieces of a jigsaw puzzle, finally losing identity among the sago palms and mangroves of the coastal swamps. No roads cross this expanse. A few feeble pink fingers crook from the coast toward the interior—temporary logging roads—but they fade to green toward the center. It can take weeks to trek from one village to the next, and it is impossible to travel in a straight line. Rivers are the natural, and often only, viable travel routes, and thus virtually all Borneo villages hang over a water highway, and the Dayak society is a riparian one.

The word *Dayak* is a generic term loosely denoting any of the more than two hundred tribal communities occupying the inland regions of Borneo. Some are the original inhabitants of the island. For centuries the Dayaks lived in splendid isolation in lowland regions, but when the Islamic Malays started to arrive on the coasts the Dayaks moved farther and farther inland, not wanting to become part of a religion that among other things prohibits the eating of their favorite food: pork. Today their numbers scratch the million mark, or so experts estimate, as a true census would be impossible—many Dayaks are still nomadic. In origin, they are of mainland Asian stock and have Mongol features, though they are believed to have migrated in waves, some centuries apart. Archaeologists have found Dayak remains dating back more than forty thousand years and have determined that in ancient times the tribes of Borneo ate the same foods and wore much the same ceremonial dress as they do today. In the neolithic period, or New Stone Age, when domesticators of plants and animals settled villages, migrants moving south from China brought with them artifacts and technology from the Chou Dynasty and the Sino-Vietnamese Dong-Son culture. From today's vantage, however, it seems to many anthropologists that the Dayak society has enjoyed a long, often sunny, sometimes cloudy day but that twilight has fallen, and soon a rich, complex, fantastic culture will be snuffed into darkness.

When Sir James Brooke—the nineteenth-century British adventurer who would claim northwest Borneo as his own, begetting a family dynasty that would rule for more than a century—first met the Dayaks, he wrote that "they are the most savage of tribes—and delight in head-hunting and pillage." Another English traveler, J. Dalton, who spent five months traveling with the Dayaks, summed it up succinctly in an 1831 essay in the *Singapore Journal*: "The most odious feature in their character is the propensity for cutting off heads."

The way some people collect baseball cards, not long ago the Dayaks collected heads. Heads were an integral part of the *adat* (traditional custom) needed for ceremonies, such as the building of a new community house and most rites of passage. They could ward off plague, increase fertility, ensure abundant harvests and keep evil spirits at bay. While the rest of Southeast Asia was suffering an exponential population boom, Borneo kept its population in check, in part because of *Koppensnellen*—Dutch for "head-hunting." When a Dayak wanted to marry, he had to show himself a hero before he could gain favor with his intended; and the more heads he obtained, the greater the pride and admiration with which he was regarded, not only by the bride but by the whole tribe. When a rajah (regional prince) died, heads had to be severed, as according to belief the victims served as slaves to the departed rajah in heaven. And whenever a male child was born heads had to be collected before the baby could be named. As that baby grew to pubescence, he was forbidden to associate with the opposite sex until he had been on a head-hunting expedition. And the most prized possession of a Dayak warrior, a damascene-bladed sword call the *mandau* (which, literally translated, means "head hunter") could not be worn until it had been washed in the blood of an enemy.

Head-hunting was originally a religious rite. The Dayaks believed a man's spirit continued to inhabit his skull after death. Whenever a family member passed away, the menfolk would go off on an expedition with the aim of catching and beheading someone from an enemy tribe. The head thus gained represented a restoral of vital energy, and its arrival in the village had the effect of an injection or transfusion. The bereaved family benefited by this new accession of strength

PAGE 50: *A Dayak warrior from Long Lebusan dressed in the full battle gear worn when forays were made to hunt human heads. (Richard Bangs)*

and was permitted to come out of mourning. The skull's power faded, however, as it became older, so fresh skulls were always needed. All this differed significantly from the ways of other so-called primitive cultures involved in head taking. In the days of Tecumseh, American Indians scalped their victims and kept the trophies taken in battle as great treasures. But the Indians did not make war primarily to secure scalps, which were merely the proof of conquest. For the Dayaks, the foremost purpose of battle in fact was not to kill; they made war mainly to secure heads. Taken heads were essential for the well-being of the community, requisite for ceremonies, necessary as oblations to certain spirits and obligatory for abiding by age-old, unquestioned customs. The Dayaks believed they needed heads as they needed food—to survive.

The heads themselves were treated like honored guests. In an effort to appease the ghosts of the decapitated, to erase grudges against the beheaders, the heads, after being drained of the brains and duly dried over a fire, were fed rice and meat; betel nut was stuffed into the cheeks; and sometimes a cigar was stuck between the pale lips. If the night were chilly, a fire would be stoked to keep the heads warm. Many acts of kindness were performed to make the spirit propitious, inducing it to show goodwill to the tribe of which it was now deemed a member. Later, the hair of the purloined head would be used to decorate the *kliaus*, gumwood battle shields, so that an enemy might think twice before striking the remains of one of his own.

In his 1902 account of an expedition to Borneo's interior, *The Home Life of Borneo Head-Hunters*, William Henry Furness related his asking a Dayak chief why such a horrible practice was pursued. The chief replied, "No! The custom is not horrible. It is an ancient custom, a good, beneficent custom, bequeathed to us by our fathers and our fathers' fathers; it brings us blessings, plentiful harvests, and keeps off sickness, and pains. Those who were once our enemies, hereby, become our guardians, our friends, our benefactors." The chief went on to recite the fable of an ancient chief, Tokong, who was advised by a frog to cut off the heads of his enemies. At first Tokong found this a very repulsive idea and did not heed the frog's advice. As a consequence, although Tokong's men were successful in battle, their village suffered badly from famine, disease and infertility. Finally he decided to obey the frog, and sure enough the crops in the fields underwent a miraculous growth, house shingles refurbished themselves, the people looked younger and healthier, babies were conceived, and, most remarkable of all, canoes would paddle themselves and rice pounders would work under their own power. The interesting point about the story is its emphasis on the fact that killing one's enemies was not enough. It was the acquisition of heads and not victory alone that offered mystical benefits.

Head-hunting survived well into the twentieth century, even lingered into the Atomic Age. Missionaries successfully converted most of the pagan Dayaks to Christianity; government punitive expeditions (often more savage than traditional Dayak head-hunting raids) and a series of tribal peace conferences brought the practice to an end. There was a last bastion of head-hunting, however, in the remote central highlands plateau, in the catchment of the Kayan River, where a tribe of Dayaks called the Kenyah eke out a self-sufficient existence. Ironically, it was a charismatic, visionary Kenyah chieftain who in the early part of this century took the bold initiative to defy generations of rigid custom and attempt to put an end to head-hunting, yet, decades after his death, his tribe was among the last to give it up. To the Kenyahs, this chieftain is their greatest hero, their George Washington, Abe Lincoln and Winston Churchill—with a pinch of Superman—rolled into one. Though the Kenyahs have no written history—only the stories passed on around the cookfires—their collective remembrance of Jalung Apui is strong, clear as rice wine. It is so clear they can act out the great moments of his life as though they were yesterday, even though the man died almost seventy years ago.

The estimated forty thousand Kenyah people of central and eastern Borneo, after centuries of static culture and unchallenged belief systems, mores and traditions, are in a state of rapid and accelerating transition. Like the tall stands of primary rainforest hardwoods that when felled cannot be replaced, the Dayak culture is being sawed off at the knees. After thousands of years of complex evolution, the Dayaks achieved a balance with their environment, became part of the natural ecology. Now, however, the harmony of that existence has been scotched by the outside world, and they've been forced to reorient their raison d'être. Most have given up loincloths, tattoos, cockfighting, gambling and alcohol; they attend church on Sundays, singing hymns in a language they don't understand; they've hung up their shields and spears and play volleyball, rugby and soccer; slavery is a thing of the past; they've renounced the spirits and idols that so long governed their lives. But they remember. They remember well.

I had the chance to witness a reenactment of the head-hunting days and of key moments in the life of Jalung Apui, the hero who dared to stem the tide of the practice that in its excesses was threatening to internally destroy his people. The missionaries would like to believe these memories have been buried, and in fact there is little trace of the head-hunting days in modern Dayak daily life. But, because of the urgings of a remarkable man, a group of Kenyahs reached into their past and pulled out moments they treasure, and they relished an opportunity to showcase their heritage.

The remarkable man is a thirty-two-year-old British expatriate, married to a Dayak Kenyah, who goes by the adopted Dayak name Taman Kahang. He was born in Ipswich, England, son of a steel buyer. He earned a bachelor's degree in geography and social anthropology, then took off to research the practical side of his discipline. He hitched and motorbiked around the world, picking up odd jobs, modeling, acting in a Hong Kong kung-fu film, peeling logs in Canada, working in a toilet-paper factory in Holland, hawking Chinese silk, teaching English, starting a book and roughnecking as a seismic surveyor in Africa for an oil exploration company. Along the way he went bankrupt, picked up dengue fever and came within a hair of dying. In 1983, on the advice of a friend, he bought a one-way ticket to Singapore, where he signed up as a seismic exploration field manager for Compagnie Générale

de Géophysique. The French concern sent him to Borneo.

Within weeks of his arrival, Taman Kahang met a pretty teenaged Dayak Kenyah girl, Anjang Alung (she likes to be called Farida, a common Moslem name more acceptable in the predominantly Islamic coastal region where she went to school). They were in the hamlet of Tanjung Manis, a lowland settlement of about 160 Lepo-Tau—a family group, or subtribe, of Kenyahs who had emigrated from the mother village, Long Uro, in 1970. *Long* simply means "river confluence," which is where many Dayak villages are situated. *Lepo-Tau* loosely translates as the "Sun Kingdom People." Taman Kahang was in Tanjung Manis doing field work; she was visiting relatives. They fell in love, and in January 1984 they married.

Taman Kahang and his bride moved to Samarinda, an old trading port on the Mahakam River in East Kalimantan that has boomed into a bustling timber town. While they were there, Farida's mother and father often came to visit, and Taman Kahang listened to their stories of the old ways of the Lepo-Tau and became intrigued. Farida's mother, Len Usat, still wears the brass rings dangling from stretched, foot-long ear lobes once considered de rigueur for the beauty of a woman and now virtually unknown among the young Dayaks. Farida's father, Panyang Alung, talked of the dances, the hunting expeditions, the music that were still a part of village life in Long Uro but which were moribund. Taman Kahang's curiosity was piqued, and when an opportunity arose to take one of the religious missions' flights into the interior to Long Uro, near the Sarawak border where Farida was born, he jumped at the chance.

Taman Kahang found the Lepo-Tau of the Apo Kayan—an area along the Kayan River— extraordinary people, proud, hospitable, hardworking, quick to laugh, ready to take him in as their own, wise to the ways of the rainforest, special. And he felt a special sympathy for their problems. One is a depletion of their numbers, especially their youth, who are needed to hunt and tend the rice paddies. They are being drawn to the coastal regions, where there are jobs,

Long Uro, a former head-hunting village on the Kayan River in central Borneo. It takes two months to trek from this village to the coast and back, so there is little commerce with the outside world. (Pamela Roberson)

money to be made, clothes to buy, exotic foods to taste and all the seductive lures of civilization. Farida and her parents had been ones to make such a migration. In Long Uro there is no reliable source of income, so none of the nectar of the outside world can be purchased. Neither was the government eager to see the Dayaks along the Malaysian border leave. Memory of the "Confrontation," the 1963 border skirmishes initiated by Indonesian president Soekarno in an attempt to unite all the Malay Archipelago under one flag, are still strong. The Malaysians, with much assistance from the British, beat back the invading Indonesians, but both sides were left with lingering suspicions that the worst was yet to come. The border has been relatively peaceful in the ensuing years, but the Indonesian government would like the Dayaks to remain in their plateau fastness to act as national security buffers in case another confrontation does arise.

The Indonesians weren't the first to utilize the Dayaks as buffers. Migration from the harsh existence of the highlands started a century earlier, as soon as foreigners penetrated the plateau and suggested that a different, perhaps better life existed beyond Dayak perimeters. When the Dutch occupied Kalimantan they realized the political and strategic importance of keeping the Dayaks along the wilderness border separating them from British-controlled Borneo. To induce the Dayaks to stay and serve as a buffer, the Dutch introduced a program to supply goods, basic commodities and some treats, to the Dayaks at considerably subsidized prices. Small quantities of salt, spices, soap, needles, thread, kerosene, fish hooks, clothing and tobacco were supplied gratis to the chiefs as narcotics. Even cattle were introduced. The plan worked, until the Japanese invasion of Borneo in World War II. The Dutch were expelled, all trade movement was prohibited, the cows died and the Dayaks were cut off from the supplies they had come to depend upon. They went cold turkey.

When the war ended and Indonesia achieved independence, the Dayaks were hopeful that the subsidized goods would again begin to flow. It never happened. The government coffers weren't as rich as Holland's and a free-enterprise climate left trading to the coastal businessmen, who made available the goods the Dayaks had come to want, but at now-inflated prices. A package of salt that costs thirty cents in the coastal towns goes for twenty times that, six dollars, in the Apo Kayan; a quart of kerosene costing fifteen cents in Samarinda goes for ninety in the upper Boh River region. Moreover, the highland Dayaks lack even seasonal income, as for example via an agent to sell their farm produce downriver (since harvests are readily available much closer to the eventual buyer). The human workforce drain has begun again, as ambitious Dayaks skip the village and head for the bright lights and the well-paying jobs in the oil fields and timber concessions. In 1958 there were around 1700 Lepo-Tau living in Long Uro; today there are 380. The dogs now outnumber the people.

The government has responded by prohibiting Dayak migration without formal approval, a bureaucratic process that makes immigrating to Albania seem easy. But the rules haven't made much difference. Those who want to leave just get up and go; there's nobody there to stop them and little incentive to stay. Many make the move for the sake of their children. Many who've made the move miss the traditional dances, music, culture and identity, but they wouldn't go back. Life is comparatively easy in the lowlands: trees are cut with chain saws, with one man accomplishing the work of ten who use machetes; rice is hulled by milling machines, rather than two-meter hand-plied ironwood pestles; washing water is warm; canoes are propelled by *ketint-ings*—long-tailed outboard motors—rather than paddles and sweat. There are hospitals, marketplaces and discos, the good life. Some Dayak emigrants dismiss their heritage. They're embarrassed by their head-hunting past. They refuse to speak to one another in their native Dayak tongue. They assume Moslem names, and they climb into the melting pot.

Taman Kahang's heart went out to his new in-laws and the Lepo-Tau, and he vowed to find a way to earn them the money they needed to keep their numbers strong, to survive, to preserve a culture on the brink. He noticed the skill of the Lepo-Tau wood carvers and admired the intricate craftsmanship of their art. So, in May 1985, he started "Dayaks—Exposition Craft Arts," and purchased a supply of their work at a locally high price, with the intent of selling it to tourists and collectors, then splitting the profits. Taman Kahang took a collection of two hundred carvings to Balikpapan, the oil capital on the coast, where he showed the work to the manager of the posh Hotel Benakutai. The art was admired but not sold. Next Taman Kahang flew to his native England and made the rounds, trying to sell the wooden figures and shields his Dayak friends and relatives had fashioned. No takers. So Taman Kahang decided to try another mechanism: tourism.

Unlike timber harvesting or oil extraction, tourism is an immediately renewable resource with comparatively little impact on the land. It can instill pride in the hosts and be a forum for issues that might otherwise remain esoteric. Tourists, often monied and influential, can become passionate about a cause they've experienced and commit to helping. It was the tourists the Sierra Club ran down the Colorado through the Grand Canyon who became the vocal critics of a proposed dam and successfully fought to defeat it. It was a tourist taking a home video of the famine in Ethiopia who got the word out and started a worldwide antihunger campaign.

In Sarawak, near the capital of Kuching, a Dayak village on the Skrang River was adapted to accommodate tourists and has achieved modest success, generating a good amount of capital for the villagers. Taman Kahang drafted a proposal for a similar living museum of the Dayak Kenyah Lepo-Tau. He proposed building a full-scale, twenty-family, traditional long house (*uma*) as a weekend tourist attraction at a newly designated forest reserve, Bukit Soeharto, outside coastal Balikpapan in Kalimantan. He envi-

Running the rapids of the upper Boh River. The Kenyah Dayaks are expert boatmen and can navigate their narrow prahus *through difficult whitewater, as they often do when hunting, fishing and visiting other villages. (Richard Bangs)*

sioned the emigrated Lepo-Tau members acting as official forest reserve rangers dressed in traditional hunting attire (loincloths, spears, blowpipies and woven bamboo headbands), stalking wild boar and deer in a fenced-off area. He pictured a wood-carving shop; a video room showing documentaries of the Dayak Kenyahs in their true environment; a zoo with orangutans, crocodiles, bears and snakes; and a restaurant serving natural jungle foods, Dayak coffee and sugar cane juice. And he proposed to supervise the project. But the proposal, to the local government, remained just that. Back to the drawing board.

On a subsequent visit to the Apo Kayan area, Taman Kahang was invited to travel with a hunting party on its way to a village that had spun off from Long Uro in 1959, Lebusan, a four-day journey trekking over a watershed and paddling *prahus* (solid tree-trunk dugouts) through the rapids of the upper Boh River. Taman Kahang was so impressed with the wilderness and guiding skills of the Lepo-Tau that he now proposed they team forces and start the "Dayak Overland Guide Service," a trekking company that could take adventurous tourists through the brutally beautiful Apo Kayan Plateau, into the razor-ridged Menyapa Mountain Range and down the cataracts of the spectacular Boh. The Lepo-Tau loved the idea of using their natural skills to generate hard currency, which in turn could perhaps persuade their young to stay. Taman Kahang printed up a flier announcing the new service, complete with day-by-day itineraries. He fea-

tured the fact that the tours would be guided entirely by the Dayaks. But no clients came. Taman Kahang took another trip to England, this time bringing Farida, and he stopped in at a British adventure-travel company. The owner wasn't interested, but she suggested that Taman Kahang contact me, as my company, Sobek, has a reputation for opening up new adventure destinations. I received a letter inviting me to join Taman Kahang on a trek through the Apo Kayan and Boh river regions, the homes of the Lepo-Tau, and I readily accepted. We scheduled the trip for late May, some six months hence.

In the meantime, the Lepo-Tau told Taman Kahang more of their folk hero, Jalung Apui, the man who instigated the abolition of head-hunting. During Jalung Apui's reign, head-hunting had degenerated from its former ritualistic status into the extremely gruesome and horrible compulsion to get heads at almost any cost. Where once only the heads of enemy warriors would qualify, by the end of the nineteenth century heads of children playing in the forest, heads of women gathering berries, even heads of dug-up corpses had all become acceptable. It was getting out of hand and threatened the existence of the Dayak Kenyah. The Lepo-Tau talked of two great remedial Peace Conferences presided over by Jalung Apui and the fantastic ceremonies that had accompanied them. Taman Kahang was curious and asked if they might reenact the ceremonies, perhaps for my visit. The *kepala kampung*, the chief of each of the two Lepo-Tau villages, Long Uro and the splinter village Long Lebusan, embraced the idea and decided to divide up the two famous Peace Conferences, each village reenacting one and its accompanying ceremonies. They even asked Taman Kahang to return in February for a dry run, which he did with video camera, capturing on tape the first attempt to rekindle what one chief called "the sad, black history" of the head-hunting era.

With photographer Pam Roberson I arrived at Sepinggan Airport in Balikpapan the last week in May, and was met by Taman Kahang. He proudly pointed out two ironwood pillars standing outside the airport VIP lounge, totems celebrating the abolition of head-hunting carved by Dayak Kenyah Lepo-Tau under a contract he helped arrange.

Our first experience in Borneo was a traffic jam, the 5:00 rush hour of Balikpapan. It took thirty minutes to get through town; then Taman Kahang drove us the 130 kilometers along the Russian-built highway north to Samarinda, past a panorama of bare trunks and branches, looking more like a New England landscape in early winter than the everlasting summer of the tropics. We were trundling through some of the eight million acres of forest incinerated in a 1983 fire that the government didn't acknowledge and somehow kept out of the world headlines. That was an amazing feat, since the smoke from the three-month-long fire forced the rescheduling of flights at Singapore's airport, across the South China Sea. The relatively unregulated logging industry had left the forest floor littered with tinder-dry wood chips and refuse, and that combined with a drought allowed a spark to ignite an area larger than Maryland and increase global deforestation for that year by 50 percent.

In Samarinda, Taman Kahang parked us at the Mesra Hotel, an overpriced, decaying property that once catered to the oil crowd but is now nearly empty. With the worldwide oil glut, many of the international operations have closed down.

After dinner, Taman Kahang took us to his home to watch videos of the dry run reenactment of the Peace Conferences and to meet his family. Taman Kahang has two sons, Stanley, a newborn, and Van, two, who doesn't yet speak—perhaps, Taman Kahang theorizes, because he's confused with so many languages spoken to him: Bahasa Indonesia by his peers; Dayak Kenyah by his mother; and English by his father, who is away for up to eighty days at a time with his current job as a drill supervisor in northern Sumatra. His wife, Farida, was there, not long back from London and looking as though she'd been properly outfitted at Harrod's. Also present was Farida's mother, Len Usat, who was impressively

OPPOSITE: *A Kenyah Dayak woman wearing the traditional copper rings on pierced, elongated lobes. This is a mark of beauty: the longer the lobes and the more rings attached, the more beautiful the woman. (Pamela Roberson)*

adorned with her full complement of fifty brass rings dangling from her pierced, elongated lobes. Len Usat's ears were perforated when she was thirteen, though many girls were started within days of birth. (Piercing is rarer among men.) At first, just wooden pegs were inserted, then small rings were attached to the perimeter. Gradually the number and size of the rings were increased and the lobe stretched, continuingly until it hung like a lasso. The longer the lobe and the more rings attached, the more beautiful the maiden, at least in the old days. Today, the custom has almost died in favor of the Western fashion of simple pierced ears with tiny earrings that seem almost a mockery of the original.

After watching Taman Kahang's fuzzy home video of some epic events, which made little sense to eyes that suffered jet lag, we retired early with hopes of catching a flight to the interior the next day. They remained hopes. The Merpati Airlines flight was cancelled because of weather, and no new one would be scheduled for several days as the following day was the last of Ramadan, and the Moslems of Samarinda would then be feasting, not working. "Nasi sudah menjad bubuk," Taman said, which translates to "the rice has already turned to porridge," a Dayak version of "no use crying over spilt milk." We were now late, and if we could not get to the highlands soon the actors in the play would return to their rice paddies.

We spent the day trying to line up a flight. The most likely source seemed to be Mission Aviation Fellowship (MAF), an alliance of different religious denominations that pool resources to serve the most obscure and dangerous airstrips in the world, mostly with single-engine Cessnas. They put us on the waiting list.

At noon the following day we received word from MAF that if we could gather everything together in thirty minutes they could squeeze in an unscheduled flight, at the unholy rate of $650. (The normal rate was $30 per person, and with Farida there would be four of us flying.) It was worth it, we felt, so as not to miss the reenactment. American Paul Lay, the pilot of the Cessna 185, has easily made a thousand flights under all conditions to the interior, yet he still got excited and pitched the plane into a steep circle as we

buzzed over two black hornbills, the huge fruit-eating birds prized by the Dayaks for their feathers and ivorylike beaks—and now an endangered species, something I felt we were about to become until Paul pulled out of his spin.

Late in the afternoon we landed at the year-old dirt strip of Long Ampung, on some maps called Muarajalan, just one degree, forty-two minutes north of the equator, a thousand meters high and steam-bath hot. Nobody was there to greet us. We were a day and a half late, and the welcoming party had given up on us. So Taman Kahang trotted the half mile to the village while we stayed behind with the gear.

In an hour a dozen small boys filed onto the strip, hoisted our heavy kits onto their backs, and marched down the trail, with Pam, Farida and me in tow. We crossed the Kayan River on a swinging bridge and passed a series of rice storage sheds on stilts (to keep out the rats) with metal padlocks on the doors (to keep out the human rats—a sign of the times and of location, being close to the air strip). Then we passed the three local churches—Protestant, Catholic and KINGMI, which is an Indonesian acronym for Gospel Tabernacle Christian Church of Indonesia. The missionaries are in keen competition here for a piece of a rich new-flock pie. And finally we came upon the main long house.

Literally a long house, it looks like a narrow warehouse on stilts, built without nails and triangularly roofed like a barn. It sits about fifteen feet off the ground to protect its residents from snakes, wild animals, flooding and, in the past, head-hunting parties, as the only access is by a notched ladderlike log that would be pulled up in the evenings. It also makes for a cooler residence than earthbound shelters. A long verandah, or gallery, runs the length of the 300-meter-long building, a thoroughfare where rice is pounded, mats woven, fishing nets repaired, rappats (leaderless, consensus-seeking communal meetings) are held and ceremonies performed. From the rafters of the porch trophy heads used to be hung like Christmas ornaments, but no longer. The government threatened to torch the long houses unless the collected heads were buried. Off the verandah are doors to separate family apartments called lamins, and inside, the floor planks, cut from giant dipterocarp trees, are covered with woven rattan mats and, in Long Ampung, linoleum strips.

The long house is a distinct Dayak tradition, but it, too, is threatened; the government has been building cheap Javanese-style single-family structures in most villages and urging the Dayaks to abandon the long houses in favor of Levittown. The official reason is sanitation and health. The government claims disease spreads faster in the communal situation, though some claim the opposite. British adventurer James Barclay, who for five months in 1978 took a *Stroll through Borneo* (and so named his book), witnessed villages that had relinquished the long houses and

> . . . found them very depressing places; it was also noticeable that many more children had skin diseases in these places than I had seen before. In abandoning the airy, big proportions of the Long Houses in favor of small, stuffy rooms, disease and germs had festered more successfully. No more general work together on the common verandah where gossip and toil could be shared throughout the day. Sense of possession was much more marked in these huts, and I noticed that they had padlocks on the doors against intruders.

Taman Kahang had another theory as to the government's campaign to eliminate long houses: Communism paranoia. The composition and order of a long house is naturally kibbutzlike, with shared responsibilities and benefits on an equal basis, and that is a bit too Marxian for a government that fended off a Chinese-sponsored Communist coup in 1965 and that maintains a fiercely anti-Communist attitude to this day.

Once in the long house we were ushered into a dark back room that turned out to be the chief's apartment. His name was Pemgbung, but Taman Kahang said most visitors call him Ping Pong. A father ten times over who chain-smoked and looked like a less-logical Mr. Spock with his hanging looped ears, he was seventy years old.

We exchanged pleasantries, and signed his newly started guest book (we were the second entry, the first in five months). Then we accepted a wad of glutinous boiled rice served wrapped in banana leaves, and some sweet pineapples, and begged an early retirement, as Pam and I still had a bit of jet lag. But Taman Kahang stayed up most of the night haggling with Ping Pong over the price of porters to carry our gear to Long Uro. When last Taman Kahang was here the price was $1.80 per person for the four-hour trek; but now they wanted $3.00 each. A Swiss tour group taking advantage of the new air strip had offered the higher price, and now the young porters refused to work for less. And, to add fuel to the fire, they presented Taman Kahang with a bill for the food we had eaten. In the not-so-old days guests could stop in and expect unbridled hospitality, including meals, but the Swiss group had offered inflated prices for the food presented, and that turned heads around. Taman Kahang, who is a sincere advocate of an improved Dayak economy, was disturbed by the precedent of short-sighted greed and pleaded that we were not tourists—our mission was of a higher nature, and they should take that into account. But the Dayaks refused to lower their price. It looked like a standoff. Then Panyang Alung, Taman Kahang's fifty-year-old father-in-law, walked in from Long Uro and volunteered to help carry the gear. Ping Pong also offered to help, and a couple of the village girls said they would pitch in for the old price. So, with a makeshift army of volunteers, we filed out of Long Ampung, leaving the young men behind with empty pockets but a certain pride intact.

It was a hot hike. The humidity squeezed like the rank coils of an unseen snake, pressing the good air from our lungs. I had a touch of diarrhea, and after I had ducked behind a bush for the third time Panyang Alung plucked some berries he called *siap bahii* and urged me to swallow them. Almost immediately I was sealed up, back on the track. We passed a cave painted with intricate curvilinear designs of birds and spirits, which Panyang Alung said was where heads were often lopped, and he did a mock demonstration with his *parang* (a home-forged, iron-bladed machete) against Pam's neck. We crossed three precarious bridges before stepping past a partial clearing where the original highlands mission was established in 1932. The American missionaries there had failed to convert the majority of the animist Kenyah at Long Uro, so they moved upriver, cleared a new site, built a new church and took their few converts with them. That outpost prospered to become Lidung Payau, thirty minutes' walk away, and eventually Christianity spread back and took over Long Uro as well.

As we were about to cross the final suspension bridge spanning the Kayan River a delegate from Long Uro ran over and implored us to wait. The welcoming procession wasn't yet ready. Minutes later they gave us the cue, and we stepped over the swinging bridge, through a cloud of black smoke from a welcoming fire and up to a procession line of the entire village. The women were spectacularly outfitted in brilliant gold and silver embroidered *kain songkets*, while the men wore their ordinary clothes. One had a polyester T-shirt that said "Bull-Shirt," while a one-legged man dubiously announced on his outerwear he was a member of the "Oregon Jogging Club"; such were the articles donated by the missionaries in an effort to evolve the habit from the traditional natural-fiber wear from the forest.

Pam and I worked the procession like politicians at a fund-raiser, pumping hands with every village member, even the babies, though neither side of the shaking wrists could communicate beyond blissful grins and vigorous head nods. Once at the end of the line we were led into another long house, this one more spartan than Long Ampung's, and over pineapple slices and bananas we were introduced to Peding Bid, the grandson of the famous Jalung Apui. Peding Bid, who walked with a limp, was an old and ailing man, but he was happy to see us, happy to know there would be a celebration of his celebrated grandfather. Peding Bid sat us down and over weak tea asked if we had any questions. Naturally, because of Taman Kahang's concerns, I wanted to know about the economy. There was little, Peding Bid explained. It would take up to two months to trek to the coast and back, and all they could sell to the Chinese merchants there was *pulut*, a sap from a local tree used for glue; *bezoar* stones, gallstones from monkeys that the Chinese believe have great medicinal properties; and the "ivory" from the hornbill's horn. The Dayak pay no taxes, and the government supplies no funds for schools, books or medicine and recognizes no

representation. The nearest radio and the nearest clinic are at Long Nawang, a full day's journey downriver.

Glancing around the long house left little doubt of the austerity of Long Uro. Except for two posters, one of Jesus, the other a cheesecake calendar for a Jakarta food company, nothing adorned the walls. The room was uncluttered, containing only an ancient Standard-brand sewing machine, a row of large, dragon-design Ming Dynasty storage vessels called *tempayans*, some brass gongs, a single-shot rifle and a white sheet that hung over a wooden frame bed. There were no tables, no chairs, no furniture of any kind. This in the middle of an island that has been called the Saudi Arabia of Southeast Asia, the greatest oil depot east of Iran. Brunei, on the north coast, distributes its oil revenue among its people, and it has one of the highest per capita incomes in the world. The joke goes, when a Brunei citizen runs out of gas, he buys a new car. But in Kalimantan, less than eighty kilometers away on the same island, the per capita income is among the world's leanest. In Kalimantan the oil monies flow to Java and to the multinational oil companies. If it stayed within the borders, the Dayaks would be flush. As we sat on the floor and traded curious looks, Taman Kahang pulled out some packages of tomato, carrot and onion seeds and handed them to our hosts. Although in Dayak there is no word for "thank you," it was clear they were overwhelmed with gratitude. They felt rich.

Long Uro was about a hundred fifty years old, ancient by Dayak Kenyah standards. Few villages make it to the century mark. The reason: swidden agriculture, which is the slash-and-burn or shifting-cultivation technique. The soil is poor in Borneo, and the nutrients are quickly leached out, leaving the ground fallow after a few plantings. This pushes the life-supporting fields farther back into the jungle every few years, and eventually there is no arable land within a reasonable distance and it's time to move. In Long Uro the nearest paddies are ninety minutes' walk away. Thirty years ago the fields were much closer, but the elders knew they were running out of time, so that was when several families packed up and moved south to the fecund banks of the

Boh River and started the offshoot Lepo-Tau village of Long Lebusan.

After a dinner of venison from a freshly killed mouse deer, it was announced there would be an evening of celebratory dancing on the long-house gallery. This is the common form of entertainment among Dayaks, like going to the opera, a concert or the movies for much of the world. At the appointed hour the entire village gathered on the floor of the verandah. From the rafters hung a *keluri*, a dried gourd shaped like a chemical retort with a hundred cigarettes projecting in a bundle from its bulb. These were peace smokes, which would be toked by the tribal chiefs in the Peace Conference later. Two men sat near the front and proceeded to play high-pitched, rattan-stringed, lutelike instruments called *sambes* in a tune that sounded like "Dueling Banjos." A

group of dancers emerged from one of the apartments and performed an elegant sun dance called Nari Preng, swaying their bodies like rice blowing in the wind. Two men, adorned in traditional battle gear, next performed Kancet Pepatai, a pas-de-deux warrior dance that in earlier times was performed before a head-hunting expedition. The men wore war helmets, woven rattan caps set with black and yellow and crimson beads and topped with six long black and white plumes from the tail of the helmeted hornbill. War coats made from the skin of the largest cat in Borneo, the clouded leopard, were worn like jerkins, taken heads placed through openings in the front of the skin. Armbands and leglets of rattan cords pinched their bamboo-colored skin. Around their waists, slung on rattan belts and sheathed in silver scabbards, were *parangs* to outshine all

Women from Long Uro perform the rice planting dance to frighten away any evil spirits that might inhibit the harvest. (Richard Bangs)

A Dayak woman performs the Enggang feather dance, one that simulates the flight of the hornbill (enggang), symbol of peace and unity. (Richard Bangs)

other *parangs*, with hilts intricately carved in horn from the antlers of the *kijang*, the Borneo barking deer. In their left hands they held elongated diamond-shaped cork-wood shields, from the center of which a huge mask regarded us implacably, its eyes red, its teeth the painted tusks of wild boar. Thick black tufts of hair hung in neat lines down either edge and across the top and bottom, tufts of hair that, in another time, would have been taken from the scalps of heads cut off in battle.

The dance began with a bow to the audience. Then the men bent and turned slowly to the rhythm, wheeling like predators, then facing each other like coiled snakes. The tinkling music grew urgent and was suddenly pierced with savage screams. The men took long strides toward one another, stomping their feet with great force.

Then, with whiplike movements, they leapt violently toward one another, weaving, dodging, lunging and striking as though cutting heads like corn. Then all at once it was over, and the crowd cheered and clapped.

Next, the women danced the Enggang feather dance, one that simulates the flight of the hornbill, the enggang bird, the Kenyah symbol of peace and unity. The dance was simple yet expressive, dignified but provocative, a delicate poem of subtle arm movements, genteel turns and graceful swoops, a ballet full of politeness. It was deliciously fragile after the violence of the men. With small, flowing movements of their wrists and fingers, all in synchrony, their arms rippling, their supple bodies undulating slightly, they appeared as leisurely birds in flight. It was a refined and elevated art, coming from one of the most remote villages on the planet. It reminded me of a scene from the Roland Joffe film *The Mission* in which an eighteenth-century Jesuit father, in trying to convince a papal emissary that the South American Guarani Indians are more than savage heathens and deserve to have their mission preserved, has a group of naked boys perform a lyric cantata chorus with a soprano that is so clean, so celestially beautiful, that it would appear no further argument as to the elevated humanity of these people need ever be proffered.

But, as in the film, those in power are not always persuaded by talent and art, especially if performed in an incongruous milieu. James Barclay dug up a letter written by a missionary in 1930 who had witnessed the same Dayak dance: "This dance is something that will be cast off very quickly once the light of the Gospel penetrates the Dayak heart . . . the rhythm and grace of these dances is undeniable, and yet they too will vanish with other heathen customs when the Lord Jesus comes into their lives." Thank God, to date, though Christianity has come to the Dayaks, the dances survive.

To bring a climax to the evening's show, one of the women dancers, a fine-featured, aristocratic-looking lady, approached Pam, took her hand and led her back into the *lamin*. Minutes later Pam emerged fully dressed in the spangled Kenyah costume, with a tuft of hornbill feathers attached to her hands, fixed like open fans. The *sambe* players immediately struck up a lilting tune. The corner of Pam's mouth twitched in nervousness as she bowed to the audience from the proscenium, but the music was hypnotic, and she was soon swept up in her own dance, mesmerizing the crowd as well. She danced with tremulous majesty, a slow, yearning, graceful dance, the long fan feathers sweeping over her body in alternating curves. When she finished, the whole village broke into an ascending chant of appreciation, called "Le-Maluck," which is similar to a standing ovation when a performer does something extra special. And Peding Bid, the grandson of Jalung Apui, hung a tightly beaded necklace with a pendant of two metallic imitation pig's tusks around her neck. Then the aristocratic, high-cheekboned woman, with the

dignified air of the Queen Mother bestowing a knighthood, stepped to Pam and pressed another necklace of appreciation into her palm. With her personal interpretation of their art, Pam had touched the Dayaks of Long Uro.

I was then asked to follow in Pam's dance steps and was donned in battle gear, complete with *kliaus* (the battle shield), and *parang* (the sine qua non sword), and asked to dance to the same tune. I could never compete with Pam's elegance, so I did my Michael Jackson imitation (he needn't worry) and then pulled out a couple of sparklers I had purchased on an impulse from a Chinese merchant in Samarinda. I lit the sparklers with a Bic lighter and did my version of a flash dance, which frightened and wowed the big-eyed audience, who had never seen such a sight and were a bit worried I might light their long house on fire. But as the sparkler fizzled to its last spark the appreciative crowd broke into applause and hummed their ultimate tribute, the haunting Le-Maluck drone-chant.

As is custom for visitors, we slept on the long house floor, in a mosquito-net tent that we had brought from the U.S. and called our "short house." We drifted off to a chorus of cicadas ringing like some carillon of tiny but insistent bells and were awakened at dawn by a tremendous cacophony of roosters crowing, geckoes chickchacking, babies crying, women pounding rice in the large porch mortises and children running across the noisy floor planks. It's near impossible to tiptoe across a long house floor, and that is by design; the planks traditionally were laid loosely so head-hunting parties couldn't sneak up on a sleeping family. There are no more surreptitious head-hunting visitations, but the clattering floorboards persist today, one Dayak custom that unfortunately doesn't seem to be threatened.

The first order of a Dayak day is a bath and a bowel movement, both in the river. (Drinking water is collected upstream.) The men go naked to bathe but are careful to conceal their genitals with cupped hands. The young women are modest and keep their sarongs tied under the armpits as they bathe, but the old ones sit contentedly in the shallows, naked from the waist up, leathery and withered, hair screwed up in graying knots. As we trotted down to do our duties, we passed a conventional-looking outhouse off the path sitting in a mud pool, looking unused and out of place. In fact, Taman Kahang with his vision to help turn Long Uro into a tourist attraction had flown it up unassembled from the coast, and in his absence the Lepo-Tau had put it together but had placed it over the wrong medium. Its off-the-beaten-track site notwithstanding, there had been no tourists to employ the facility, and the villagers certainly preferred the alfresco circumstance of the river.

After a breakfast of pea soup and bamboo shoots mixed with rice, we were led to a path outside Long Uro, where the Lepo-Tau reenacted, for the first time since the real thing, a head-hunting raid. What they didn't show was the preparation that used to go into such a raid. Before going into battle, the Dayak Kenyah warriors were not allowed to have sexual intercourse for at least a week; they slept together in a special room apart from their women; and during the day they trained outside the village so they would not even see a female. Even their food, which was cut back to half-rations with just one cup of water a day for a minimum of seven days, was served to them by boys. On the actual day of battle they were not allowed to eat or drink anything. It was believed the Spartan practices would sharpen their awareness and increase their discipline during the actual attack.

In the play we witnessed, a group of Ibans, a rival Dayak tribe, was walking down the forest path to their fields and paused for a lunch break. Then from out of the bush on all sides the Kenyah Lepo-Tau ambushed the Ibans. Some of the attackers wore genuine battle gear, passed down from grandparents, consisting of vests fashioned from sun-bear pelts, hats with war feathers, and mother-of-pearl breastplates. Others, less fortunate in their inheritances, wore cardboard vests painted with feathers, kitchen colanders as breastplates, and Western-style shorts and T-shirts, one announcing the warrior was a "break-dancer." *Parangs* flashed, arms flailed, throats screamed and bodies fell. There was much parrying, feinting and dodging, and one Iban escaped in flight. It was all too real, with blood lust clearly etching the faces of the Lepo-Tau and fear coursing through the Ibans. After the last of the

Ibans was struck down, the victims, who collapsed with backs toward us, buried their heads in their chests, so that from our vantage it truly looked as though they had been decapitated.

When the dust of battle cleared, the Lepo-Tau picked up the bodies and started to carry them back toward the village. "Cut!" the director seemed to yell, a village elder watching the show from the sidelines. "It's all wrong. Take two." It appeared the Lepo-Tau had committed a grevious script error when they started to cart back the bodies, something that was never done in real head-hunting raids. So they started from the top and ran through the entire scene again, but this time, once the Ibans were dead, the Lepo-Tau pretended to bury them in shallow graves in the brush adjacent to the path. It was a take. Cut and wrap.

We next followed the victorious warriors as they paraded home after a long day hunting heads. As they climbed up onto the long house porch the women lined up, dressed in their finest, and congratulated their men folk with gong banging and singing. Then the men broke into games of celebration, including one in which rounded rocks and a huge gourd were bowled back and forth down the gallery planks amongst a riotous chorus. The rocks and gourd were supposed to be heads.

It was time for a respite. We sat down to a long prayer, one that precedes every Christianized Dayak meal, then supped on shredded wild boar with rice capped with bites of the posterior of a formerly flying insect so big that anywhere else it would have required a pilot's license. After a brief siesta, the villagers wanted to continue with their celebrations of the head-hunting era. With small bamboo sticks substituting for spears and wads of clay for rocks, they demonstrated how they would train young boys to prepare for a head-hunting expedition. An anonymous 1909 account in the *Sarawak Gazette* also declaimed how the young were prepped for the rigors of head-hunting:

Justly are the Dayaks called head-hunters, for during the whole of their life, from early youth till their death, all their thoughts are fixed on the hunting of heads. It is the first thing for the Dayak grandmother to teach her grandchildren—it is the last thought of the dying Dayak. The child, unable to speak, scarcely able to walk, is addressed by his grandmother in the following way: "Listen well, my rice, my rice-basket, we put all our confidence in you, for you have to avenge us. For the head of your grandfather or some other member of your family is hanging somewhere over the fireplace, and you have to avenge us. Let us not confide in you in vain, let it not be in vain that we educate you and carry you to the river to bathe; let us not have given you our milk in vain." This is the daily admonition the boy receives till at the age of fourteen or fifteen, he reaches manhood. Then comes the time for marriages, and this makes him go out for the first time for human heads. Of course, he wants to get a good wife, but he cannot unless he can show a human head to the women. And so it goes through the whole of his life; the women, in their cruelty and blood-thirstiness, are the cause of this head-hunting. At every festival the old skulls are taken from the fire-place, where they are preserved and smoked from generation to generation, and carried through the house by some women. A monotonous song is sung by the women in honor of the hero who cut off the head, and in derision of the poor victims whose skulls are carried round; and again and again and again the infernal chorus is heard: "Agi ngambi, agi ngambi" (bring us more heads).

A very affecting ceremony takes place when the heads come home for the first time. This ceremony has to be performed before the sun has reached its zenith. The whole house is decorated, mats are spread, and as a substitute for flags they hang blankets from the roof. Suddenly a war-whoop is raised in front of the house, and the warriors approach to the bottom of the ladder. Then mats are spread, and they sit down whilst the women sing the nimang (an epic song) in honor of the heroes. This song alone makes such a tremendous impression on some young men that they forthwith descend into their boats to go for the purpose of capturing another human head; others get furious, slashing at trees and other things, and in the utmost frenzy. Then the men ascend the ladder and go to the verandah of the house. There a pig, just butchered, lies in a pool of blood; every man steps in this blood, and then onto a certain stone, ready for the occasion. This means health and long life for them, for the antu (spirit) of the victim is supposed to follow them. After that the women take possession of the fresh head and start at once their horrible dance with it. I have seen them myself with heads, dripping with blood, and exhaling an awful stench; with devilish joy they were taken by the dancing women, who in their rage—for they get enraged over it—bit the head and licked it, whilst they were dancing through the house like mad women. Horrible! A special kind of food is prepared to feed the heads; they fill the mouth, nose, ears, and eyes with rice, and dancing they express the wish that it will enjoy its food. At last, exhausted with dancing and yelling, they roast the head above the fire, till the smell becomes intolerable, even for the women. For seven days and seven nights the feasting goes on, and during this time nobody is allowed to sleep, especially the night, and this is always kept up very strictly.

Fresh heads were integral to good harvests, but other now-defunct rituals were equally important, and the Lepo-Tau tried to bring them back. They performed a stick dance, wherein they pounded planting poles on the floor, symbolically striking the birds and diseases that might otherwise destroy a crop. And they planted bamboo stalks flayed at the top, where raw eggs were placed, offerings to the Kenyah goddess Bungan Malan who has a fondness for chicken embryos.

At last it was time for the main act: the life and times of Jalung Apui. The year was approximately 1890, though nobody knows for sure as no records were kept, birthdays were not observed and the Dayaks were not on the Gregorian calendar, nor any calendar for that matter. The chief of the Dayak Kenyah Lepo-Tau was a great man (some say he was 240 centimeters tall), handsome and magnetic. He was recognized as the first and only king of all the Kenyah peoples. Jalung Apui was disturbed, however, with the anarchical atmosphere reinless head-hunting was creating. Heads were taken indiscriminately, and everyone lived in fear. He wanted to do something about it.

Then one night Jalung Apui had a dream. A black ghost named Jelimpam visited him and assured him his instincts were correct about head-hunting and that together they could abolish the hideous practice. Jalung Apui awoke and found a black stone inside a hanging basket near his head, left by Jelimpam. He fashioned it into an armband and wore it through his remaining

years. After his death, Jalung Apui's son wore it as an amulet, and after the son's death, Peding Bid, the grandson, wore it as a belt buckle, so that the missionaries wouldn't recognize it as a non-Christian spiritual symbol (in Jalung Apui's time human kneecaps were often used as belt buckles). In 1961, a Coastal Malaysian trader slept next to Peding Bid and had a powerful dream about a black snake. Suspecting the black stone might have something to do with the dream, the trader offered to barter a bolt of cloth for the talisman. Peding Bid hastily agreed to the trade and soon afterward found himself inexplicably paralyzed in one leg. And the Malay trader went on to become one of the richest merchants in Kuching.

The above act was performed by Peding Bid, the grandson playing his grandfather, and Jelimpam was played by a village elder, wearing a

Peding Bid, grandson of the Dayak folk hero Jalung Apui, who started the movement to end head-hunting, reenacts the seminal dream of his grandfather. (Pamela Roberson)

black garbage bag as the black ghost. At the end, Peding Bid told me his dream now was to reclaim his grandfather's sacred black stone, and every day he wondered if there might be some way to go to Kuching and fetch it back.

Next was the actual Peace Conference. In reality there were two, about twenty years apart. For reasons beyond me, we would be witnessing the second first. Perhaps because memories were stronger of the latter and Long Uro had first pick.

Before the review could begin the village had to kneel in prayer, asking God's permission to bring back their unholy time for the benefit of the visitors. Then it began in earnest with a procession of women slowly shuffling to the beat of a gong down the verandah of the long house, carrying a continuous length of chain at their sides. The chain symbolized their unity and linkage in the Peace Conference. I couldn't help but notice that the women, even the young ones, had the traditional looped earlobes hanging on their shoulders, and it wasn't until I looked closely that I could see these weren't flesh at all—rather, flesh-colored strands of rattan doing an excellent impression of ears from that era. Marching around a huge effigy of the enggang bird, the bird bigger than an eagle that doesn't eat meat, the symbol of peace, the women wrapped the chain around a Chinese jar and covered it with a gong. Inside the jar were the souls of all the Kenyah peoples, and the gong placed on top was a lid of protection.

Jalung Apui had persuaded the leaders of eighteen neighboring subtribes to attend this Peace Conference, a miraculous achievement considering the times. Each leader sat around Jalung Apui and took a sip of *tuak* (rice wine) as an oath of allegiance. Then, one after another, each leader rose and spoke passionately about the evils of head-hunting and stomped his foot to indicate he would do all in his power to crush it. After each speech, the crowd would show approval with its trademark ascending-staircase drone—Le-Maluck—with three downward notes at its end. Jalung Apui, draped with a necklace of tiger's teeth traded inland from Sumatra (there are no tigers in Borneo), watched the ceremony passively, without expression. When the last speech

was made, the gongs sounded, the leaders surrounded Jalung Apui, and together they cut off the head of a chicken, symbolizing the last head to be severed among them. They dripped the chicken's blood on a bamboo paintbrush and smeared the blood paint over Jalung Apui's body, the last blood to be spilled.

The blood was also a protective shield for Jalung Apui, as he next was carried in a sedan chair down to the river and carefully positioned under a thatched-palm-leaf awning in the middle of a *prahu* that would paddle him on a dangerous peace mission to the northern coast. As he departed, the village women lined up on the bank and gave him a hardy bon voyage by waving, in unison, their brightly colored patchwork umbrellalike hats. He traveled with 100 armed men, as it was no mean feat to try and impose peace in a region rampant with headhunters. Along the way he would engage in several vicious battles trying to impose peace, and the river would flow red. Dayak Kenyah oral history tells that on this mission Jalung Apui visited "Tuan Rajah," the White King of Sarawak—Charles Brooke (son of Sir James)—at his palace in Kuching on the Sarawak coast. They agreed to work together to eliminate head-hunting, and Brooke sealed their accord with several gifts, a few of which were on display in Long Uru, such as a Sumatran tiger skin, a tarnished bronze Victorian fruit bowl, and two *maniks*, precious lacquered glass beads believed to have been traded from Venice, via China, in Marco Polo's time. In November 1924, a little more than a decade after Jalung Apui's last Peace Conference, Vyner Brooke, Charles's son, held what he called "The Great Peace Council" in the village of Kapit on the Rajang River in central Sarawak. It was attended by a Dutch civil/military delegation, British envoys and hundreds of Dayak tribal chiefs. It was heralded worldwide as the conference that ended head-hunting in Borneo, and Western history records Rajah Brooke as the humanitarian hero who orchestrated the watershed event. In the articles of the time, and in subsequent books and accounts, there is no mention of Jalung Apui, the Tensing Norkay to Brooke's Hillary, a local hero who quietly stood in the shadows but who may deserve the lion's share of credit.

Of course, head-hunting didn't just disappear after Brooke's Kapit conference. As a practice it ebbed in the 1940s, perhaps dribbled into the 1950s. Ironically, perhaps the last heads taken—in the early 1960s—may have been taken by the British when troops were sent into the interior to defend Malaysia from Indonesia during the 1963 Confrontation. Incited by the fierce reputation of the Dayaks, the soldiers made a preemptive strike and took four Kalimantan Dayak heads. The story goes that the heads were brought back to headquarters in Kuching and the commanding officer was so incensed he ordered the soldiers back into the jungle to sew the heads back on, so the victims could rest whole in peace.

Sometime around 1920, a few years after Jalung Apui safely returned from Kuching, the black ghost Jelimpam appeared in another dream. But this time Jelimpam brought bad news: that Jalung Apui would soon die, and that three days after his death the black boulder known as "Batu Buring" in the middle of the Kayan River would split, as a sign of Jalung Apui's lasting power. Sure enough, shortly after the dream, Jalung Apui died. Thousands of Dayaks from all over the island came to pay their respects as the leader lay in state for eight days. And, as predicted, on the third day Batu Buring split, and it sits today in front of Long Uro, a cleaved polished piece looking like the back of a giant sleeping sea monster or, perhaps, a fallen tombstone.

After the ceremonies, all the players changed to normal attire and squatted around the porch critiquing performances. I, not being able to follow, pulled out Redmond O'Hanalon's instant classic *Into the Heart of Borneo*, a book about a spurious quest for the Borneo rhinoceros, which hadn't been sighted in decades, and read a passage that in turn had been pulled from a 1956 volume of *The Sarawak Museum Journal* describing a peculiar Dayak custom called *palang*:

One of the exhibits that excites the most interest in our museum is that of the palang. This is the tube or rod of bamboo, bone, hardwood, etc. with which the end of the penis is pierced among many inland people. In each end of this center-piece may be at-tached knobs, points or even blades of suitable material. Some men have two palangs, at right angles through the penis tip.

The function of this device is, superficially, to add to the sexual pleasure of the women by stimulating and extending the inner walls of the vagina. It is, in this, in my experience decidedly successful.

We also have a "natural" palang, exhibited alongside. This is the penis of a Borneo rhinoceros. In the natural state this powerful piece of anatomy has, about four inches behind the tip, a similar sort of cross-bar, projecting nearly two inches out on each side. When tense, this becomes a fairly rigid bar, much like the human palang in general implication. As such, these things were included among the esoterica of inland Long-Houses, along with sacred stones, beads, strange teeth and other charms mainly in connection with human head and fertility ceremonies.

Many who have handled this pachyderm device have been unable to credit that it is "genuine." However, in the untouched state it can be even more impressive. The penis of another male in our possession measures over a foot and a half (relaxed), has a longer tip and cross-piece than the Museum's displayed one.

I had seen this rhinoceros *palang* some months earlier in the Kuching Museum, and now reading this passage my curiosity was naturally roused. I looked up at the crowd of men in animated discussion and asked through Taman Kahang if any had a *palang*. To my complete surprise, the assistant chief of Long Lebusan, Pelenjau Serang, who had trekked for five days to witness the Peace Conference, looked at me and nodded "yes."

I was astonished. This seemed the sort of fantastic apocryphal custom that would filter out of the jungle and be embellished to large type, like the "discovery" of Michael Rockefeller's ingester in New Guinea. And, if the practice had existed, it would have been one of the first to go under missionary dominion, like the annual let-off-steam drunken, wife-swapping orgies the Dayaks used to organize, now history. Yet Pelenjau looked at me innocently and asked if I wanted to see his *palang*. I hesitantly replied yes, and when no women were looking he indicated I should follow him to the schoolhouse.

Once inside the schoolhouse, Pelenjau locked the door and checked the cracks in the wall to make sure nobody was peeking. He was clearly nervous, and before the unveiling he explained that he was among the last to undergo the operation, that the church and state had indeed persuaded the Dayaks to discontinue the custom, with the promise of a five-year prison term for disobedience. Then he pulled up one side of his shorts and displayed what looked to be the results of an extremely painful operation. Near the tip of his uncircumcised penis a three-inch-long dowel of rattan pierced the flesh. Various materials were used for *palangs*—deer horn, wood, pig bristle, gold, silver, copper wire, and in modern times the sheer pins from outboard motors were favored. The accoutrement is supposed to bring great pleasure to the women, a sort of troglodytic French tickler, and for the men it was a private statement of bravery. It is never displayed in public and is one of the reasons the men cup their privates when bathing. If the wife tells of her husband's *palang*, it is grounds for divorce, though in the old days no woman of any esteem would condescend to marry a man who was not properly decorated. The crossbar was usually inserted postpuberty, often just before marriage. If the intended was a virgin, the first bar would be the length of the thumb from the middle knuckle to the end of the thumbnail. Then, after a time a larger one would be inserted, one the length of the little finger from knuckle to nail. And finally, for the ultimate satisfaction, usually after the wife had borne a child or two, a crossbar measuring knuckle to nail on the ring finger would be inset.

The operation itself, performed riverside, could be self-executed by driving a six-inch-long sharpened bamboo spike through the flesh just below the glans of the flaccid penis as it was clamped into an instrument shaped like a small bow. There could only be one try. If one couldn't face the self-infliction, he could hire an expert to do the deed for about $35. It didn't seem to affect

fertility—Pelenjau had six children—but it very often festered into a serious infection, and many Dayaks died postoperatively of septicemia.

It was finally time to leave Long Uro. The men had to get back to the fields; the women had rice to pound. The Dayak Kenyah Lepo-Tau are in a period of dynamic adjustments to changing environmental, social and economic pressures, transitions that are lightning fast by their standards, but they still have to work as they have for millennia to maintain on the frontier of survival. We packed up our dunnage and climbed to the long house porch for goodbyes. There were hardy handshakes, wide grins and a hundred dollars passed to the *kepala kampung* as a gesture of gratitude for the performances. The noble-looking woman who had given Pam the necklace after her dance a few nights previous, and who looked to be about her age, took Pam's arm and brushed her nose against the back of Pam's hand in a gentle gesture. Then her dark eyes began to tear and cry.

We then headed to Long Lebusan, Long Uro's splinter village, where a reenactment of the first Peace Conference was scheduled. The route would take us up the Kayan River close to its source, then southeast, up a pass over a watershed divide and down into the Boh River basin, part of the Mahakam catchment. It was an old headhunting trail.

Not a mile into the journey, we stopped at a *kubu*, a resting lean-to, and bowed in a long group prayer asking for a safe trip. Then we trudged along in the afternoon heat, bent like beasts of burden, until late in the day we stumbled into the village of Long Sungai Barang, the uppermost Dayak Kenyah village on the Kayan River. We were told that Sungai Barang was forty years old, and it once housed more than 2500 people. Yet today fewer than four hundred people call the place home; the rest have given up on the poverty and remoteness of the highlands and sought greener pastures across the border or down Mahakam-basin way. Closer to civilization than Long Uro, Sungai Barang is a bit richer, with a per capita income of about sixty dollars a year; and it is a bit looser, with stashes of *tuak*, a couple of bottles of which were pulled out to celebrate our visit. It was also a bit cooler, this being one of the highest villages in Borneo, somewhere up around fourteen hundred meters.

Next morning, as the heavy mist from the Kayan was still rising, giving Sungai Barang a primeval, dawn-of-mankind look, we took to the trail. This would be the long trek day. We continued up the Kayan for a time, then turned south and followed a hint of a jungle trail up the pass. The rainforest closed in on us with an airless gloom, as we thrashed through a creepered world of endless twilight, slogged through mud troughs and bounced over rank, springing vegetation, all part of the oldest, richest, most stable ecosystem on earth. The heat seemed insufferable, an all-enclosing clamminess that radiated from the damp leaves, the slippery humus, the great boles of oaks and chestnuts. At the first stop I pulled up my pants leg and found a fat leech, his unctuous head buried in my calf, drunk and happy with the drink of my blood. I hadn't felt the sucker because the bite of *Haemadipsa zeylanica*, the common ground leech, is painless, containing an anesthetic in its saliva as well as an anticoagulant. Nonetheless, it was no fine time watching the turd-brown, rubbery, segmented three-centimeter worm suck my blood, becoming globular and wobbly in the process. I tried to pull the grubby little parasite off me, but his head was anchored deep, and he successfully resisted my efforts. I had heard of all sorts of leech removal techniques—salt, burning, alcohol, drowning, amputation—but before I could resort to any attempt Pelenjau was hovering over me with his *parang*, and he shaved the bloodsucker right off. Then he pulled out a wad of tobacco from his pouch, mixed it with spittle and rubbed the concoction all over the exposed skin of my legs and feet, the Dayak leech-protection formula. For double protection he tied tight strings of rattan around my upper calves, little Berlin Walls for the red-baiters. That was the holistic part. For post-attack, he quickly carved an exact replica of a buck knife from a bamboo stalk and stuck it in my belt. I was ready for the lousy scoleces.

For hours we walked through an enchanted forest, any one ten-hectare plot of which hosted as many as eight hundred different kinds of trees.

Most trees were linked to neighbors by fairy chains of pendulous festooned lianas, making it seem as though we had stumbled into some well-decorated hall ready for a celebration. Sometime midday we crested the pass, marked by the call of a gibbon on a high branch whose gray, furry back was cast with a lattice of sunlight. The going got easier as we dropped into the streambed of the Muse River, with delicate hanging plants and vines looking as though they'd been professionally arranged alternating between lovely little cascading jewels of tributary waterfalls.

We slogged along, stopping every now and then for a suck on an orange and a leech check (the tobacco juice washed off in the first creek crossing). Pam, who had set out on the trek wearing long, thin cotton harem pants, by afternoon had had them shredded to shorts by the forest thorns. Puluck, who was a fit sixty-seven, always stayed out front, trail blazing in his calloused, spatulated bare feet and once whacking off the head of a sleek, green coral snake, just before Pam stepped on it. Borneo has the richest snake fauna of Southeast Asia, with some 166 known species, though only eight, such as the coral Pam almost got to know, are deadly poisonous. This snake, I was later told, was the same kind responsible for the condition of the man in Long Uro with the "Oregon Jogging Club" shirt, the man with one leg.

Near twilight, after seven-and-a-half hours of hard trekking, we passed from the somber bluish-greens of the primary forest to the yellowish-olive hues of an expanse of secondary forest, the dregs of now-fallow swidden rice paddies, and down to the confluence of the Muse and Dumu rivers. Another *kubu* provided shelter. It was the only remains of a once-prosperous village, Dumu, which had been abandoned five years ago, now reclaimed by the forest. This was also the farthest point *prahus* could be brought upriver, and two from Pelenjau's voyage from Lebusan ten days previous had been pulled up next to the *kubu*. The area was also buzzing with a blizzard of sweat bees, obnoxious critters that suck body sweat and sting if irritated. So we all fled for the river, stripped and soaped up, leaving a pile of sweat-soaked clothing on the bank to feed the frenzy. Once washed, we had to move slowly, deliberately, so as not to perspire, as the smallest bead brought the hordes. Perhaps, I thought, this was the real reason the people of Dumu left.

That night, safely tucked under the mosquito net, downwind from the campfire smoke, Puluck slipped a viscous wad of unidentifiable mush into my hand and indicated I should eat it. I did—it tasted fine, something like spinach—and so he passed me another wad. This time I pulled out my flashlight and examined the snack—sweat-bee embryos. Puluck had somehow raided a sweat-bee nursery and grabbed what he considered a delicacy and what I now could not.

Before departure downstream the following morning, Pelenjau recited the obligatory prayer for safe passage. Then we piled into the two ten-meter *prahus*, each hewn from a single tree trunk, and started poling downstream. Three Dayaks stood in the bow of each boat, two in the stern. In the middle, Pam and I sat on duck-boards sandwiched between the duffle on one craft, while Taman Kahang and Farida took midship on the other. As feeder streams found ours, water depth increased, and within an hour our guides took seated positions and traded their poles for paddles. We glided along through a dark, blended-colored, narrow canyon, as though passing through paradise. William O. Krohn, in his 1927 book *In Borneo Jungles*, described a similar voyage: "There is no more beautiful sight than a Dayak boatman . . . always combining perfect poetry of motion with greatest physical efficiency." It was cool, pleasant, effortless, and the scenery was stunning. From the upper branches of a crocodile-tooth tree a rhinoceros hornbill rustled, then wheeled off downstream, as though showing us the way. We ran the moderate-sized rapids, but some were just too steep, requiring portages. These too were executed quickly, deftly, as ours was a route traveled many times, dating back at least a century when the Apo Kayan Kenyah would paddle these waters on head-hunting expeditions.

At one point, while cruising down the river, there was a sudden lurch of the *prahu* and a stir of commotion, as the boatswain frantically pointed to a black blur on shore and the rest of the crew shifted paddles into high gear. Craning to get a better look, I watched the blur slip into the water and slither toward us at an astonishing speed. "It's a king cobra," Taman Kahang yelled to me from the other boat, which was several lengths ahead. Fine, I thought. The king cobra, or hamadryad, is the largest venomous snake in the world—up to six meters long—and has a reputation for aggressiveness. Pelenjau had lost three dogs to a king cobra the month before. James Barclay described an incident on a similar downriver excursion in which a king cobra swam out to his boat, then crawled on board. He was barely able to knock it away with his umbrella. We didn't have umbrellas, but one of our guides pulled out a single-shot rifle and readied his aim. We were quicker than the snake, however, and sailed around the corner before there was damage from either side.

With the rifle ready, though, the crew decided to drift down the side of the bank and look for *babi*, wild boar, the Dayak delicacy. Almost immediately one appeared to emanate from the thick green leaf matting and at once disappear back into it like flowing mud. No meat for lunch, it seemed, but we paddled up a tributary, tossed weighted conical nets called *jala* into the currents and pulled out a big flat fish resembling a sole. We wouldn't go hungry.

Our little river merged with the larger Boh, and the *prahus* were moored with their rattan painters to a buttressed tree. Up the bank was a food cache of bamboo tubes crammed with boiled rice and the rank, sun-baked jerky from a bearded pig that had been speared on the upriver journey ten days ago. A fire was started, the fish roasted, and we sat down to a respectable meal in the middle of the Borneo rainforest. Over bites of the putrid-smelling *babi*, one of the guides told us his father had been killed by Ibans in a head-hunting raid near here some years ago. He remembered the retaliatory expedition launched against the Ibans, one in which after nine days of tracking six were caught and decapitated, and as the trackers had no food, they ate two of the victims. Our storyteller told us he remembered the men from his village returning after the avenging hunt with the taken heads, and that he and the other village boys in their Rousseauean inno-

An herbalist at Long Lebusan displays the rainforest plants and roots he uses to cure illness in his village.
(Pamela Roberson)

cence were kept amused playing with the skulls for weeks around the long house.

That night we pitched camp on a broad beach on the western bank of the Boh, less than a mile upstream from Ternak, the most dangerous cataract of our journey. Huge dark clouds were piling up across the river, so the guides unsheathed their *parangs* and set to work building waterproof lean-tos out of bamboo and wide succulent leaves. It poured hard all night, dropping a significant percentage of the five meters the area receives a year, but we all stayed dry.

The next morning, Pam's birthday, a saffron butterfly floated onto her toothbrush, then fluttered off downstream toward the great rapid. We arrived an hour later at its entrance, a gray-walled gorge that took a sharp turn so the guts of the cascade couldn't be seen, though the ominous

noise of arguing currents ahead could be heard. Pelenjau and crew unloaded some of the more precious gear and took off on a thirty-minute portage around the kilometer-long rapid. Pam and Farida followed, deciding not to risk running the rapid in the tipsy *prahus*, one of which had capsized and almost been lost on the earlier, upstream journey.

With a blue grip on the gunwales, I answered, "I'm ready, I think," to Pelenjau as he shoved us into the swirls, and we were swept toward Ternak. It was a violent descent. Through the thunder of incoming water I could hear the frantic, staccato commands of Pelenjau, who was ruddering the rear. Through the curls of spray, rocks reared up and shot past as the boatmen feverishly struggled to keep a purchase on the current. There were three distinct falls in Ternak, and at each it seemed the canoe was about to spear itself into a rock when at the last instant a coordinated flash of paddles would swerve us into the rebounding water. The craft rolled left and right, bobbed up and down as we hurtled through the white, churning water, until suddenly we had all purled into an eddy, where Pam and Farida were waiting, plucking leeches from their jungle portage.

An hour downstream, we passed fields of beans and maize, the good works of the village Long Lebusan. At the insistence of Pelenjau we pulled over and walked through a sugarcane field to survey the prospects of a partially razed patch of level ground—a new airstrip being cleared by Lebusan with hopes of attracting larger and more frequent aircraft than does the current mudway that the mission flights occasionally drop into.

A few more paddle strokes downriver and we met the Lebusan River, clear and shallow. It was raining, a good sign for arriving guests, said Pelenjau. Paddles were stowed, the poles once again pulled out, and our crew powered the *prahus* up some riffles and parked in the waterfront lot of Long Lebusan.

It had been almost two weeks since our ten-member team had seen their friends and relatives in Long Lebusan, but it was not a happy reunion. The first news was that a fever had been going around, and just yesterday two baby girls had died. Most of the villagers were wearing pink headbands in mourning, and an exuberant arabesque-designed structure was festooned with red, yellow and white cloth—a mausoleum for the deceased children.

Despite the pall of grief, the people, upon seeing our arrival, quickly slipped into their ceremonial clothing and lined up for a welcoming procession. They draped colorful leis around our necks, flashed gold-toothed smiles and told us we were the first nonmissionary Americans to ever visit their village.

Long Lebusan lies in a beautiful dell between the razor-toothed mountains of the Menyapa Range to the south and east and the hanging spurs of the Apo Kayan Plateau to the north and west. Before its current incarnation, the Lebusan valley was inhabited by a tribe of Dayaks called Busang. But Kenyah raiders so frequently launched successful head-hunting expeditions to the area that the Busang finally abandoned the site and moved down to the Mahakam proper. In 1958, when the dry rice fields close to Long Uro were turning barren, a plan was hatched to move half the village to the fertile soils of their old head-hunting grounds at the confluence of the Boh and Lebusan rivers. Now some 437 residents with six long houses and two churches make up the village. That's down some 50 people in a year, lost to the irresistible lures of the lowlands, including lifesaving medicine, doctors and hospitals.

The riches of Long Lebusan are another problem altogether. The Dayak Kenyah Lepo-Tau of Lebusan have discovered placer gold in the Boh River. They know it is a blessing but sense it could be a curse. To date the government has not recognized land sovereignty for the Kenyah, and in fact no highlands Dayak village in East Kalimantan has received a land title. The Dayak Kenyah of Lebusan believe that in the not-too-distant future outsiders, entrepreneurs, carpetbaggers and foreign companies will be awarded contracts and concessions to mine the gold of the Boh River, and the people of Lebusan will lose out—not just in the monies they feel should be their own but in the rape of their culture, inevitable if a rush for gold began. To stay ahead, the Lepo-Tau of Lebusan would like to find a way to trade their gold before it's too late. It takes too long to trek it to the coast, and MAF has no regular service and frowns on employing their higher-purpose planes for crass commerce.

One solution Taman Kahang has put forth is to convince an American whitewater rafting team to come to Lebusan with some whitewater inflatables and make the first descent of the eighty-kilometer-long Boh River gorge, which begins just downstream. To trek around the gorge can take weeks; but no *prahu* has ever successfully navigated the narrow, twisting canyon that spills the Boh off the plateau, the obvious whitewater boating skills of the Kenyah notwithstanding. The rapids in the gorge are just too big for the heavy, unwieldy *prahus*. Below the gorge the Boh flattens out, becomes navigable, then joins the Mahakam, which in turn runs to Samarinda before emptying into the Makassar Strait connecting the Sulawesi and Java seas. Taman Kahang's idea is to persuade a group of adventurers to undertake this expedition, bringing along the best of the Lebusan boatmen as crew, teaching them how to pilot the rafts, then leaving the rafts behind for the Dayaks. They could then use the boats to bring their gold and other goods—such as the aloe wood found in the area—to the coast in a reasonable time frame. To get the rafts back, since they are lightweight and roll up to the size of a large backpack, river taxis could be hired, taking the crews and gear to the bottom of the Boh gorge, and then the gear could be trekked the final distance up to the plateau. It could cut the trade time 50 percent—and, if MAF would fly the rafts back, even more.

It was an intriguing, enterprising idea, and I warmed to it, telling Taman Kahang I'd like to organize such an expedition and return. Funding, as always, would be a problem, as rafts and air tickets don't come cheap, but I promised to give it a try.

After the welcoming procession, Baya Udau, the chief of group ceremony and *adat* for Long Lebusan, led us to a three-room structure across from the soccer field and said it would be ours for the duration of our visit. It had been the house of a Moslem Bugi trader who had privately flown in cooking pots, steel tools, the coveted salt and other items and set up shop to trade for gold. He made his fortune and left. Baya Udau gave us a padlock and key and offered to have a guard watch the place while we were out. This seemed odd, in a small, remote village in which crime of any nature would be difficult to achieve and more so to conceal. Yet Taman Kahang took me aside and said that one of the young Lepo-Tau who had emigrated to the lowlands had become a renowned professional thief, and he was presently back in Long Lebusan visiting relatives. Taman Kahang himself had been ripped off in lowland Tanjung Manis by the thief, who was especially clever with his craft. We were obvious targets and had to take extra precautions. In Taman Kahang's view, the thief was a casualty of civilization. In the recent past, when the *adat* of the

Kenyah was the highest principium and rubric of village life, such behavior would have been unthinkable. But the codes of the coast, including material success at all costs, were encroaching.

After we settled in, crushing a dozen giant spiders on the walls of our little house, we bolted the windows from the inside, locked the door and stepped out to the soccer field where the villagers were preparing their reenactments. In Long Uro we had witnessed the second great Peace Conference organized by Jalung Apui; now we would see the first one, and several related events of that era that have survived to the present. It all began with a tug-o-war. In Jalung Apui's years, when it was near harvest time, all the villagers would gather in an open field and stretch a rattan rope, the men on one side, women on the other. With a signal, both sides would pull, and if the men won, it meant a good yield; if the women overpowered, it meant bad crops. The whole setup seemed to guarantee the correct outcome, the natural size differences of the sexes even more so, but we watched the contest, cheering like basketball fans as the rope went taut, twenty-five men on one side, eighteen women on the other. Then it snapped, sending both sides collapsing back into human piles. "What does that mean?" I asked Pelenjau, who was judging the match. "It means there will be no disease on the crops," he snapped back, as fast as the rope.

Next we witnessed a series of demonstrations: how the Dayak Kenyah made a two-and-a-half-meter blow pipe; how they boiled the sap from the *upas* tree, turning it to a potent strychninelike poison, and cooked it on darts. They displayed fourteen different herbs and plants gathered from the surrounding forest and told us how they were used for infections, swellings, itching, backaches, muscle cramps, coughs, exhaustion, congestion and other ailments. They demonstrated the Dayak deep-tissue massage; basket making; and the setting of animal traps, placed around the paddies to keep rodents and civet cats away. They showed how they inspected the nipple positions of newborn dogs (wrong arrangement and the pup would have to be drowned). They took us to Pelenjau's eighty-nine-year-old mother, Iring Alung, who was the last in their village with the traditional indigo tattoos decorating her legs. A series of concentric rings meant to be part snake, part bird and part plant design, they identified her tribe, family and station. She had it done when she was a young bride, the pattern punctured into her skin with brass needles hammered with a stick, the ink a mixture of tree sap and black ash from cooking pots. It was a torturous process, and once completed it took three months before she could walk again. The Kenyah men of the past would tattoo their hands, one imprint for every head taken. The church had put an end to tattooing, but Iring Alung was still proud of her markings, flattered we wanted to see them.

That evening, while the wet air was filled with the sounds of vibrating membranes of thousands of cicadas, we were visited by Pekuleh Bilung, the seventy-year-old shaman who was the chief of tribal group ceremony and *adat* for the whole of the Boh region. He was also a wizard of much repute and once performed his good magic for Soekarno, or so he said. Such sorcerers were once among the most powerful and esteemed personages in the Dayak cosmology. They had to be consulted for every major village decision and were sought after for healing magic, fertility blessings and general advice. The missionaries stripped the shamans of their potency, telling the villagers that to practice magic was unholy and would not be tolerated. However, there are those who still believe, and Pekuleh operates a sort of underground magic service, offering us a demonstration for three dollars.

By the scant light of an oil lamp, Pekuleh sat down and produced two dark polished rocks—one with a doughnut hole, the other curved like a small scimitar. He told us that thirty years ago the first rock was left under his pillow by Anying Ibou, the other in his field house by Lihan Lilling. Both his benefactors were ghosts. And with the rocks he could call the ghosts at will. First he bent his head in prayer and crossed his chest. Then he launched into a crazed chant and seemed to lose himself in a trance. He emptied rice from a tin cup—an offering to the spirits—then showed us that the vessel was empty, using

the same melodramatic gestures Las Vegas lounge prestidigitators employ. Then he dropped in the two rocks, rattled them around a bit, and walked outside to the porch. A minute later he returned—with water in the cup!

Pekuleh explained that the water was left by the two ghosts; that it was magic healing water, sought by the whole community and other villages as well. If a sick person came to him, and he asked the ghosts for the water and it didn't appear, the sufferer would die. With its manifestation, all would be hunky-dory, as long as the missionaries weren't told. He sprinkled the water on my head, then blew through his fist that held the rocks, then touched my cheeks. It was over. I was cured. I hadn't felt bad in the first place, I confessed to Taman Kahang, but one never knows.

A powerful rain kept things quiet the next morning, but by noon the sun was shouldering the clouds, and in Long Lebusan warriors were gussying up. The first reenactment was an "open war" on the muddy football field, replete with war masks, argus-pheasant feathers in plaited-fiber, toquelike helmets (worn only by successful headhunters), panther-skinned girdles, flashing *parangs* and dropping bodies. They refused to say which battle they were reenacting, except that it was intertribal, because it might prove embarrassing. No human blood was spilled, but to give verisimilitude an enormous bleating pig was speared to death, and the field ran red.

At last it was time for the first Peace Conference, Jalung Apui's seminal council that put the brakes on runaway head-hunting. Dayak Kenyah legend has it that head-hunting started about four hundred years ago. The Apo Kayan was then a Garden of Eden. It was a time of never-ending peace and prosperity. They didn't have to grow, harvest or pound rice—they'd just boil forest leaves in a certain closed pot, and voila, a banquet of rice. There was no sickness, no war; everyone was happy, until a curious girl, Asiung Liyang, decided she wanted to look inside the magic pot. This was forbidden, as it would be a breach of faith, a statement of doubt in the order

OVERLEAF: *The villagers of Long Lebusan reenact a famous battle from early this century when their ancestors were trying to convince other villages and tribes to give up head-hunting. It was a bloody conversion process. (Pamela Roberson)*

The Kenyah Dayaks of Long Lebusan perform a skit in which they mimic a visit by Westerners. The fish basket represents the airplane on which the visitors arrived; the actors whiten their skin with chalk and wear Western garb. (Richard Bangs)

of the universe, of nonbelief. Yet Asiung Liyang couldn't resist, and one day she lifted the lid of the Dayak Pandora's box, and evil was released. Head-hunting began.

It wasn't until the late nineteenth century that a campaign was launched to end the evil practice. In this first conference, Jalung Apui invited the four leaders of the four closest Kenyah subtribes to join him.

For the reenactment, all of Long Lebusan gathered on a long-house gallery, in front of a wall mural depicting two tigers flanking a Chinese vase. Over the vase hovered a hornbill. As in Long Uro, the vase was supposed to hold the souls of all the Kenyah people; the hornbill protected the vase from above, while the two tigers, representing Jalung Apui and his cousin Pingam Sutang, guarded the sides.

An effigy of an enormous hornbill with tinder, a symbol of fire, in his beak, hung from the ceiling joists; it also represented Jalung Apui. The fire would burn to death any chief who didn't stick to the peace pact. Four smaller hornbills ringed the large one, representing the four subtribe chiefs. The reenactment began with Jalung Apui and his fellow chiefs stooping over a trough and slopping up rice, as though they were dogs, to indicate how as headhunters they had reduced themselves to animals. An old woman wearing blue then called the chiefs as though they were mongrels, and they turned and rose as humans. They then cut themselves and dripped their collective blood into a cup, which was passed around for each to take a drink, a blood-brother peace toast. Then five tiger's teeth were dipped into the cup, meaning that if the chiefs didn't keep the peace pact, a tiger would come and eat their hearts out. This was the beginning of the end. They would return to their respective villages and start the process of winding down the hunting of heads, a conversion that would take more than half a century to realize.

That evening, our last, we were called to the porch for another dance. We expected the graceful Kenyah performances we'd witnessed in Long Uro, and we got them but a bit more as well. As the *sambes* were tuned, a man emerged from the shadows down the gallery dragging a big fish trap with a propeller attached. Inside was another man, who spun the propeller as they moved into the light, amongst gales of laughter. The man inside the ersatz plane stepped out and next to the other. They looked like Taman Kahang and myself, Westerners. They had white chalk covering their faces and hands; they had sharp Western noses, fashioned from cardboard. Their hair was slicked back. They were wearing jeans and backpacks, and one had a fake beard. The other had a tin can slung around his neck, which he pointed toward the audience as though a camera. The burlesque was uncanny, a keen mimicry of their visitors, with mannerisms and tics to a tee. The man playing me would stoop and point his camera at a winsome young girl in an exact impersonation of me. The village was convulsed in laughter, and I as well, though I also felt I had been dissected and was being held up in a beaker for the class to see. But this was exactly what I had been doing to them for the past two weeks, and what missionaries, colonialists, anthropologists, humanists and moralists had done for decades before me. I was probably abetting the process Taman Kahang so wanted to arrest—the Westernization and moral deterioration of the Dayaks.

Yes, head-hunting was evil. The taking of any human life is evil, the paramount crime against humanity. But, it could be argued, the Dayak Kenyah headhunters had a higher moral philosophy than our own. Our methods of warfare allow us to forget our enemies have names and faces. Although the headhunter on a raid was a treacherous and indiscriminate killer of men, women and children, there were at least some human as well as technological limits to the brutality of the system. His wars were waged against people who could provide links with the eternal powers of the gods and ancestors. Our wars are fought over an economic system, or oil, or politics, or reasons nobody really understands. And they're fought electronically and with the same strategies used to eliminate vermin.

As the skit was winding down, I looked over to my British host, Taman Kahang, and his Dayak wife, Farida, and noticed something with little significance. After his two weeks in the highlands, Taman Kahang was now beginning to look like a Dayak hunter—he was unshaven, unwashed, his face dark with dirt and he wore the same stained, ripped and wrinkled clothing he'd started with. Yet Farida, seated next to him, wore a freshly pressed cotton dress, meticulously applied nail polish, a new Seiko watch and a chic gold necklace. Somehow they'd switched places, and each was striving for what the other had had by birthright.

BALI

Walking the Demons' Paradise

A FAIR, frail mist wreathed the parrot-green mountain to my right and pulled on my attention. But the sunset on my left, illuminating the gentle rolling waves with long purple forms like actors in ancient plays, seduced my eyes. The air was warm and scented. The wet sand felt cool between my toes as I stepped over a little woven dish of banana leaf ritually filled with flowers, fruit, a dollop of rice, a lump of pig fat and a chili pepper. The sensory load was manageable, the route clear, until I rounded the bend and was presented *en tableaux* with a gliding parade of sloe-eyed, cocoa-colored women in brocade blouses, batik sarongs and jasmine or gold-leafed tiaras seemingly suspended from a uniform layer of brightly colored umbrellas. This formal procession was by the water's edge. A bit higher on the beach incongruously sprawled a string of nubile, fair-haired and -skinned, bare-breasted women, glistering in lotion, lolling in the last rays of the equatorial sun. I walked between the two spectacles and for a moment lost all sense of place and time. As a feeble effort to fetch reality, I glanced at my wrist.

Anywhere else, at that moment, I would have blown my top. But it somehow seemed appropriate when, on my first day in Bali, my watch broke. I smiled with the discovery. Time seemed useless here. Some say, though, that Bali is running out of it.

Bali is paradise, many claim, including the hawkers who make relative fortunes on the tourists. Bali is rigid custom and religion, a spiritual mote with more than thirty thousand temples for its three million people, the most popular of which, one tour guide told me, is the Colonel Sanders outlet. Bali is a place where the native girls now cover themselves with high-necked puritan modesty but the tourists go topless. Its culture is renowned for its peaceful ways, yet, like the island's two volcanoes, it erupts periodically, unpredictably, in deadly violence. Bali is a modern-day Eden replete with pristine beaches and lush vegetation but also hookers, magic mushrooms and tourist stings. It's an island of Hinduism floating in the middle of the world's most populous Moslem nation; it's a lifeboat of extraordinary natural beauty, of true wilderness, that is so overcrowded it seems ready to sink. It has extreme poverty backfenced against excessive wealth; the serenity of a back-eddy village contraposed with the island's history of tumult and violence; the cultivation of native music, dance, poetry and art competing with discos, comic books, plastic bric-a-brac and black-market video and music cassettes. And this yin-yang of cultures and of centuries is precisely what makes Bali one of the finest, most intriguing places on the planet for a walk—and one of the most perplexing.

A keener irony of the island plays and battles on its beaches. The soft sand and sultry sunsets of Kuta and Legian beaches are legendary, and now over a half-million foreigners a year spread their towels above the tide. Yet, for the Balinese, the coast is anathema—evil incarnate. It's not the place to hang out or take a stroll.

Bali is probably the only island in the world where the villages turn away from the sea to face the mountains. No one lives on the beach. It's haunted by the spirits of the departed. Their ashes are tossed into the sea, a sea that has proven unkind. It has provided no natural harbor for the tiny island, its currents are deadly, its coral reefs sharp and host to sharks, poisonous snakes and mythical elephant fish. And the sea brought the invaders, first the Dutch, then the Japanese and now those in cruise ships, who have relentlessly chipped away at one of mankind's richest cultures.

The doctrine of the Balinese-style Hindu-animist religion involves a ceaseless striving for balance between the forces of good and evil. Good (*kaja*) is represented by the holy mountains, the rising sun, the right-hand side and life. Evil and death are represented by the sea, the setting sun and the left-hand side, all of which belong to evil spirits (*kelod*). The temples and homes face the tip of the island's highest volcano, Gunung Agung, above which the gods live in a many-tiered heaven topped by Bali's supreme god, Sanghyang Widi Wasa, or Tintia, while cemeteries, animal barns and garbage pits face the sea, the abode of the demons. This conception may appear simplistic, but in fact it is quite natural, as the realm of man stands between two extremes: the peaks of the volcanoes and the depths of the sea. The *kaja/kelod* duality is a constant in Balinese life and appears in its art, dance and the performance of sacred rites. Lustral or heavenly rites appeal to benevolent powers, whereas the object of the rites with a focus on the underworld is to drive evil away. An offering for

purification is always placed on high ground, reaching toward the gods; other offerings, such as the one I stepped over my first day on the beach, are laid on the ground to repulse the demons of hell.

By local interpretation, then, a walk along the coast of Bali would be a traverse across the razor-edge bridge between *kaya* and *kelod*, a tightrope act between coexisting antipodes. And, if this coastal walk were on the left-hand side of the island, on the side where the sun sets, it would be a taunting walk on the wild side, a trek along the demons' gate. This also would be a walk along the same stretch extolled in the tourist brochures as paradise nonpareil. How could I resist?

That Bali, in the midst of a swath of thirteen thousand islands, many with wider, whiter beaches and milder surf, has become a tourist mecca is practically an accident. Some put the blame on Bob Hope and James Michener. Hope's 1953 movie *The Road to Bali* was filmed on location in Burbank and depicted an island with oversexed maidens in grass skirts. No such skirts exist in the real Bali. And the model for the mythical Bali H'ai in the Michener book that became the musical *South Pacific* is thousands of miles away. Yet these fictions helped put Bali on the map and planted a conception in the crawl space of popular consciousness. Hawaii, Tahiti, Fiji and, lumped with them, Bali. Interchangeable sun, sand, easy sex and tall drinks with bursting tropical fruits and tiny umbrellas. Until recently it would have been a travesty to put Bali in that category. Now, it's partially true.

Bukit Badung ("Hill District") is a bead of land on the extreme southern tip of Delaware-size Bali, connected to it by an isthmus. The isthmus is a bridge between extremes; a passageway between cultures, between fabulous wealth and inhumane poverty, the ethereal and the hard assets. It's this chiefly barren pearl-shaped pocket that the Indonesian government has set aside for tourist development, and forty-million-dollar

PAGE 82: *The split gate at Nusa Dua on the Bukit Peninsula in southern Bali. It is said that the two halves of the gate will come together to crush any evil spirit that tries to intrude. The split gate is found at the entrance to all temples in Bali. (Richard Bangs)*   OPPOSITE: *A Balinese dancer reenacts the story of the Hindu epic the* Mahabharata, *which relates the conflict between good and evil. (Pamela Roberson)*

properties have sprouted, lavish hotels designed to appear like Balinese temples but with $300-a-night rooms, speedy room service with cheeseburgers or champagne and dance troops that nightly perform on the grounds. In fact, the visitor never has to leave the hotel compound; everything he needs can be purchased in the lobby shops, or brought to him, even an ersatz sampling of the culture. Ronald Reagan stayed here in 1986, in a room with a private pool and bulletproof windows. It can be the perfect retreat for a man who wants to be out of touch.

However, at the far southwest tip of Bukit Badung is a real temple: Puru Lahur Uluwatu, one of the two great sea temples of Bali. And if you trace a route on a map up the "evil" western coast, up the isthmus, past the international airport, past some of the most infamous tourist beaches, onto the body of the island and along unnamed sections of coast, after a few inches (about thirty-five kilometers by the key on my map) you come to Pura Tanah Lot, the second great sea temple of the island. Walking between these two temples, or *puras*, would seem to be a walk between worlds. As it turns out, it is one of the great walks of the world.

Both temples are best seen at sunset, yet neither has overnight facilities, so I decided to break up the walk into parts that would allow sleep between clean sheets. In an area with more than four hundred tourist hotels and ten thousand rooms, ranging in price from four dollars a night to the price of a used BMW 320i, I couldn't find the spirit to camp. So I based at the Pertamini Cottages, a sprawling, twenty-five-acre concrete complex built by the national oil company in 1973 and looking like something prefabbed on the North Slope but transplanted to the southern tip of Kuta, just a hundred meters from the airport, and positioned exactly midway between the two sea temples. For continuity and concept's sake, the walk should be taken in linear fashion, from one temple to the next, spending the night in whatever beach hotel suits fancy and wallet. But that all seemed a bit too tidy and straight on an island where chaos is an art, and no road is straight. So I would start at the cottages each morning, walk all day and hitch back to my clean sheets each evening.

Early morning and late afternoon are, not suprisingly, the best times to walk in coastal Bali; not just for the diffused light but to escape from the heat, which can be brutal midday during the hot arc of "mata hari," the "eye of the day." Also not surprisingly, succumbing to the lure of languorousness that is Bali, a land whose motto might well be "Never do today what you can put off several days hence," I didn't get started until 10:00 A.M., the beginning of the hot arc, the most intense hours of the day. Stepping past the golf course, the tennis courts, the convention hall, the Ayodya Disco, the sea-blue pool and the security guards I evaded the strictures and attained the beach, attached to a pool-blue sea. I was at the bottom end of Kuta, at the rim of the Indian Ocean on a sand spit too narrow and rocky for beach life, so for the first couple hundred meters it was quiet.

It didn't last long. After a few minutes, I was approached by my first hustler, a woman selling cheap T-shirts and shorts emblazoned with a stylized logo of the island's name. She started low in her asking price, by my standards, and got lower, and as she was my first I was civil and actually ended up buying a pair of shorts, for three dollars, which didn't last beyond my first kneebend.

The next merchant was vending massage. Most Balinese women are on the cinnamon side of cappuccino, tiny boned with round, delicate orchidlike features, flat epicene noses, long sweeping eyelashes and heart-shaped lips, yet this woman was chocolate colored, thick and hard looking. It turned out she was Madurese, a native of the island of Madura off East Java, famous for its bull races and prostitutes. And in fact, because the beach is still *costa non grata* for the traditional Balinese, trades including fishing, merchandising, scamming and soliciting have been picked up by those with different theology and fewer scruples. This offering was a genuine coconut-oil massage, however, for two dollars, and she was part of an organized force of more than three hundred, wearing her uniform of a long-sleeved T-shirt and blue mushroom-head peasant hat, with her number on the front (in case I wanted a reorder or to complain?), and, as I scanned farther down the beach, I could see dozens of these

The Barong, a sacred mythical creature with the face of a lion, protects villages from unrelenting demons. Two men dance in the Barong costume, magnificently adorned with flowers, mirrors and leather carvings. (Richard Bangs)

bobbing blue hats, working the white-skinned crowds. They made good money, by Balinese standards, and each contributed six dollars of her earnings each month to a fund that attempts to keep the beach clean. Like all good travelers, I dove in to feel the culture, succumbing to a long, sensuous massage. An hour later, legs wobbly with relaxation, I started down the beach again.

After a few more steps, I was into it—the throbbing, sybaritic heart of Kuta. The circus had come to town, or I to it; brown-skinned barkers, hucksters and traffickers were everywhere. I couldn't walk more than the length of a woven bamboo massage mat without being accosted by peddlers of practically everything, including cowrie necklaces, Tijuana-quality art, bad bone carvings, erotic carvings fashioned from fake ebony (veneered with Kiwi shoe pol-

ish—a company spokesman told me Kiwi does banner business here, even though nobody wears shoes) and batiks, cold drinks and Baliburgers, gaudy postcards, tie-dyed blankets, drugs and flesh (thirty-five dollars). One popular service was hair braiding and beading à la Bo Derek, offered by the masseuses to all sexes and all filaments, including beards and moustaches. It was the "Kuta look," and fully a quarter of the lounging foreigners sported the style. The crash of the surf competed with the roar of ghetto blasters and 125cc Japanese motorcycles (the largest allowed on the island), piloted by bearded, neck-pendanted Javanese in designer jeans ready to hawk round-the-world tours.

But there were other rings in this circus. By the score, Australians, Europeans, and the odd American sprawled along the sand, tossed Frisbees, hung ten on the tubes, knocked back the brew, turned up the volume, dogeared the pulp and poured on the oxybenzone. A *mise en scène* from Anybeach, U.S.A., except for a couple of points—virtually every woman on the lighter side of the pigment scale, that is, each visitor from foreign lands, was topless, while no Balinese woman followed suit. This seemed some weird inversion of morality. It wasn't long ago that documentary films were being cranked out calling Bali "The Last Paradise" and featuring endless voyeuristic shots of innocent-looking, naked-from-the-waist-up Balinese women going about their daily routines oblivious to the camera and to any sense of impropriety. But the Dutch, who ruled Indonesia for four hundred years, finally put feet down, and shirts on, during World War II, believing the native girls in their natural state would entice the soldiers and inhibit the performance of their duties. Christian morality prevailed, even though missionaries, after centuries of attempts, were never able to convert the Hindu-animist Balinese to either the cross or crescent and were often murdered for their efforts. The white man issued an edict that no Balinese woman could bare her breasts in public, but beyond the beach villages, and the eyes of the colonialists, it was ignored. The torch was then passed to one of the first Javanese governors of the island after the revolution, a certain Major Salim, who decreed that all Balinese women, wherever residing, were to cover their breasts. He even went so far as to have two thousand long-sleeved blouses distributed among the women free of charge. These garments puzzled the ladies of Bali, who did not quite know how to wear them. Realizing, however, that their main purpose was to conceal their bosoms, they hung the blouses loosely over their breasts, drew the sleeves under their armpits and tied them in a knot in the middle of their backs. They've long since adopted the proper method of wear, and now, while the Dutch and other visiting Europeans and Australians bare it all in Bali, the Balinese suffer the heat under polyester T-shirts, paradise tossed.

Kuta has before been a Satan's Alley. For more than two hundred years, Kuta's chief export was flesh—slaves shipped off to Java and points beyond. The women, valued for their beauty and artistic skills, were a part of the human cargo and were often bid off the block to become wives. At its height, toward the end of the eighteenth century, Bali was exporting about two thousand slaves a year, most shipped from Kuta, where unsavory merchant types were controlling the trade. Kuta became a hermitage for pariahs, scamps, lepers, practitioners of black magic and other undesirables. Malaria and marsh fever were endemic. The settlement earned a Casablanca reputation. Kuta's coastal waters were shallow, and when steamships began replacing the slight-draft masted schooners there was no place to park, and as a port Kuta dried up. It declined then to one of the poorest fishing villages on the island, and only a keen prophet could have predicted the disco inferno it has become.

Some credit for early initiation of the influx belongs, perhaps, to the first white settler, Mads Johansen Lange, a Danish trader and adventurer, who built a copra factory near the beach in 1840. He invited his friends to come vacation on his beach, and word spread of his special spit of sand with the grand sunsets. He also may have been the unwitting father of Kuta's sense of international intrigue, as after visiting a local prince he was found poisoned to death on the beach, and the murder remains unsolved. (His grave still stands above the high-water mark near Lange's Lane, the only street in Bali named after a foreigner.) The first hotel, Miss Mank's, a series of thatched bungalows, opened to poor business in 1930, though it soon had competition in the Kuta Beach Hotel, a series of native-style cottages opened by an American couple, Robert and Louise Koke, in 1936. Robert Koke, a former photographer for MGM in Southern California, introduced surfing to Bali, and he is also responsible for changing the Dutch name of his private paradise, "Koeta," to "Kuta," so Americans wouldn't mispronounce his hotel. In a *Fortune Magazine* article of the day, Robert Koke told

OPPOSITE: *A carving of the head of Bhoma, child of the earth, whose bulging eyes, fangs and threatening grimace are meant to scare away any evil spirits that might enter a temple or family compound. (Pamela Roberson)*

how he discovered the site of his seminal hotel: "One day, when we were exploring the island on our hired bicycles we pedalled through a coconut grove and came out on the most beautiful beach in the world: clear surf lapping miles of white sand fringed with palms, and no trace of human habitation as far as the eye could see."

By 1940 Bali averaged about two hundred fifty tourists a month, and as the first aircraft landings on the island were made on the broad beach at Kuta, the few who dared arrive by air often stayed at the adjacent properties. Tourism limped ahead, until the Japanese invaded. The hotels were leveled, and locals were conscripted to fell coconut palms along the beach and to build bunkers and other defenses. Robert Koke went on to work for the CIA and never returned. But the hotel did, reopening under new proprietorship and fewer coconut palms in 1955. Then in the 1960s the hippie caravans discovered the beach, and it became part of the hip triangle—Kathmandu, Kabul and Kuta. Now Kuta is thick with tourists, tawdry types, thieves, trash and even a few walkers, or beachcombers, as they were once romantically called.

Weaving between hard bodies and hawkers, I reached the Legian Beach Hotel, just north of Kuta, and stopped for an *air jeruk* (lemon juice). My table was positioned between two robust, leering guardian statues, common throughout the island, each swathed in a mantle of simple black-and-white check cotton. The gingham was symbolic dress, meant to remind believers of the continual options of right or wrong, good or bad—in the case of my lemonade, sour or sweet. As neither good nor evil can be allowed to prevail in Bali, the black and white must be of equal shape and size, and I poured sugar into my drink.

It was a timely respite. After a few sips I heard a shower of crystal notes, a spinning kaleidoscopic web of sound in minor keys—the tinkerbells of the gamelan—and a procession began to file past, through an arcade of *penjors*—decorated bamboo poles—and onto the beach.

Every day is a holiday for the tourists in Bali, but for the locals every day brings a celebration, somewhere. Most are devised to somehow appease the fickle gods, with elaborate costumed rituals, dances and parades, all with ample offer-

ings to the higher-ups. Every life passage has a rite, such as tooth filing for puberty, whole-body egg rolling for weddings and animal sarcophagus processions for cremations. Every phase of the moon, every rise of the sun seems to be an excuse for a party for the gods. Urs Ramseyer, author of *Art and Culture of Bali*, commented that "Pious Balinese go through a life full of rites whose purpose is to cleanse what is unclean, reconcile what seems irreconcilable, compensate, worship and appease, avert danger, obtain nourishment and secure a happy life and a good rebirth beyond this one."

Virtually all of these rites and ceremonies take place away from the evil sea, either in the village *puris* (shrines) or the mountain temples, such as Pura Besakih, the mother temple, Bali's highest and holiest, on the upper flanks of the brooding, 3142-meter-high volcano Gunung Agung, the mountain Balinese believe to be the navel of the world and the abode of the supreme god, Sanghyang Widi Wasa. But once a year, at the spring equinox—the end of the troublesome rainy season—the whole of Bali spills onto the beach for "Melasti," a fantastic purification ceremony designed to rid the people and gods of the evil spirits before the start of the new lunar year three days hence. By sheer coincidence I was making my walk during Melasti, the eve of the year 1909 by the Balinese Saka lunar calendar.

From the Legian Beach Hotel, I followed one of what were called the *melis* processions and found myself in the middle of Mardi Gras, Chinese New Year and the Rose Bowl parade. Thousands filed onto the beach, then broke off into miniceremonies, all presided over by the *pemangkus*, the high priests, all having something to do with casting out evil. High altars were brought to the sand and filled with offerings of confections, fruit, colored rice and incense to the Bhutas and Kalas, the evil ground spirits who try to interfere with man's activities. Pendet dances, with arabesque posturing and fingernails vibrating like bees, were performed by women in gold headdresses; waist-sashed, bare-chested men performed a *kris* dance, in which they worked themselves into a trance and seemed to stab their chests with the curved blades, but without drawing blood. Tinkling music rose like

A melis procession during Melasti, a purification ceremony designed to rid the people and gods of evil spirits before the start of the upcoming new lunar year. (Richard Bangs)

smoke from all quarters. Groups of somber-faced men and women knelt by the water and bowed in prayer, cupped hands held over their heads, gestures meant to achieve a temporary unity with God. Incense wafted over the kneeling files, and priests wove through them, sprinkling holy water as a blessing and purification on the bowed heads.

Other groups worked into a frenzy, then walked into the sea water, where they sacrificed pigs and chickens by whacking off the heads. As this ceremony is performed at the cusp between the wet and dry seasons, the sacrifices are meant to purify the earth, which was soiled by the rains. The rains are believed to have unbalanced the harmony between the *bhuwana alit* (microcosmos) and *bhuwana agung* (macrocosmos), and only the hot spilled blood of living creatures can restore the balance. Promenades of gongs, tall flags and frilled umbrellas covering *pertimas*, the wooden statues that serve as vehicles for deified ancestors, were transported in line down the beach to the breakers for a symbolic cleansing, and vendors cropped up selling five-cent *satay* (barbecue) and sugar water. *Anjings*, stray dogs, had a beggars' banquet lapping up the thousands of personal demon offerings, little square palm-frond dishes filled with flowers, salt and food scraps left on the beach for still other bad spirits, such as the sorceress widow Rangda, the incarnation of evil whose mission is the destruction of the universe. When the food is devoured by the dogs it is a sign that the bad gods have accepted the offerings, and worshipers can look forward to a trouble-free period.

I joined one group marching in my direction

Sacrifices of pigs, chickens, dogs and other small animals are made into the ocean at Kuta Beach, along with the demon offerings of foodstuffs and flowers, during Melasti. (Richard Bangs)

carrying huge stylized puppets of mythical beasts, moving to the beats of liturgical chants, mystic incantations, resonant drones and wooden *kulkul* drums as they walked. Other processions from different *banjars*, the village organizations, on both sides of me wound their way to the sea for the symbolic cleansing. The whole spectacle was, for the Western walker used to the solitary beach or wilderness track, rather bizarre and quite extraordinary. But perhaps the most extraordinary aspect of it all was that, while this religious extravaganza played, a good many of the Caucasian sun worshipers never took off their Walkmans, rarely looked up from their paperbacks, didn't move from their terrycloths. It was as though two wildly disparate cultures were colliding on the same beach but in no way connecting. Then something somehow symbolic

happened: warship-gray clouds came crashing in and let loose a cannon of rain. This was the one heavenly force that would persuade the hedonists to move, and they ran for the air-conditioned shelter of the restaurants and hotels and left the sand to the processioners. The rain, it seemed, had purified the beach.

After a time I knew I had to continue walking if I were to complete this expedition, as I knew the next component of the annual exorcism was Nyepi, the antipode to the cacophony of Melasti. Nyepi was the "Quiet Day," the birth of the New Year in the Balinese Saka lunar calendar, and would take place three days hence, March 31. On that day from sunrise to sunset there could be no activity, just meditation and silence. By island law there could be no reading, working, talking, cooking, eating, smoking, sex, drinking, driving—or walking. The rules of the day are summed up in four divine decrees: 1) *brat amati geni* (no fire or light); 2) *amati karya* (no work); 3) *amati lelungan* (no movement); and 4) *amati lelangan* (no desire). The idea is that if any of the evil spirits survived the ordeals of Melasti and were still around, they would think the island had been deserted and would leave as well. And the Hindus themselves could start their new life with nothingness, a clean slate.

I knew I'd be stuck with nothingness if I didn't complete my trek before Nyepi, so I trudged on northward, a warren of hotels on my right, a couple of surfers pumping two-meter rollers on my left, and a black and white *anjing* staking out territory on my path. One of Mads Lange's hobbies while overseeing his Kuta empire in the mid-1800s was importing and breeding Dalmatians, and today less pure descendants, such as the one frolicking on my itinerary, still pad the beach.

Soon the pandemonium was behind me, and I passed the last hotel along Legian, the Oberoi, built and originally designed by Pepsi Cola as an executive retreat and now the most expensive resort on the western side of Bali. It is also near the notorious Kerobokan Jail, the "paradise prison" consisting of not-so-plush accommodations for those convicted of drug dealing and use in the regency of Badung, which includes Denpasar, Legian and Kuta. Sentences are stiff in Bali: two years for smoking cannabis; ten for possession; life for dealing; death for hard drugs. Wives can get up to a year for not reporting their husbands. And skin color makes no difference; the cells are filled with Australians and Continentals as well as Balinese. I stepped quickly past the watchtowers, and took a turn around a *kris*-shaped beach and was met with a glorious sight. As far as I could see, a beach as smooth and white as an *anjing*'s tooth, and not a soul sullying it. The beach here was called Seminyak, and because the coastal road turned inland at the Oberoi, this stretch was distinguished by its utter lack of development. This was the Bali of centuries past.

I strolled along humming and taking in the paradisiacal scenery. At sand's edge palm trees leaned seaward as though listening for the muted crash of breakers spilling over the reef. Tiny crabs etched delicate mosaics in the wet sand. Mahatma Ghandi is said to have called Bali "the dawn of the world," and now it seemed as though I was walking along earth's first beach. This was how the Dutch saw Bali on their first voyage to the isle in 1592, and it was easy to understand why a couple of the sailors jumped the trading ship, taking Balinese wives, going native, believing they'd found paradise on earth.

After an hour I waded across a tributary and was on Petitenget Beach, black sanded and soft. Here, again, were small signs of civilization: a thatched garage of thirty fishing catamarans; a lone man herding his flock of ducks to the fresh water stream; an old, bent woman picking lime from the exposed reef with the low tide.

For hours I walked in peace, sometimes stepping along coral or passing through a limestone arch and always drinking in the shimmering scenery of the China-blue ocean on one side and the rice-terraced misty volcano on the other.

Toward twilight I rounded a bend and came across another set of seminude bathers and simultaneously ran into a small procession carrying a gold box on a *djempana*, or sedan chair. The women of the party wore spray coronets of frangipani and jasmine, and the men were wrapped in bright red cloth. They stopped beneath a small split-gate temple, carved from coral, and a thin, elderly woman faced inland, away from evil and toward the holy mountain, shut her eyes and began to scream and writhe in apparent pain. The rest of the group just laughed and sprinkled water on the entranced woman, who continued her fits and cries. Then a second woman held up a live yellow chick, and a man handed the first a *kris*. The older woman held the *kris* above her head and, with a kung-fu yelp, brought it down to the chick's midsection, slicing it neatly in two. Then she was free of her trance and started up the stairs to the temple, as another in the proces-

OVERLEAF: *Sunset at Tanah Lot, the great sea temple of southern Bali, built in the sixteenth century. Today, Balinese come here to pay homage to the guardian spirits of the sea, and tourists visit by the busload to watch the spectacular sunsets. (Pamela Roberson)*

sion stepped out and over to me and asked for money.

Yes, I must be near Tanah Lot, I thought. For although the sea temple is one of the most revered on the island it is also one of the biggest tourist attractions. And with tourists comes the plaintive cry for money.

I waded across another feeding stream and stepped over a meter-long green snake, which then slithered toward me in a menacing manner and had me briefly break into a run to escape. Legend has it that a huge snake dwells inside one of the shrines at Tanah Lot, guarding it from infidels. Maybe I'd just encountered a relative in training or, perhaps, a rookie outlying guard. Then, as the sun dipped its toe into the sea, I took the turn that presented Tanah Lot.

Suspended on a limestone pedestal, sculpted by the tides, Tanah Lot is spectacular, particularly at sunset when its black, pagodalike towers stand in silhouette, and it is a wonderful spot to finish a day's walk. It is probably the most photographed of all Bali's temples, and busloads of tourists arrive at the guardrailed overlook each twilight to witness the stunning light show. At my arrival there were already hundreds gathered for the performance, though I dare say I was the only one to arrive by foot. It's one way to avoid the ten-cent admission fee.

Tanah Lot looks like an ancient Oriental watercolor. It is ancient. In the sixteenth century much of Indonesia was Hindu, and the religious center was the Majapahit Kingdom in East Java. With the onslaught of Islam, imposed by Arab traders, Majapahit fell, and the devout fled to the fastness of nearby Bali and established what would become the greatest Hindu enclave outside of India. One of these refugees was a charismatic priest named Danghyang Nirartha, who, by legend, crossed the tempestuous strait between Java and Bali riding on the leaf of a Keluwih tree. He then traveled my proposed walking route along the coast of southern Bali. The story goes that Nirartha arrived, as I did, early evening and was impressed with the beautiful setting and decided to spend the night on the rock isle. Some fishermen saw him and brought gifts to his perch but tried to persuade him to come ashore and sleep in a more sensible place, such as in one of

their huts. Nirartha refused, citing divine guidance, and suggested the villagers take a cue from him and build a shrine on the rock. The villagers complied, and Tanah Lot became one of the great sea temples where Balinese come to pay homage to the guardian spirits of the sea and to purge *kelod* from their shores. And it became a great tourist draw, which many see as an unexpected blessing, bringing much-needed hard currency to the villagers who run the shops, restaurants and food stalls. But others say tourism is just another form of *kelod*, a demon that has devised a clever way to compromise their culture and pollute their religion through the seductive agent called money.

"How did you get here?" a Javanese tourist inquired as I climbed the stairs to the official photo stop with the last rays of the fiery sunset.

"*Jalan-jalan*," someone replied for me who had watched my unconventional approach from the south.

"Sounds good. What does it mean?" I turned to the Indonesian who had spoken for me.

"Walking," he smiled, and I nodded with a grin, then fetched about to hitch a ride back to the hotel.

From my window I could tell that the walk in the other direction to Uluwatu, on the southwest corner of Bukit Badung, the dot on Bali's exclamation point, would be tougher, and longer, than that to Tanah Lot. Soaring limestone cliffs sliced directly into the sea, making a waterside walk impossible. I took the day off to scribble notes and to see if I could locate someone who might offer advice on hiking to Uluwatu. "It's a bad road, but you can make it," most would reply. But they were referring to the seventeen-kilometer rutted road running from Kuta down the middle of the peninsula to the temple. I wanted to make a coastal walk, and nobody had ever heard of such a thing; and some said it was simply not possible.

Late that afternoon I decided to check out as much of the route as possible by taxi, and I ended up at Jimbaran, the southernmost beach accessible by road. There I met Wayan, who invited me to his thatched hut for tea.

As we sipped there was a soft rustle of the ban-

A prahu, or fishing vessel, used by the Balinese to make all-night harvests of mackerel, shark, turtle and crayfish. A mythical elephant fish is carved into the bow to fool real fish into visiting and to please the sea goddess. (Christian Kallen)

yan outside his door and a subtle change in temperature. The *kulkul*, the village drum, was struck with particular insistence. "It is time," he said. Wayan was ready to enact a role his grandfather's father had performed, and he expected his grandsons would as well.

Wayan stood, stretched, tightened his sarong, grabbed his kerosene pressure lamp, the blue nylon gill net in which his wife had just finished repairing a rip from the night before, his matching blue "toadstool" helmet and, perhaps most importantly, his demon offering, a little woven dish of palm frond filled with flowers, ginger, a wedge of rice and a betel nut. And he walked onto Jimbaran Beach.

I followed Wayan as he walked to a long hut above the high-water mark and helped him pull out two four-meter-long, brightly painted bamboo poles. Slinging both over his left shoulder, he

walked toward the water's edge, then paused in front of the open mouth of a carved giant, mythical elephant fish propped on coconut-log chocks. As he stared into its yawn, Wayan noticed a paint chip in the trim of the jaw and indicated he would have to soon fix it. He didn't want to offend the gods.

Then Wayan raised his head over the gaping mouth and scanned the horizon. In a minute his father strode up beside him and then, on his other side, his grandfather. His two sons, Made and Nyoman, gamboled in the mud at shoreline. The scene was one depicted a thousand times by Wayan and generations of his family, and except for loud subsonic thunder overhead, the lone sound, it was unchanged for millennia. Wayan's eyes followed the noise, and a hint of a frown formed on his face as he watched the Garuda Indonesia DC-10 growl its way out of the sky and

A Balinese fisherman with his monofilament net at Jimbaran Beach in southern Bali. (Pamela Roberson)

onto the runway just a kilometer north of his half-moon bay. In the old days, it was the position of the falling crimson ball against the blue horizon that gave the cue. Now the twilight roar of Rolls Royce engines was a signal it was time to move.

Silently, with timing tempered by their overlapping seasons, the three men pulled back a blanket of coconut-leaf mattings, picked up the sleek *prahu* with the oscitant forepeak and turned its nose around, toward the sea—away from the volcano it had bowed to the past twelve hours.

Then the men attached the bamboo poles as outriggers to a pair of spindly arms arching over the body of the *prahu*; Wayan hung his lantern off the mast, set his offering on the bow and unfurled his simple two-boom triangular sail. And with the help of his father and grandfather, who shoved, then rebounded to shore, he launched the skinny boat into the surf and bounded into a forest of sprouting sails and the raving sunset.

Wayan would spend the night, as he does every night the weather permits in the nine-month dry season, fishing from his one-man boat with his tiny monofilament net. He would pull in oil sardine, frigate mackerel, Eastern little tuna and the occasional shark, sea turtle, red snapper, grouper and other coral fish—including crayfish, which he would sell to the resort restaurants, who would in turn feature such as high-priced lobster on their menus. He would drift among a score of similar Lilliputian *prahus*, his little mantle light burning a hole in the darkness of the isolated bay in southern Bali. Just a few flaps of a seagull's wings north, hundreds of tourists daily from all over the planet spill onto Wayan's island, spending in a day what he makes in a year. But the foreigners never see Wayan or his boat or those of his neighbors. They're whisked directly to the resorts of Sanur, Nusa Dua or Kuta, just a few kilometers away but worlds apart. The airport runway is the demarcation line, a Balinese likeness to the Korean Thirty-Eighth Parallel.

The *prahu* is the Malay name for any small-to-medium-sized sailing or fishing vessel in Island Southeast Asia. Some, such as the *mayang*, built of teak and capable of holding twenty sailors, are used for long-distance sailing, and these boats were carrying spices and sandalwood to China, India and beyond as early as the second century B.C. On the other end of the scale are the little one-man *prahus* called *jukung*, small enough to navigate the tight coral passages of Bali and light enough to be hauled up on the beach after a night's harvesting.

Wayan's *jukung* is the sports car of the Bali Sea. Lean, sleek, spritely, with good mileage, it can turn on a tuna. It's called a *penunggalan* and is hand crafted with axe and adze from a highlands hardwood called *punyan ganggangan*. The elegant personality painting and detailing were effected by Wayan himself, with special attention to the elephant fish fashioned into the prow, a figurehead meant to fool the real fish into visiting a brother and also to please Baruna, the goddess of the sea. The surrealistic eyes painted on the countenance are believed to be able to see at night and guide its sailor through the blackness. They are also supposed to frighten away wicked ocean spirits. As an extra measure, to keep the evil spirits at bay, or at least away from it, and to ensure safety and a bountiful catch, Wayan or his wife will position a demon offering on the bow of the boat each evening at launching. To the inhabitants of Pandemonium, the little things can make a difference.

Skittering among the waves, working his delicate water spider of a boat, Wayan would spend a lonely twelve hours casting his net, singing into the ebon darkness and pulling in his product. I watched Wayan's boat spin into the sunset, then hitched back to the hotel for some much-needed sleep.

This time I decided it best to start my walk a bit earlier, and since I still had no working timepiece, I arranged for a wake-up call—admittedly, one of the decadent little perks of hotel civilization, along with mints on the pillow and little bottles of egg shampoo in the bathroom.

In spite of lingering jet lag, or perhaps because of it, I was on the beach by 4:00 A.M., this time heading south. The immediate obstacle was the runway of the Ngurah Rai Airport, named for a twenty-nine-year-old commander of nationalist troops in Bali who led a suicide guerrilla raid against the Dutch forces in 1946. (The Dutch had been ousted by the Japanese during World War II but, after Indonesia's declaration of independence at war's end, had to be ousted again.) The airport extends off the natural isthmus at Tuban onto an artificial jetty, and the walker has to carefully step over the quarried landfill stones to make the traverse.

The airport behind me, I was again on Jimbaran Beach, the five-kilometer gentle curve of powdery sand that has been called the finest unspoiled beach in Bali. Backed by the fishing village, book-ended by a coral reef, blockaded by cliffs to the south, Jimbaran hides from the hedonists, gives wide berth to the headlights. In fact, as I strolled the predawn beach, the only lights I could see were the oil lanterns of dozens of *prahus* as they bobbed like fireflies offshore against the rising night curtain. On my other shoulder, the moonlight lapped at the face of the great volcano, like a dog rousing a master from sleep. The mountain looked drowsy, creased from a long sleep. It was not easy to envision this quiescent Olympus letting loose one of the most violent eruptions of this century.

Gunung Agung had been dormant for more than a hundred twenty years and was thought to be inactive when in 1963 it screamed and vomited fire and ash, affecting the entire island, damaging some 22 percent of the agricultural land, killing more than fifteen hundred people and leaving another hundred forty thousand homeless. Catastrophic, but more than a natural phenomenon, or so the Balinese believed, as the eruption occurred during the purification ceremony of Eka Dasa Rudra, the once-every-one-hundred-years purification ceremony that is the most important ritual of all. Dedicated to the eleven sacred directions of Balinese space, it is conducted to restore the harmony between the forces of nature and man. Just as the ceremony was beginning, high on the slopes of Gunung Agung at Bali's most sacred temple, Pura Besakih, the holy mountain blew its top, just above the worshipers.

Many interpreted the explosion as divine retribution for the past sins of the people. Accepting the calamity as punishment by the deities on high, they assumed a fatalistic attitude, and even those below in their homes simply awaited death passively as the lava rolled in and hot ash rained down upon them. It was an attitude assumed again just two years later when another violent eruption occurred, but this time it was entirely of man's doing. An unsuccessful communist-backed coup in Jakarta incited a frenzy of savage reprisals throughout the young nation, and Bali saw some of the worst. Many who were communists passively turned themselves in, knowing the sentence would be death but believing in the sanctity of a rich afterlife. Thousands of others, who weren't communists, also died, as opportunists used the chaos of the moment to settle nonpolitical disputes and enact personal vendettas. Whole villages were wiped out in the witchhunt; individuals were hunted like boar and slashed, clubbed and chopped to death. This was another side of the Balinese character. By some estimates, more than a hundred thousand died in the bloodbath.

Although just seven kilometers from the crater rim, Pura Besakih suffered little damage from the 1963 eruption. Lava flows seemed to split at the holy ground, avoiding the mother temple. The ceremony of Eka Dasa Rudra was mounted anew sixteen years later, in 1979, and a new century was hailed. Gunung Agung, the supreme mountain, has been slumbering peacefully ever since, and it didn't look as though it was about to be aroused just now.

As I walked, the night pulled back, then blushed to an opal dawn. The great mountain tinted to a delicate pink. On my right I could make out the *prahus*, looking like a flock of mythical beasts, as they trimmed their sails and started paddling to shore. While stepping along the wet sand I recognized Ktut, Wayan's wife, umber skinned and naked from the belly up, eyes locked in the middle distance, waiting patiently for her husband to roll in with the bacon. On her head she balanced a silver bucket, the container she uses to carry Wayan's catch to the market a kilometer away. "*Selemat pagi*," good morning, we exchanged.

Then we both looked up to see Wayan's thin, tiny boat aim its wide-eyed bow toward us. Just before entering the surf, Wayan dropped his bird's-wing sail and pulled out his paddle. He waited until the precise moment when he could catch a modest swell, then dug his blade deep into the heaving water and furiously paddled to shore, leaping out as his outriggers struck the sand.

Wayan gave his diminutive wife a broad, gap-toothed grin. It had been a good night: the narrow-beamed *prahu* was filled with six basketfuls of fish, and the net hadn't ripped on the coral. After paying the five percent commission to the government auction house Wayan would come home fifteen thousand rupiah richer, which in someone else's terms would be about nine dollars. For this, he was happy, and as he dragged his little boat above the high-tide mark he stopped and gave it a thankful pat on its sea-soaked and glistening belly. We passed smiles, and as he disappeared into the palms I extracted my feet from the sucking sand and continued my walk.

By sunrise I had reached the end of Jimbaran Bay and had to climb the fifty-meter-high corrugated cliff to continue. On top, it was a different planet altogether. The Dutch had called this region "Tafelhoek," the "Tableland," and it is a limestone plateau that looks much like the Dalmatian coast of Yugoslavia. Unlike the rest of the island, it is arid, dusty and desolate, with prickly pear cactus and euphorbia instead of palms and rice paddies. I quickly discovered it was impossible to walk along the rim, as I had hoped, as the farmers had constructed a series of living fences of thorn bushes to protect their bean fields from cattle. So I had to follow labyrinthine cow paths that would detour sometimes a kilometer or more away from the cliffs, and occasionally I would bushwack back through the paddocks. Other times sheer gorges blocked passage, and

OPPOSITE: *Rice is the staple that feeds the overcrowded island of Bali, and terraced rice fields are marvels of hydraulic engineering. Streams are dammed far uphill from the fields, with water flowing in hand-built aqueducts to the fields below. (Richard Bangs)*

I'd find myself mountain climbing rather than walking. This was quite the contrast from the casual saunter of two days previous—and in other ways as well. There were no tourists, no hotels, no palm trees. And there was very little sand. Occasionally I'd look down upon a little cove dusted with white unfootprinted sand and scramble down the escarpment to a perfect private beach. It was hard to believe such beaches existed after having crossed Kuta, and it was hard to believe such spots would remain pristine for long.

After a dip, I tried to continue the walk at tide level, but the beach soon petered out, and I was faced with a blockade of limestone boulders that had spilled from the rim. It appeared a route existed through the rubble, as scant footprints appeared in little pocks of sand along the rocks, so I hoisted myself up and proceeded to negotiate. Ducking through water-bored arches and scrambling over the broken, surf-polished karst, I made good headway and was convinced I could make a fair distance on this route without having to climb back up and continue along the hard dirt in the hot, harsh environment of the plateau. The sea breeze was tonic, and the view looking back across a spangled bay to the palms of Kuta was out of a Gauguin. Sometime around noon I found a sand-dusted bench notched in the cliff about four meters above the water. Positioned beneath an overhang, it offered shade and a soft place for a respite. I pulled off my pack and sat back to suck on an orange and pull on my canteen. I was making good time, the tide was neap, so I figured I could afford a small recess from the walk. As I leaned back, my pack felt like my favorite pillow. The sand was soft as down, and the rhythmic billowing of the surf below was hypnotic. I closed my eyes for a couple of minutes, at most.

A cold, salty slap on my face was my next sensation. I sprang up and rubbed my eyes. The sea was less than a meter from my bench, and the sun had dipped several degrees. My couple of minutes must have stretched to a couple of hours, and the tide was coming in. With much haste I saddled up and started once again southwest, but I could make only a few meters before meeting a crashing comber. The high water now covered the route. I could see no way to continue, so I turned back and worked my way over the boulders and across a scalloped shelf back toward the beach where I had originally descended from the plateau. But, as I shimmied around a rock and clutched to a crag, I saw there now was no beach. The rising tide had covered my retreat. And, worse, the tide hadn't peaked. I fixed my attention on a black rock and watched as each flux of the surf left a higher stain. My first instinct was to leap in and swim for it, but a second thought—remembering my pack full of camera gear—dampened that plan. I decided to get back to my bench and survey the options, quickly.

The situation didn't look promising. The water was now half a meter from my resting bench and rising. With every swell my chamber was spewed with spray and foam. With the ebb, however, I noticed some exposed rocks to the southwest. And, stretching my neck from my roost, I thought I saw a hint of a trail just fifty meters southwest that zigzagged back up to the plateau. It appeared the only option.

So I watched the undulations, the ebbs and flows, for several stanzas, and mentally charted my course. Then, with a reflux, I jumped into the millrace and sped for safety. I slid over the slippery sedimentary rocks, pitched myself up on a boulder and dropped down onto a sand shelf; then the waves rolled back in and wrapped around my waist. With one hand I held my day pack above my head; with the other I desperately gripped the haft of an outcropping, and the water tugged on my balance, calling me out to sea. As the currents sucked and swirled, a sea turtle poked his head through the spume and eyed me curiously, as though empathetic with my predicament. I watched the distorted shape of his underwater body as he was swept away with the receding water, and I made another dash—over the scree and straight to a dead end. The cliff curved upward like the wall of a parabola, and its surface was satellite-dish smooth. The tide was still rising, and I was on a perch that evidently would not exist in a matter of minutes. Preserving the safety of my camera and lenses now lost some priority, even knowing they were not insured. Still, I took them from the pack and held them high above my head with my right arm, then jumped into the maelstrom. The swirling water reached my neck but no farther, and I could half-swim, half-hop southward, hanging onto cracks and notches as the surges pulled at my body. Then I reached a vertical notch in the cliff. It looked as though it had been created by running water and worn into a trail by people. Grabbing a tussock of grass, I pulled myself from the water and was on the steepest trail I had ever seen but most certainly a trail. The camera and lenses were spotted with water but still functioning, and I was safe. As a final wave fired a splash of foam at my face, I spat back and turned to get to where I belonged—on the plateau.

It was a thirty-minute haul, up switchbacks that would intimidate Edmund Hillary. The final pitch was sheer and required negotiating a makeshift bamboo ladder left by some guardian angel. Then, at last, I was back on top.

The path was more distinct here, winding through bean fields and fruit orchards and past the big eyes of skinny cows. In the last century, Bukit Badung was a hunting preserve for royalty, since wild animals—wild boar, deer, tigers and leopards—fled here as cultivation blanketed the rest of the island. Now only domestic animals inhabit the dry tableland, the others having long been hunted out. At one turn, the paths split, and I took the smaller tangent. It was now a quiet stroll. I passed a black butterfly, like a velvet bow, poised on a waxy white orchid; then a row of trees from which were suspended minute brown, barrel-shaped beehives made from *idjuk* fiber. Since there is no winter, and thus no rest for Balinese bees, they go on producing their honey year round, and each month a hive like the ones hanging on the plateau would yield about half a kilogram of wild, exotic honey. The dusty path led to a compound of three dried-mud huts fenced in by a hibiscus hedge. I wandered in and found chickens and pigs, a white-haired man sharpening his machete and two golden-skinned, half-naked women washing their *kebayas*—long-sleeved village-style bodices. At the sight of my entrance, the women dropped their laundry and scampered into the darkness of one of the huts; the old man raised his machete in a defensive gesture, then lowered it when he looked into my eyes and saw I meant no harm.

My presence in this little compound was clearly an unusual circumstance, and I felt as though I had stumbled back a century or two into the Old Bali of romanticized literature. Though the fertile body of Bali is packed with people, the rangy hanging tail of Bukit Badung is practically empty, a desiccated tableland spotted with subsistence homesteads and people who rarely, if ever, interact with Westerners. All this will change, of course, since Bukit Badung is the district marked for tourism development, and the northeast side at Nusa Dua has already undergone the multimillion dollar metamorphosis. How all this affects the Balinese, and their culture, is the big question.

Back in 1930, photographer André Roosevelt contemplated the same issue in the introduction to Hickman Powell's *The Last Paradise*: "Nowhere in the world has the aborigine been able to resist the invasion coming from the West. The age of steel, as typified by this country [America], has crept into the lazy, happy, contented East, leaving behind a trail of unhappiness and sorrow. Can Bali, which stands in a peculiar geographical and economical position, be able to resist and retain its individuality?"

The renowned Mexican artist Miguel Covarrubias mused on the question in his 1937 classic book *Island of Bali*:

In adapting foreign ideas to their own culture, the Balinese have shown unusual logic and an intelligent power of assimilation. It is to be hoped that those in control of the island's future will see that progress comes to the Balinese naturally and gradually and that they shall be permitted to decide for themselves what they want to absorb without losing their essential qualities and becoming another vanishing race of coolies. The Balinese deserve a better fate; they are too proud and intelligent to be treated with the prevalent arrogance and patronizing attitude of colonizers who regard the native as a shiftless and treacherous inferior whose contact pollutes the "superior" whites and who regard those who show deference to the native as a menace to the prestige of the often bigoted and insolent whites. . . . The

Balinese have a great culture that cannot be saved by the admiration of the outside world . . . if this principle is disturbed, the foundation will be knocked from under the structure upon which the culture, the law and order of the Balinese are based, and social and economic chaos will eventually descend upon the happy and peaceful island of Bali.

Then cut to the 1980s. Bali has been besieged by tourists. There is mechanized mass production of erotic carvings and wooden salad spoons with handles fashioned in the shape of pineapples, and other objets d'art. There are twice-weekly flights on the national airline, Garuda Indonesia, from Los Angeles direct to Bali and a greater frequency from most major European and Australian cities. David Bowie, Mick Jagger, Hollywood glitterati and marquees of celebrity trendies vacation here, along with millions of pretenders. It's a well-oiled holiday destination, and as such the culture has been stained.

"Prices are getting higher, money-minded people in the tourist ghettos like Sanur, Kuta and Denpasar hassle you, the sound of motorbikes is constant, quality of paintings and carvings is declining," wrote Bill Dalton in his 1983 opus *Indonesia Handbook*, which is banned in its subject country for its sometimes critical look at politics, policy and the dark side of reality. "People who were here during the 30s can't bear to go back. It's too painful to see." And German author Kurt Huehn, who penned the 1985 *Hildebrand's Travel Guide to Indonesia*, in his chapter on the "Island of Gods and Demons" wrote: "Those who knew the island before will today notice a change for the worse in all sectors. The commercialization of temple rites and dances has taken on dubious forms, and the daily life of the Balinese, which is characterized by colorful ceremonies, may appear to some as a staged holiday attraction."

There are those who believe, however, that Bali has not been corrupted or compromised by the West. In 1938 Beryl de Zoete and Walter Spies coauthored a book called *Dance and Drama in Bali* in which they claim the Balinese have "a suppleness of mind which has enabled them to take what they want of the alien civilisations

reaching them for centuries and to leave the rest." That is certainly true to a degree, as the walk through Kuta during Melasti demonstrated, with thousands of Balinese lost in a centuries-old ceremony amidst pale-faced surfers, paddleball players and sun worshipers. A New Zealand writer, Hugh Mabbett, self-published a 1987 book entitled *In Praise of Kuta* in which he quotes a young Balinese who converted to Christianity while in jail: "Before that my gods were Harley Davidson bikes, fighting, dope, women, drinking." Curiously, Mabbett uses the quote to show that Kuta is changing, certainly, but for the better. He believes that, like his Christian convert, the scene at Kuta is being born again, and old values and customs are replacing the celebrated decadence that made Kuta infamous in the 1970s. He also argues that *banjars*, the village co-op organizations that oversee marriages, tooth filings, burials, festivals, temple ceremonies and cremations, have such a ripstop coating on the fabric of Balinese mores and societal behavior that they have prevented the tears and punctures that have shredded other cultures. The *banjars*, he believes, have kept a rich culture strong enough to resist the alluring debaucheries of the West. What is indisputably true is that in some sectors a fundamentalistic movement is washing over Bali, calling for a return to ancient values and religious rule, and some of the village *banjars* are leading the way. When crime seemed to be getting out of hand in the late 1970s, several *banjars* organized vigilante groups, starring karate students, to run all-night patrols and do battle with the hoodlums. Some would question the use of violence to preserve a culture, contending the violent act itself compromises and invalidates the peaceful spirit of the Bali they seek. Others condone it, submitting the doctrine of ends justifying means.

Beyond the strong-willed character of the Balinese and their self-sustaining ability to hang on to their heritage, Mabbett and others posit that tourism has pumped life into a cultural rebirth, giving an economic incentive to preserve and refine ancient dances, plays and art. A new prosperity along Kuta cannot be denied, but how much of it has come from the dismal science of underbelly commerce is unknown. There are

A view of Sanur Beach, in southern Bali. (Andreas Bender)

tourists who want dances and museums and traditional music; and there are those who want Bintang by the case, cannabis by the kilo and flesh by the hour. Tourists, Mabbett further proposes, with their excesses and absurdity, may help to preserve the Balinese way of life, as the islanders see through the nonsense and want nothing of it. Only, all too often, all too many instead of shunning the ridiculous are attracted to it and join the carnival.

Much has been made of the refractoriness of the Balinese character and its mulish resistance to unwelcome change. The historical citation is an incident at the turn of this century, on the other side of Bukit Badung near Sanur, when a wrecked Chinese cargo ship was looted by the Balinese, a salvage operation that was traditional practice for the islanders. To that point, the Dutch had pretty much ignored southern Bali

because of its lack of spices and ivory and the shortage of safe anchorages along its craggy and cliffed coasts. But when the raja of southern Bali refused to pay a bill for the plundered goods, the Dutch used it as an excuse to move in and impose their power. In September 1906, Dutch soldiers landed at Sanur, marched inland and lined up outside the palace of the raja of Badung. Preferring self-destruction to the ignobility of surrender, the Hindu prince and his court and family, wearing white cremation garments, charged into the lines of the Dutch armed forces, ritually killing themselves, often by driving their own swords into their own hearts amidst the murderous cannon- and gunfire of the Dutch.

The Masadalike mass suicide at Sanur, called *puputan* (Balinese for "the end"), was repeated up the coast in Klungkung in 1908, when the Dutch launched a similar punitive expedition

The monkeys at Pura Luhur Uluwatu, the second sea temple founded, according to legend, by the wandering priest Nirartha. (George Fuller)

over local interference in the opium monopoly. This time the traditional leader of the entire island, Dewa Agung, as well as more than two hundred Balinese men, women and children, chose death before dishonor, engaging in self-immolation and mutual fatal stabbings as the Dutch fired into the mayhem. When the smoke cleared, Bali was officially part of the Dutch East Indies. This second *puputan* marked the end of Balinese independence, and, some say, the end of classical Balinese culture, as the Dutch formally and completely took over administration of the island. Almost forty years later, in an eerily reminiscent incident, the young military officer Ngurah Rai, whose bravery is commemorated in the airport's naming, led ninety-five of his ragtag guerilla soldiers on another *puputan* mission

against the Dutch colonial forces, although this time the mass suicide was a significant domino that led to the fall of foreign rule and the emergence of Indonesia as a nation. *Puputan* is popularly cited as the true show of the depth of Balinese tenacity. And some are hoping for a renewal of that spirit to fend off the new Western invasion of twisted values. Nobody expects martyrdom, but some are hoping for a fight to the finish—a rigid, almost inhuman resistance to the blandishments of the future. But the tomorrow of Bali has already crept onto the southern beaches, and many hearts and minds were taken without a struggle, barely a squeak. The rituals, routines, celebrations, ceremonies, offerings and prayers still exist, and exact a strong influence over the people, but more and more the ceremonies are performed solely for the amusement of a visiting audience, and prayers are made to the bars, neon and tourist wallets.

The little compound I had tripped into on the remote outer region of Bukit Badung was out of synch, out of place and running out of time. Bureaucrats in Jakarta whose Kiwi-polished shoes will never be scuffed by the potholes of this compound have already decided its fate. It will be turned over to the tourists, and the simple, shy family I had encountered will probably change, becoming hard as the Bukit dirt, covetous as the rest of us, their *banjars*, traditions, *puputans* and rebirth notwithstanding.

I smiled and bowed deeply to the now-friendly old man, who, if lucky, would live out his days in the nineteenth century, then turned to take up again on the main path. By midafternoon I had negotiated enough up-and-down relief to have climbed the Matterhorn. I needed a drink and looked down to see Padang Padang, a protected shallow reef that has earned the reputation as one of the best advanced surfing spots on earth. And sure enough there were scores of boards plying the breakers, skidding through the spray. And on the narrow strip of beach there was a tiny thatched hut with a little, wrinkled Balinese man out front holding a plastic bucket full of soft drinks. I reached for change and glissaded down the slope for the exchange. The label talked of caffeine and caramel, but the taste was like champagne.

Another hour along a surfers' path and I reached my goal: Pura Luhur Uluwatu, meaning "the temple that is located above the stone," the other great sea shrine built, according to legend, by the wandering priest Nirartha. And, so the lore goes, this was where Nirartha came for his final sunset. Hung like a Malibu beach house over the two-hundred-meter-high precipice, it seems precariously balanced, ready to dive with the first earth trembler. The rock foundation, however, has held the temple for four centuries, and it is believed to be the petrified ship of Dewi Danu, a goddess of the waters.

The temple itself, however, hasn't fared as well. Like all Balinese temples, it has no roof, so that God might drop in whenever he gets the urge. So the interior coral has been worn by weather, and the upper tiers were struck by lightning a few years back. The troop of sacred monkeys allowed to run amok through the temple have stained most of the surfaces. Nevertheless, it is a grand temple, with a Chinese motif, pagodalike, and when the sun goes down the sight of Uluwatu in exotic relief is breathtaking and inspirational at once.

It was easy to see, as I watched the colors pulse through the split gate, why Nirartha came here to die and how he achieved Moksa, the Balinese equivalent of Nirvana, the place of eternal bliss, where the human spirit is united with the spirit of God.

At the risk of sounding trite, I too felt delivered, upon reaching Uluwatu by foot and watching the sun sink in a glorious pageantry of technicolor. I too waited here and, after the last licks of red on the horizon, found myself alone. The tourists, who had driven here from the resorts for the witching hour, had headed back for cocktails. Even the monkeys, one of whom had pinched my sunglasses, had repaired to more interesting endeavors than hassling humans. I was left with the spirit of Nirartha and the recollection of an oft-cited chestnut about the Balinese and their ultimate tribute to the balance of life that is forever unobtainable in this earthly incarnation: that the Balinese believe heaven to be just like Bali, only without trouble and illness—and, some add these days, tourists.

NUSA TENGGARA

Sailing the Savu Sea

OVERSHADOWED by the passionate histories of Java and Sumatra, the wild interiors of Borneo and Sulawesi and the graceful culture of Bali, the links of the island chain to the east of Bali have sometimes been called the forgotten islands. They scatter like beads from a broken necklace, following the arc set down by Sumatra and Java, reaching eastward toward New Guinea. Upon them can be found megalithic tombs, remnants of ancient Hindu kingdoms, the palaces of Islamic sultans and Catholic cathedrals. There are rainforest and desert, tree ferns and eucalyptus, enormous volcanic craters still warm from recent explosions. And there are rainbow-colored lakes, submarine floral gardens and lizards large as lions. This is the province known as Nusa Tenggara—literally the Southeast Islands of Indonesia.

To the uninitiated, the names of the Lombok-to-Timor span of islands—Sumbawa, Flores, Sumba, Savu, Roti and others—do not evoke a romantic past of piracy or spice trade or religious fervor. Yet here in the islands of Nusa Tenggara—especially in the scattered lands surrounding the little-known Savu Sea—the art of *ikat* weaving has evolved to a level that approaches the mystical. The people of these islands wear more than just sarongs and shawls: they wear a cultural history, a genealogical record and social statement, woven into the fabric of their daily attire. Certain pieces are said to bring good luck; some are said to bring bad. The oldest cloth of all, the most valuable and magical, is hidden and protected, almost never revealed.

Collectors of the *ikat*-weave cloth of Flores, Timor, Savu and Sumba usually buy the cloth in Bali, Java, or farther afield in Singapore or Hong Kong; only rarely do they make the extended journey to Nusa Tenggara. Perhaps in part to serve the serious collector, there exists a twelve-day tour of the islands, including Timor, Sumba, Flores and Savu, all of which enclose the Savu Sea. Via Spice Islands Cruises' forty-meter *Island Explorer*, passengers visit the weaving villages where *ikat* is woven and worn—and see the fabled dragons of Komodo, the multicolored lakes of Keli Mutu and the diving reefs of the tropical seas—without sacrificing the comforts and luxuries of a cruise ship lifestyle.

Huge lizards and scenic wonders are appealing lures to any traveler; I signed up suspecting that among these lesser-known islands of Indonesia there might also be sensed the calm beat of the archipelago's pulse, long since accelerated by modern stimulants on Java and Bali.

Nearby Bali is a natural point of departure for

a tour of Nusa Tenggara. In fact, Indonesia's original political divisions included Bali among them. Bali is geographically the westernmost island of the Lesser Sundas; the Greater Sundas are the four largest islands of Indonesia—Borneo and Sulawesi on the equator, Sumatra and Java to the south. From Bali east, the archipelago breaks up into smaller islands, fragmented in the geological zone between Asia's Sunda Shelf and Australia's Sahul Shelf. Although the human societies on these smaller islands are isolated by currents of history as well as navigation from the modern age, it is the region's biological and geological distinctions that may be its most notable characteristics. Nusa Tenggara is a zone of transition, as first noted more than 130 years ago by Alfred Russel Wallace.

Wallace postulated what is today known as the Wallace Line, the demarcation between Bali and Lombok that distinguishes the flora and fauna of Australia from Asia. It is not a firm and impenetrable barrier but a border of convenience—in general, certain plants, birds and smaller mammals indicative of Australia are not found to the west of the line, and the life forms of Asia are found in decreasing numbers to the east of it. (The region of transition where Asian life forms give way to Australian is known as Wallacea.) A prime example is primates: the gibbons that inhabit the forests of Bali (and who steal watches, wallets and peanuts from the tourists who visit the "Monkey Forests") are not found across the Wallace Line, in nearby Lombok. Meanwhile, the colorful birds of New Guinea and Australia, including cockatoos, parrots and birds of paradise, are almost never seen in Bali or Java. Biologists believe that tree-dwelling monkeys make it more difficult for colorful birds to survive—their display is attractive to predators as well as to potential partners.

Lombok, the westernmost link in the chain of the islands of Wallacea, was to be the first cruise stop within Nusa Tenggara. Such was the original intention of the *Island Explorer*, but the ship had developed engine troubles and was therefore unable to leave Bali's Benoa Harbor on schedule. So I spent an extra afternoon at Sanur Beach, purchasing souvenirs of Bali and staying cool in the shade of a papaya tree. Perhaps next time I would see Lombok; this time I would content myself with reading about it.

Lombok, which means "chili pepper" in Java's Malay dialect, is an almost circular 5435 square kilometers of terrain radiating from the volcano Gunung Rinjani. One would not expect to find one of Indonesia's highest peaks on this relatively small island, but here it is, at 3726 meters the highest besides the Carstenz massif of Irian Jaya. Near the top is a crater lake, Segura Anak, formerly one of the holiest sites on the island, where kings became pilgrims in pursuit of longevity.

There is, not by accident, another holy lake on this island at the summer palace of the raja of Karangasem—the name of a Balinese family that ruled over western Lombok in the nineteenth century. Here, near the market town of Narmada, one of the later rajahs built an elaborate complex of tiered gardens, fountains and arbors, courtyards and pavilions, all focused on a manmade lake. The king sadly informed his subjects that he was too old to make the annual pilgrimage to Rinjani, and he had built this lake as a substitute; his rationale accepted, he encouraged young women of Narmada to bathe in its waters. From his palace windows, the aged king would point out the most beautiful and have her introduced in his quarters. It was certainly a lot easier than a long hike and may have served longevity equally well.

Spring-fed pools, percolating from the aerated volcanic soil, are one of the characteristics of Lombok. The range crested by Rinjani on the north is paralleled by a low-lying, arid, nonvolcanic range on the south, and the narrow corridor between the two—some twenty-five kilometers at its widest—is as fertile and terraced as Bali. This rice-growing region is filled with ornate Hindu temples, Islamic mosques and lush sacred springs. The springs were worshiped long before either Hinduism or Islam (or, later, Christianity)

PAGE 108: *Pinneate palms stretch to catch the sunlight's last glow on the coast of Lombok, guardian island of Nusa Tenggara. (George Fuller)*

came to Lombok in the seventeenth century; prior to that, animistic beliefs prevailed among the Sasaks, the island's native inhabitants.

Some believe the Sasaks, with their dark skin and wavy hair, came from India or Burma; some believe they migrated by bamboo rafts from Java. Lombok was certainly under the control of Java's great Majapahit Empire by the fourteenth century. In fact, the ancient *lontar*-leaf book *Negar-akertagama*, one of the most important sources of information about the ancient empires of Java, was uncovered on Lombok. Whatever the early history of Lombok and the Sasaks, it all changed dramatically in the seventeenth century.

From the east came the Makassarese, by way of Sumbawa, bearing the sword of Islam; from the west came the Hindu Balinese, ostensibly to assist the Lombok overlord Datu Selaparang defend himself against the Makassarese. When Datu was killed, however, the Balinese took over the western valleys for themselves, enslaving the native Sasaks. The Makassarese were finally driven out, but the message of Islam had been adopted by the Sasaks of the east, who successfully held out for more than a century against the Balinese. Finally, in 1849, Bali's raja of Karangasem unified the island under his rule. The Dutch came along in 1894 to unsettle matters anew, wresting control of the island from the Karangasem rajas in a bitter, bloody but brief war.

Aside from Islam, the Makassarese imported one other significant cultural feature to Lombok, one which has since become familiar to the world at large. Alfred Russel Wallace, writing about his 1856 visit to Lombok in *The Malay Archipelago*, took note of this curious phenomenon:

One morning, as we were sitting at breakfast, Mr. Carter's servant informed us that there was an "Amok" in the village—in other words, that a man was "running a muck." Orders were immediately given to shut and fasten the gates of our enclosure. . . . A short time before, a man had been killed at a gaming-table, because, having lost half a dollar more than he possessed, he was going to "amok." Another had killed or wounded seventeen people before he could be destroyed. In their wars a whole regiment of these people will sometimes agree to "amok," and then rush on with such energetic desperation as to be very formidable to men not so excited as themselves. . . . And what that excitement is those who have been in one best know, but all who have ever given way to violent passions, or even indulged in violent and exciting exercises, may form a very good idea. It is a delirious intoxication, a temporary madness that absorbs every thought and every energy. And can we wonder at the kris-bearing, untaught, brooding Malay preferring such a death, looked upon as almost honourable, to the cold-blooded details of suicide, if he wishes to escape from overwhelming troubles, or the merciless clutches of the hangman and the disgrace of a public execution? . . . In either case he chooses rather to "amok."

I closed my copy of *The Malay Archipelago*, packed up my beach towel and headed back to Benoa Harbor. The sun was just going down as I arrived, and the news was good: the engine trouble had been fixed, and we would set off soon. The *Island Explorer* gleamed white with blue and yellow trim at its berth, bright in the setting sun. I tugged my luggage up the gangway, eager to meet my shipmates and begin an adventure in culture and history.

One by one—or two by two, more often, like the animals to the Ark—the other passengers came aboard or appeared from the cabins below. There were a handsome French couple in their late fifties; a like-aged English pair; a German husband, Chinese wife and their two boys, aged eight and nine; and two single women—an elderly inquisitive American from Florida and a German in her midforties, dressed in a blue and red sailor suit with rainbow platform shoes. There was also a couple from Java, a chubby husband with a comical splay-footed walk and his wife, quiet and slender. The group was rounded off by Nikki, a small dark woman from Jakarta, cute as a button and engaged to the cruise director; and Brenda Unseld, the American-born shipboard lecturer for our cultural travels. Only fifteen of us, then, on a boat outfitted for thirty-six. Plenty of room for all.

I was shown to my cabin, number nine, on the port side just aft of amidships. (I had originally thought it was room number nine on the left but was soon set aright.) It was small, but by no means cramped, with space for a pastel-pink sofa, a standing closet, a vanity table and bathroom with shower, as well as a bed. I unpacked my bags and brought out the souvenirs I had bought in Bali. The blue and white batik sarong draped nicely over the end of the bed; I propped the frog mask on a light fixture and hung a small carved monkey from an air-conditioner. Then I went up to the lounge just as the engines revved into action. The *Island Explorer* left its berth and headed slowly out of Benoa Harbor. For the next week and more we would cruise across the Lombok Strait to archipelago's end, bound for the mysteries of Nusa Tenggara and the weaving meccas of the Savu Sea.

Upstairs, a thin bearded man in a white uniform—with three white stripes on the epaulets, high civilian rank—was introducing himself as our cruise director. Alex Durrant struck me at once as efficient, proper, perhaps a little punctilious, every lean inch the Englishman despite the dozen years he had spent in Jakarta.

Alex filled us in on shipboard ritual: breakfast was served from 7:00 A.M. on, and lunch from 12:30, but both were casual and buffet style. Dinner, on the other hand, did require our prompt attendance at 7:30, and dress should be a bit more formal—"smart and casual" being the international phrase for evening wear, with clean shirt, long pants and shoes preferred over shorts and sandals. There was even to be an afternoon serving of coffee, tea and biscuits, which relieved whatever fears I had that a full day's encounter with the goat-eating dragons of Komodo or the rolling seas of the tropics would be quite unbearable. There was nothing a cup of tea, served with porcelain and stainless, couldn't cure.

Alex also filled us in on the ship's engine problems and noted the changes in our itinerary they had forced. Our delayed departure from Benoa had allowed the crew to partially if not completely repair the starboard engine, and we were underway at last. However, due to the time lost in repair and the slower speed at which the still-crippled ship was traveling, the *Island Explorer* would not call at the two easternmost destinations, including Kupang on the island of Timor. Until 1975, Timor had been half-Indonesian, half-Portuguese; a still-controversial Indonesian army takeover of East Timor (Timor Timur, or "Tim-Tim") unified the island at the cost of thousands of lives. But the indigenous culture of Timor was rich and ancient, and the colorful *ikat* cloth woven there is among the most valuable in the world.

Since I knew little about weaving I was far more unhappy about our other missed stop—Lembata—and its small fishing village, off the east end of Flores. On Lembata, prehistoric methods of whaling are still practiced. Villagers sail their ten-meter catamarans to within striking distance of the leviathans, keeping pace with oars to allow the harpoonist one leaping shot off the front prow. It is literally a leaping shot—the man hurls his weight down on the lance to drive it home, then swims frantically for safety. This made me think of Pip, his fearful jump from the *Pequod*'s whaling boat and Stubb's forceful argument—"*Stick to the boat*, is your true motto in whaling; but cases will sometimes happen when *Leap from the boat* is still better."

Dinner was served as we passed into the Lombok Strait. Small photocopied menus were set, two to a table, along with your typical three-fork, three-spoon, double-knifed cutlery. I consulted the menu: shrimp salad, asparagus soup, rack of lamb or chicken sauteed in white wine, vegetables and potatoes, chocolate cake. And two varieties of wine—a Haut-Médoc and an Australian chardonnay—by special order of the cruise director. I decided there was every reason in the world to look forward to the rest of the cruise aboard the *Island Explorer*.

Dawn found us still off the coast of Lombok, the ragged majesty of Rinjani just ahead of our starboard bow. The currents were strong, progress was slower than expected and our new first day's destination, Palau Moyo—an island off the north coast of Sumbawa where we were to have enjoyed a day of snorkeling and water skiing—was at first delayed, then canceled. We would continue on through the day in hopes of reaching Komodo, home of the giant lizards, early the next morning.

So we become enforced companions for the next thirty-six hours, without the possibility of landfall to relieve our company. The long day of cruising became the opportunity for us to find out about each other, an effort that revolved most readily around the issue of langauge. The French couple, Nicole and Bertie Morel-Journal, spoke a quiet and intimate French to each other, while Bertie's gentlemanly conversations with the rest of us in his quirky English were articulate and enjoyable. Kurt and Judi Dimter—he a German engineer, she a Cantonese artist—seemed to be of the world's citizenry, knowing German, French, English and even a bit of Malay. (They now live in Singapore and will soon move to Beijing.) Their bilingual children spoke German and English. The Supranas, the Javanese couple, spoke English, German and a bit of French in addition to their native Bahasa Indonesia. Frau March, a librarian from Germany, had her native tongue, a bit of French and less English. For that matter, no one could converse with me or Mrs. Sweeney, a Coral Gables matron, except in English. My *turista* Spanish did me no good in these tropics. No one knows Esperanto; English is today's universal language, in business and tourism at any rate, and it became the public language of lounge, dining cabin and sun deck.

We went our separate ways after breakfast, some disappearing into cabins, some climbing up to the sun deck before it became too hot. By the middle of the day, the *Island Explorer* had left Lombok behind and begun to churn along the north side of Sumbawa; by midafternoon, the island's blasted crater of Tambora appeared. It was one of those odd corners of the world that most people have never heard of but that once exercised an enormous impact on the lives of its neighbors and whose influence was felt around the globe.

Prior to 1815, the conical peak of Gunung Tambora dominated the skyline of Sumbawa, towering more than 4000 meters high to exceed Rinjani as the region's highest summit. Then, one day in April 1815, a tremendous eruption obliterated the top fourth of the mountain, casting some eighty square kilometers of ash and rock into the skies. Villages and rice fields nearby were bombarded; perhaps twelve thousand people on Sumbawa died in the eruption, which wiped out almost the entire western half of the island. Worse still, the ash that settled on Sumbawa and Flores to the west destroyed livestock and farmland, and another eighty thousand lost their lives to famine in the coming years, making it the deadliest volcano known to history.

The scale of the eruption is almost incomprehensible. It was considerably larger than the recent eruption of Mount Saint Helens in Washington, which ejected less than one square kilometer of ash and claimed sixty-one lives. It was about twice as large as the 1912 eruption of Mount Katmai in Alaska (which, because of its isolation, may have killed no one); and it was even four times larger than the famous eruption of Krakatau, to the west of Java, in 1883. The ash from Tambora entered the upper atmosphere and circled the globe, leading to the so-called year without summer of 1816. Yet now the 2850-meter summit of Tambora is just another dormant volcano in an archipelago littered with both quiet and smoking cones, and yesterday's catastrophe is today's footnote.

In the early evening Brenda Unseld, our lecturer, presented an introductory lecture on the weaving of Nusa Tenggara. At this point I was not interested in weaving and expected to be bored. But Brenda, a tall, slender woman wearing a floor-length native sarong for the occasion, had surrounded herself with samples of colorful, elaborately decorated cloth. They were all traditional Indonesian *ikat* weavings, sarongs and shawls and decorative panels, most of them from islands we were scheduled to visit in the next week. Their colors were muted earth tones—maroon, brick and other shades of red, as well as deep indigo blues, browns and blacks; the patterns were geometric, boldly banded or deeply detailed, some of them showing representations of fantastic creatures such as lions, elephants, dragons and trees sprouting skulls. In the antiseptic atmosphere of the ship's lounge, its VCR and compact disk player at the ready, its well-stocked bar quietly open for callers as the ship bounded over the waves of the Flores Sea, these weavings breathed of ancient arts and secrets.

Ikat means "to tie" in the Malay languages. The technique of *ikat* weaving is usually based on dyeing the warp thread into patterns, which are then bound on the backstrap loom and woven into heavy shawls. The *ikat* process itself takes place as a skein (formerly of handspun cotton thread, but now increasingly commercial cotton or even synthetics) is strung up on a frame, and the design to be woven is tied onto the thread with bindings of palm fiber, grass or coconut leaf. When the thread is dyed, the bound portion resists the dye because of its tight knots. "Dye-resist" is the generic name for this sort of dyeing; batik is also dye-resist but uses wax instead of bindings to create its design elements.

Subsequent immersions in different colors of dye, with different patterns of bindings on the thread, creates the multicolored design. Usually this is executed on the warp thread, the material running the long way on the backstrap loom of Southeast Asia; the weft thread is dyed a single color, the dark background of the pattern, and it is passed through the warp thread by the shuttle to complete the weave. In some areas, the weft is the *ikat* thread, and the warp the background color. In a very few isolated regions—including the Indian town of Pattan, the Japanese island of Okinawa, and the old Balinese village of Tenganan—both warp and weft have been patterned by *ikat*, and the resulting double-*ikat*, style creates extremely subtle designs of great beauty and worth.

As well as being artifacts of great immediate appeal, these weavings provide a kind of cultural overview of Indonesia, a material window on history that is almost geologic in its historical revelations. The backstrap loom, and possibly *ikat* dyeing itself, were probably introduced into the Malay Archipelago between the eighth and second centuries B.C. by migrants from northern Vietnam—the kingdom the ancient Chinese called Annan. These Proto-Malay immigrants brought with them what is known as the Dong-Son culture, said to be the source of the isolated Neolithic and megalithic cultures of Indonesia. Decorated traditional houses, rice cultivation, stone graves and animistic magical traditions in-volving head-hunting are other characteristics of these Proto-Malay people in Indonesia.

The Dong-Son culture was the most dominant culture in Indonesia for at least a thousand years. Traces and effects of the Dong-Son can be found throughout the archipelago, except where completely obliterated by later influences. In fact, the Dong-Son culture was so widespread that it provides a cultural background against which further developments took place; people on the less accessible islands or in hard-to-penetrate interiors were insulated from succeeding influences, and they still display an essentially Dong-Son culture in the present day. Among these are the Toraja of Sulawesi, the Batak of Sumatra's Lake Toba region, the Dayak of Borneo's interior and some tribes among the scattered islands of Nusa Tenggara.

The first major influences to affect the Dong-Son cultures in Indonesia were the Hindus and Buddhists from India in the second to fifth centuries A.D.; some of their artistic motifs still survive in remote areas of the archipelago as secondary strata, frequently without local recognition of their origin. But it was not until arrival of the later Indian traders who introduced Islam to Indonesia during and after the thirteenth century that the extraordinary influence of the double-*ikat* style known as *patola* came to be felt.

Probably originating in the Indian city of Varansi (Benares), *patola* spread across the subcontinent to reach its height in the northwestern district of Gujurat, where it is still found in the town of Pattan. Although it is known as *cindai* or *cinde* in Java and Sumatra, *patola*—the word used east of Bali—still describes variegated silk cloth in many dialects of modern India. *Patola*'s double-*ikat* weave of silk creates textiles of bright colors, soft texture and great beauty. These were certain to have been highly prized characteristics among the Indonesians of a thousand years ago, when the dull colors, rough texture and simple designs of single-*ikat* weave were prevalent. Ironically, the bright colors of the *patola* were possible only by using water-soluble dyes; to wash the cloth was to ruin its appeal. Hence, the cloth was impractical for everyday use, and it necessarily became ceremonial.

As a result, *patola* cloth became the most valued textile of Indonesia. *Patola* became the royal wear—kings on Savu wore it in ceremony, those on Roti when they were buried; priests and aristocracy as well as royalty signaled their importance by their possession of *patola*. As time went on the original *patola* cloth began to disintegrate in the hot and damp climate of equatorial Indonesia. Pieces of it were patched into ceremonial garments, and even today fragments of the original double-*ikat* cloth are sometimes seen woven into wedding clothes. The value of the cloth has been transposed into magical power: what fragments remain are rarely shown to strangers, being kept in taboo baskets under the care of priests or shamans.

As the original *patola* cloth became rare, the native weavers of Nusa Tenggara copied Indian designs and incorporated them into their own traditions. Foremost among these is the *jilimprang*, an eight-pointed floral motif. This design is found almost without change from one end of Nusa Tenggara to the other, and variations of it are at least as widespread. On Flores, the large island nucleus of the Lesser Sundas, the *jilimprang* has been deliberately combined with the snakeskin motif of traditional animistic symbolism, while in Flores's Sikka region all memory and traditions of the *patola* have been lost, but the *jilimprang* motif is faithfully rendered on nearly all native wear.

Other *patola* motifs are also found in Nusa Tenggara, including interconnected rhomboids, stars, elephants, hearts and the "spearhead" shape used frequently in borders. These are often combined with indigenous motifs, such as the Neolithic-style human figures, horses and "skull tree" used on Sumba. But so widespread has been the influence of *patola* on the native weavings in Indonesia that non-*patola* textiles are by far the more rare.

Brenda concluded her presentation by showing us some supplementary weft material from Sumatra, with a pattern that had been added into the developing weave by an additional weft of gold thread. These pieces are, as you might suppose, extremely valuable; but to my eye they looked somewhat showy—garish cloth in which material had precedence over technique. I realized that my ignorance of weaving had turned quickly into opinionated interest, marked by a distinct preference for the traditional subtleties of the *ikat* of Nusa Tenggara.

"Dinner is served," announced one of the stewards. We filed in to seat ourselves at the linen-covered tables, where a meal of air-dried beef on papaya, tomato cream soup, pepper steak or lobster thermidor and Black Forest cake awaited us. I sat with the English couple but could not turn my attention to their conversation, even when it touched upon the best cheap wines of the world. As it happens, good cheap wine is one of my own areas of expertise, but I had to force myself to pay attention. Instead, I found myself contemplating the patterns on Brenda's sarong at the next table and examining the weave of the napkin in my lap.

I was awakened just before midnight from a dream of public rail lines built of bamboo: Brenda called my name from the corridor. I dressed and went up to the sun deck—now a star deck, basking in the glow of the equatorial night. A small group had gathered to watch our progress past Palau Sangeang, an active volcano off the northeast coast of Sumbawa. We passed within about three kilometers of its shore, watching as the distant glow resolved into a fiery fan of molten lava. There was a late-rising waning moon behind us, and making out the jagged summit of Sangeang was possible only when it was crowned by the flame of ejection. Shortly afterward a clotted surge of rubies would pour down, spreading out until it turned a corner of terrain invisible in the darkness and was hidden. Behind the ship's bridge the Southern Cross tilted up from the horizon; before us the lava river flowed, a galaxy of its own, various magnitudes of red stars concentrated in a dense steep avalanche of burning. From the silhouette of the summit, pale smoke rolled slowly eastward through the night over the Flores Sea, toward Maluku, New Guinea and the South Pacific.

When the *Island Explorer* shut off its engines early the next morning we were anchored in Liang Bay off the coast of Komodo. The dry, hilly island between Sumbawa and Flores should be unremarkable in an archipelago of more than

The dreaded dragons of Komodo, at more than three meters long the largest of the world's monitor lizards, converge on a goat offering. (Christian Kallen)

thirteen thousand islands; it is only 5200 kilometers square and boasts but one village, a score of bamboo huts inhabited by the descendants of exiled prisoners. The reason they were incarcerated on this particular island is the same reason the fame of Komodo has spread out of all proportion to its size, for here live the world's largest lizards, the dragons of Komodo.

Neither dragons nor dinosaurs, these are the largest of the monitors, the biggest genus of lizards alive today. There are no fossils of Komodolike lizards from the Age of Dinosaurs; whatever evolution the monitors have done they have done since the mass extinction of dinosaurs at the end of the Mesozoic era 65 million years ago. Some sauriologists believe that the modern *Varanus komodoensis* is only a few million years old, not much older than the apelike species *Homo*

sapiens. Once more wide ranging, in the present era these lizards have found their niche only on these tide-isolated islands. What makes them remarkable is not their antiquity or their isolation, but their size: more than three meters in length, up to nearly three hundred pounds and maybe as much as a century old.

Now three meters is not big for a whale, or a living room; but it's a heck of a lot of lizard, especially for those of us who jump at the sight of a gecko. They have other disconcerting characteristics, too—like their swift speed, which allows them to catch small deer, pigs, goats and the occasional preoccupied human, and also their saliva, wherein dwells a bacteria so potent it can poison the bloodstream of their victims. So escape is only temporary: sooner or later the bitten game will collapse, and the dragon will be not far behind. They also eat smaller members of their own species, and should an adult dragon become wounded, why, no sense in letting all that good reptile flesh go to waste.

Their main source of nutrition, however, is carrion. Wandering solitary through their island domain, a lizard might happen upon bird eggs or a stillborn goat, though such easily caught prey as a broken-winged cormorant or a busily rooting pig will not be passed by. It doesn't take too much time for the prey to be completely consumed, shell, feathers, fur and all; and a little meat goes a long way in their cold-blooded metabolism. Since the modern discovery, in 1912, of the dragons of Komodo, the habit of offering sacrifices to these nightmarish beasts has evolved into the more sophisticated practice of stringing up slaughtered goats so tourists can take pictures of the congregation of reptiles. This has changed the behavior of the lizards to the extent that the formerly solitary animal is now found in packs, which converge upon the suspended offering and consume its dangling limbs in a feeding frenzy.

The dragons of Komodo are protected by the government of Indonesia in a national reserve composed of the island of Komodo as well as several of the neighboring islands where the lizard is found. Most visitors to Komodo land at Loho Liang, a small government-run camp on the bay, where guides are willing (for a modest fee) to sacrifice and string up a goat at a favored viewing spot; you are requested to supply the goat. Fortunately the arrangements had all been made by the cruise ship company, so all we had to do was dock, walk and focus. Thinking that we might be able to watch the slaughter of the goat (and beat the crowd), Nikki and I left without breakfast to catch an early landing-craft run to Loho Liang, where we joined a guide on the two-kilometer walk through the quiet morning.

Or almost quiet: cormorants and cockatoos screamed, cicadas sawed, and in the distance there was a deep heavy growling. At first I thought it was the roar of a dragon, and I scanned the horizon for the smoke. Somewhat regretfully, I decided it must have been only the lowing of a water buffalo. Soon afterward we met another guide, who held a dark, sticky machete at his side.

Although it was not yet 9:00 A.M., the day was already hot, and we were sweating by the time we reached the fenced viewing area, a roofed cabana set on a bluff seven meters above a ravine. We were not surprised to see the brown-and-white goat already dead and suspended from a tree, a blue rope running between the branches to a carabiner clipped through its pierced ankles. The dragons were already converging, their thick long bodies covered with dust in the dry ravine below us. The first thing that struck me was the silence. There was no roaring, no squealing, no fiery exhalation (some believe their forked yellow tongues, half-meter-long organs of touch and smell, were the inspiration behind Chinese legends of fire-breathing dragons), just the scratching of their claws on one another's scaly skin, and every now and then a soft, sinister hissing.

The goat had been hung out of reach of the lizards; it would be gradually lowered once the rest of the visitors arrived, to spread the feeding out so we would have ample opportunity for photographs. But even now nine of the beasts swarmed below, climbing on each other in an attempt to reach the bait, and two more joined them as we waited. By clambering up on another's back and lifting himself until his forefeet barely supported his weight, one of the smaller lizards—a mere two meters—was several times able to latch onto the head of the goat. When he fell he stripped off its skin, till a bloody skull hung by the strength of its vertebrae above the frustrated beasts below.

Finally the other passengers came, and the goat could be lowered into feeding range. While the lizards were thus occupied with their meal, Alex asked if any of us would care to hike down into the ravine for close-up photos. "Care to" was perhaps the wrong choice of words, but the opportunity was an unusual one, and half a dozen of us followed Brenda and Alex down the short trail to the ravine floor. Two more lizards came crawling out of the forest after we arrived, making thirteen in all, but they, too, quickly became involved in the meal. We stood within five meters of the reptilian carnage, snapping photos of bloody jaws, torn carcass, flickering tongues, the savagery, the horror.

Horror or no, I shot through a complete roll of film, and only the need to reload—that and the fact that the lizards were just about finished and now turned their beady eyes in our direction—prompted our retreat to the fenced observation compound. The fence itself seemed like a joke, a series of fragile stakes little more than half a meter high, linked together by baling wire. But though the dragons live in trees for up to the first year of life, those more than one meter long rarely climb anything; so when a couple of the creatures casually crawled just a couple of feet away from the fence, we felt somewhat safe. If they were big enough to be scared of, we reasoned, they were too big to climb in and get us.

One of them, nearly three meters, lingered awhile just outside the gate and watched young Stefan Dimter with a hungry eye. Or perhaps it was just curious—there seemed to be a glimmer of intelligence stirring in that primitive gaze, as I stuck my telephoto lens into his face and snapped a portrait his mother would be proud of. Or perhaps it wasn't intelligence at all: look what changes the intellect has brought our own particular branch of the ape family tree, in just a million years, from our fertile origins. The Komodo dragon has lived more or less unchanged for at least as long, and if his range is now confined to a few islands in the Flores Sea and his numbers reduced to several thousand, his homeland is ground zero only to volcanoes.

When we returned to the ship, I stretched out for a quick rest; our midnight volcano-watch, the morning's excitement and the tropical heat all combined to sap my strength. When I awoke more than an hour later, the boat was deserted, or almost so—the *Island Explorer* had moved out of Liang Bay to a nearby cove, and the other passengers were all on shore for a picnic lunch. I managed to get a steward to run me in on one of the landing craft and was snorkeling before fully awake.

It was only appropriate, really: I was again reminded that snorkeling is a dream state, a world revealed of strange colors and shapes, populated by bright quick denizens who flit into and out of vision; a world with luminous images that evaporate once one is back among the wakeful, on dry land. Corals shaped like tubes, trees, trunks, the undersides of mushrooms, like nothing in the dry world of normal sensations. A huge pink anenome with a cluster of tentacles the size and thickness of forefingers stood swaying translucent in the subtle currents. It was surrounded by clown fish, angelfish, needle-nosed fish—so many kinds one is speechless and gives up on knowing their names, though never upon seeing them all.

Still, for some reason I could not relax in these waters and gave up my snorkeling after only a few uneasy minutes. As I swam toward shore, I realized why. Komodo dragons too are able to swim—how else could they inhabit the remote islands in this archipelago? And it was such a nice hot day, even a lizard must have thought it fine weather for a dive.

The most wasted landscape I had ever seen greeted us at sunrise, a huge crater still smoking from who knows what eruption. Nothing could grow in its blast zone, which fanned out directly toward us from the jagged maw, bearing with its long-since spent violence the scene of sulfur across the sea. It was not without a certain beauty, in its colors of radioactive cloud and polluted sunset, but surely we could be near no inhabited land. Then we passed around the east side of the volcano and entered the sheltered harbor of Ende, capital of Flores.

The volcano, Iya, had indeed erupted recently, in 1982; but its energy swept out toward the sea, leaving the town untouched. The narrow peninsula that Iya has created over the centuries extends from land right at Ende, so the town has two harbors, one on each side of the volcano. Ende's connection with the interisland trade of Nusa Tenggara, and with the traditional weaving villages of the interior, has not rendered it a town of any great fascination. The Dutch exiled the upstart Soekarno here in the 1930s, hoping to kill his dreams of independence with boredom.

Flores is the largest of the Lesser Sundas; in Nusa Tenggara only the nonvolcanic island of Timor is larger. Its name came from the first European surveyors, the Portuguese, who in 1512 dubbed its easternmost extension "Cabo das Flores." Cynics believe the Portuguese were embellishing a stark, very unfloral landscape; romantics think they named the cape for its submarine coral gardens, still among the most beautiful in the tropics.

Like Lombok and Sumbawa, Flores had been part of Java's Mahajapit Empire of the fourteenth century. Following its collapse, the sultan of Gowa (on Sulawesi) took control of the west, the sultan of Ternate (in Maluku) of the east; both attempted to convert the inhabitants to Islam. That the island is now some 90 percent Catholic indicates that they were unsuccessful, or that three centuries of Portuguese Dominican missionaries eradicated their efforts. The missions began with the concession of Ternate's territories to the Dutch in 1683 and the resulting Dutch dominance of the island's trade in wild cinnamon, sandalwood and sappan wood (for spice, perfume and red dye, respectively). When the Dutch finally gained complete control of Flores, in the 1940s, they replaced Dominicans with Jesuits, and the spread of Christianity continued unabated.

But the island's animistic cults survived it all, and that they did is the most compelling reason to visit Flores: that, and the multicolored lakes of Keli Mutu. It was ostensibly to see Keli Mutu that we docked at Ende, but here my growing interest in *ikat* was rewarded: two young women appeared as we stepped down the gangway, wearing traditional sarongs whose rusts, blacks and blues set off favorably the brown of their bare shoulders. I raised my camera, asking them to pose and smile. They did so readily and professionally, and I realized that they must have been engaged by some local tourism authority to welcome us. Even though I was disappointed, I realized that we could not exactly hide our rather grandiose arrival in a gleaming white jet boat forty meters long. Nonetheless, they were beautiful, and seeing the *ikat* sarongs of Flores worn on living bodies was worth being a tourist for.

We didn't spend long on the dock; our destination, Keli Mutu, was sixty-six kilometers away, and the roads turned out to be among the worst in Indonesia. Riding in a small bus whose shock absorbers had long since been amputated, we bounded, bounced and bumped our way through a deeply chasmed landscape along the rocky drainage of the Wolowaro River. Waterfalls slid down sheer volcanic walls, tiny sawah fields decorated the steep valleys, thatched-roof settlements passed by and, beneath the trees—sugar palms, *lontars*, cocos, and even *kapoks*, their pods exploded into white fibrous balls—walked the people of the Lio district. On the thatched walls of the houses I noticed animistic patterns of diamonds, mazes and even human figures; the old beliefs still seemed to be alive here. On the sarongs, muted reds and blues in narrow strips, the white patterns were too small for me to see in our quick passage.

Keli Mutu is not a particularly high mountain—some 1600 meters—but in climbing the steep road to its summit we made a quick transit of several vegetation zones. From the tropical lowlands we slid imperceptibly into a cloud forest, where tree ferns rose above the forest floor and epiphytes clung to hardwoods; then, abruptly, we broke into an open region almost alpine in appearance. The ground was nearly barren, due in part to the volcanic origin of the mountain. Naked ridges sprawled over the summit, hiding in their depths three lakes—each one a different color.

On the drive up, Brenda and Alex had been debating with each other what color the lakes would be. Tradition has it that there's a red, a green, and a black lake, but landslides, earthquakes and even heavy storms have been known to change the mineral content of the waters and thus the colors. On their last visit, the two lakes that are side by side—the third being several hundred meters away—had turned the same green after a landslide.

When we finally arrived, Brenda was first out of the bus, and she raced up the nearest ridge. "It's red again!" she shouted, excited. We trudged up the rocky trail, and it was true; the nearest lake was a deep burgundy color, though along one bank a green hue remained. Its immediate neighbor was bright blue-green, almost turquoise, and their juxtaposition—separated by a high narrow ridge that cut like a knife between them—was surreal. Even more eerie was to see familiar pines and blueberry bushes clinging to the cliffsides, like a luridly retouched photograph of alpine lakes in the Cascades or Sierras.

I took my time walking along the dangerous

Two of the three colored lakes of Keli Mutu, in the caldera of a dormant volcano on Flores. (Christian Kallen)

rim of the red lake, photographing it and its green sister with wide-angle lenses. The rest of the group walked up to the summit of Keli Mutu from where all three lakes are visible. However, it is impossible to photograph all three lakes at once. The black lake—nearly circular, deeper within its well than the other two—is too far away from the others, and no lens can encompass the three lakes together. I consoled myself with a tedious count of the many stone steps leading to the summit of the high observation point (273, in two pitches of 152 and 121); by the time I arrived at the summit, most of the rest of the group was ready to leave.

Our local guide remained at the top with me—a school teacher, whose classes had exams that day. I asked him about the significance of the color of the lakes, for I had heard that the spirits of the dead are said to inhabit them. He denied all knowledge of this, until I made an attempt to explain the stories: "Don't the souls of sinners live in the red lake, the souls of young men in the green, and those of virgins and children in the black?"

"Oh, no, that's not right," he answered. "The good go to the green lake, the old go to the red, the unmarried go to the black."

"What about the people here—do they ever come up to the lakes, to make offerings or anything?"

"Oh no. These are just stories. Nobody believes them." Later, I read that the Lio villagers in the Keli Mutu region do in fact shun the volcanoes, since they believe the souls of the dead live there. In any case, there was something otherworldly about Keli Mutu, with its stark terrain and vivid waters; whether or not that other world is the world of the dead was not for me to decide.

"That lady seems sick," mentioned the guide. I looked down the mountain to the end of the stairs, where a woman—I could not tell who it was—was lying supine on the trail. When the other passengers gathered around her and we saw the bus sent for it became clear that something serious was afoot, and quickly we headed down. Afoot indeed: Nicole Morel-Journal had twisted her ankle on the rocky trail, and it lay at a horrible angle, a bruise beginning to form. Our visit to Keli Muti cut short, we drove back through the band of cloud forest to the nearby town of Mone, where Alex had heard of a mission nurse.

While Nicole's foot was being splinted with a short piece of bamboo and wrapped in a gauze bandage, I joined Mrs. Sweeney, the Coral Gables matron, on a short walk back up the road to a stand of clove trees. Perhaps seventy, still intensely curious and well informed, she turned out to be the curator of the Florida estate of botanist David Fairchild, whose tropical travels led to his establishing a garden known as the Kampong near Coconut Grove. The Kampong is slated to become the eastern part of the National Tropical Botanical Gardens, whose first site is located in Hawaii as the Pacific Tropical Botanical Gardens. Even on this brief walk, Mrs. Sweeney's knowledge was impressive; she identified nearly every plant we saw by Latin and familiar names, and kept in her notebook lists of the native names as she discovered them.

Our presence in Mone had not gone unremarked. Back at the bus, a crowd had gathered, and many of them bore *ikat* cloth for sale. Brenda led the way in asking questions, feeling and bidding on pieces; Alex bought one, then Judi and Kurt Dimter also began to ask prices and barter. Brenda was able to identify the village where several of the cloths had been woven, for in Flores the ancient traditions of clan and village design are still followed, and one can tell where someone is from by the sarong. In Lio—the district that includes Mone—the most important motif is the snake, or *naga*. Good luck and good news are said to be brought by snakes, and pregnant women wear a snakeskin-patterned sarong to ensure healthy offspring.

Nicole could have used a little *naga* luck—the nurse was fairly certain the ankle was broken, not just dislocated, and the drive back to Ende was a long and painful one for her. In Ende, we left Nicole and Bertie at the hospital—an unimpressive compound of peeling paint, open doors and dusty walkways—and reached the ship just as the sun set. After much discussion, one of the stewards was left with the French couple and arrangements were made to fly them the next day back to Denpasar, in Bali, and from there to Singapore, to set the bone in the best hospital in Southeast Asia.

The sudden tropical darkness had descended by the time the *Island Explorer* hauled anchor and set its course due south, across the Savu Sea, for our next port of call. But the loss of Bertie and Nicole had left us subdued; our group had been reduced to an unlucky thirteen, and our uneasy mood seemed to affect our appetite. Vichyssoise, lumpia (Indonesian egg rolls), glazed ham or seafood in lobster sauce—not even the chocolate mousse tasted quite right. There was no lingering over dessert, but some of us did gather in the lounge to compare the day's purchases of *ikat*.

The relatively large size and steep terrain of Flores has made it an ethnographic treasure chest with dozens of distinctive cultures secluded in its isolated districts. There are a large number of dialects spoken, of the two different language groups—Melanesian in the east, Malay in the west. It is in such a diverse cultural realm that the importance of traditional wear is most clearly felt: as a means of identifying the home of a stranger. To know one's village, and to advertise it, prevents conflict by presenting one's lineage openly. To hide one's origin is to facilitate betrayal. Clothes become, more than mere ornamentation, the very texture of social communication. In this, who is to say that the people of Nusa Tenggara are any different from the style-conscious citizenry of Europe or America, whose wardrobes are a clear cultural signal—the basis for first impressions, the visible assurance of social place.

This traditional language of textiles is changing in modern times: patterns are being shared that once were exclusive, trends develop and die, new influences are displayed. Formerly, for instance, there were eighteen kingdoms on the small island of Roti, just west of Timor, each with its own variations in textile motifs. Even the materials of which sarongs were woven reflected status—the softer cottons in East Sumba identified nobility; rougher weaves, common status. Color has also been one of the most prevalent dignifiers of status, the difficult-to-produce bright reds being reserved for royalty in several traditional cultures. With modern synthetic materials, chemical dyes and better communication between villages, many of these ancient distinctions are being compromised.

At Mone, I had bought a single panel of cloth, new from the loom—not yet mated with another identical piece to form a sarong and not fringed at its end to form a *selimut*, or wrap. It was nothing valuable, I knew; it cost about five dollars, and had I been a more astute bargainer it might have been mine for less. But among its small white patterns were deer, rhomboids, stars and patterns of prehistoric antiquity, symmetrical shapes that spoke a language I did not know. I draped it over the chair in my cabin, and it warmed the close pastel decor far out of proportion to its size.

You grow used to the steadiness of a ship's motors, especially if your cabin is at waterline, only a few feet above the spinning engines. The sound is loud but not so loud you don't become accustomed to it; the vibration seems to adjust your pulse rate to its own frequencies, and you almost become a part of the ship's propulsion. Sometime in the night after we left Ende the pitch of the engines changed, and the new noises and vibrations were raw and exposed.

When I came up from my cabin at daybreak, Alex was already scurrying about looking harried. "What's up?" I asked.

"Unfortunately it seems that the starboard engine has given up. We hope to get it working, of course, but I have to admit that again our plans may be changed."

Glumly, I sat down to a cup of tea next to the Supranas, the couple from Java. We compared stories of waking in the middle of the night and realizing that something was wrong. We felt adrift in the Savu Sea, running on damaged propulsion and out of luck. At first we spoke quietly,

then as others joined the table our fate became a matter of general discussion.

We had had a string of ill omens thus far: the initial problem with the engine and our change of plans in not visiting Timor and Lembata; the heavy currents in the Lombok Strait, and the necessary sacrifice of the Palau Moyo stop on the very first day of our cruise; finally, and most unnerving, the broken ankle at Keli Mutu. Now, although we were still scheduled to arrive at the island of Savu around 8:00 A.M.—after thirteen hours of cruising from Flores—we were down to thirteen passengers, the same number of lizards we had seen at Komodo. And it was Friday the thirteenth. Hesitantly, I wondered aloud how many crew members there were.

A half-hour later, Jaya Suprana came waddling up to me in his Japanese flip-flops. "I have asked Rudi how many crew there are. There are not thirteen. There are twenty-six." He giggled. "And Alex told me that the same thing happened to the port engine during the America's Cup finals in Australia. A month ago. On Friday the thirteenth."

Like the Bermuda Triangle, the Savu Sea is a three-cornered body of water, a sixty-four-hundred-kilometer-wide basin bound by Timor on the eastern side, Flores to the north, Sumba to the west and the barely noticeable five-hundred-square-kilometer island of Savu at the southern apex. I could imagine strange vibrational forces at work within these waters, ancient animistic spells that protect the old gods from dangerous intruders and careless tourists, spells sealed perhaps by sacrifice. The fated voyage of the *Titanic* rode the waves of my imagination. Uneasily I went up to the sun deck, to keep watch for icebergs.

Instead, I saw the approaching island of Savu, palm trees fringing its green hills, slender *prahus* radiating from the harbor beneath blue sails. Known on some maps as Sabu, and pronounced (and often spelled) *Sawu*, the island is almost never visited by casual tourists, as it lacks hotel facilities. There is only one flight a week to this mote, in a small Twin Otter out of Kupang, Timor. The most common approach is by sea, which has for centuries isolated its inhabitants from the vicissitudes of history while at the same time linking them with the stabler trades and traditions of their Nusa Tenggara neighbors. Although I had never heard of Savu before this cruise began, I had the day before looked it up in Bill Dalton's *Indonesia Handbook*, and what little he had to say about it was tantalizing: "An island like the Garden of Eden 100 km N.W. of Roti."

The cultural traditions of Nusa Tenggara—*ikat* weaving being the visible manifestation, the fabric of their culture—suggest common origins. One of the windows into the past of preliterate cultures is mythology, tales passed down orally from generation to generation of world creation, cultural formation, social birth. On Sumba, to the northwest of Savu, they tell of a family that sailed from India in the distant past. The father, mother, son and daughter followed the winds east, until they reached Bali. Here the daughter chose to remain for life, and the rest of the family continued eastward. When they reached Sumba, the son stayed among the people, and the parents sailed on. When they reached Savu, the father and the mother settled at last in their own new home.

But this seminal ship brought more than settlers to its ports of call. The daughter brought to Bali her talents in dance and music; the son taught the Sumbanese the martial arts of battle. Finally the parents, at the end of their lives of wandering, bequeathed to the Savunese all their knowledge of magic. On Sumba, they still tell of the war just a few generations ago when the troops of Savu marched all night across the waters of the Savu Sea to surprise and conquer the Sumbanese villages.

The basic premise of the myth, that Savu was inhabited by immigrants from the west, is supported by linguistic evidence. Savunese speech is of the Sumba-Bima group of languages common to the west, whereas the inhabitants of Roti a hundred kilometers to the southeast speak a language in the Timor-Ambon group. Wallace noted the strong physiognomic resemblance of the Savunese to the people of Bali. That Savu has remained an island alone, outside of the winds of change brought most forcefully by the Dutch, is due in large measure to its economic and historical isolation, an isolation that has preserved many of its ancient cultural traditions and led to its reputation as a Garden of Eden.

The island was, and is, strategically unimportant: no valuable spice grows here, its situation is not significant in naval passage, and its people, noted through history as excellent warriors, were not suitable to subjugation by slavery. Aside from its warriors' notoriety, Savu was so remote from the concerns of the European explorers and merchants that one of its early visitors made an impulsive stop to reconnoiter simply because the small island was not on his charts. Capt. James Cook, on his globe-girdling voyage aboard the H.M.S. *Endeavor*, put in at the port of Seba in September 1770 and was at once struck by the island's barren beauty. Cook recorded many of its unique aspects of life, including its cultivation of *lontar* and betel palms, its social organization into five principalities, its emphasis on genealogies and its excellent palm wine. When he left Savu after several relaxing and productive weeks his fresh supplies included buffalo, sheep, hogs, dozens of fowl, limes, coconuts, eggs (half of which proved to be rotten), garlic and several hundred gallons of palm syrup. Not bad for an unscheduled stop at an uncharted island.

Unique among the islands of Nusa Tenggara, Savu is an island society held together by ceremony. Each of its five territories or states has its own calendar and its own rituals, but they are all parts of a larger ritualistic whole—a complex lunar ceremonial cycle that embraces the whole island. Every state has its own ritual leaders, determined by clan alliance; their duties are prescribed by, and reinforcing of, the state's specific place in the island-wide lunar calendar. There are local clan and village chiefs of some power, and when the Dutch came, they chose their rajas from these secular leaders rather than religious leaders. But the secular leaders were so less valued that the title "raja" devolved in a very short time, and within a century it was said that there were on Savu more rajas than houses.

The rich ritual life of Savu is more than just the counting of days—it is also marked by the sacrifice of animals, and by events that empha-

OVERLEAF: *The life-giving lontar palm spreads across the green spring landscape of the island of Savu. (Christian Kallen)*

size physical prowess and confrontation. Cock-fighting has long been the most popular manifes-tation of ritual—cocks signify individual men, men represent their lineages, and lineages in turn represent spirits. In some territories, the end of the lunar year was marked by rock-throwing bat-tles. This emphasis on physical confrontation led to the high regard the Dutch—and their Nusa Tenggara neighbors—held for the might of Sa-vunese warriors.

Much of this social and ritual organization has survived to the present day. The Indonesian gov-ernment's prohibition against royalty has cer-tainly affected the Savunese nobility: the last king of the most powerful territory, that of Seba, died in the 1950s. But his widow is still known as "the Queen of Savu," and her friendly advice is sought by everyone from quarreling families to *ikat* spe-cialists. However, the priestly class seems to re-main in existence. The highest ranking priest is the *deo rai*, the "lord of the earth," identified with the agricultural cycle; the secondary priest is the *apu lodo*, "descendant of the sun," whose func-tions are linked to the *lontar*-tapping season. Sa-vu's survival in relative isolation and the enforced simplicity of its economy in large measure center on this single tree species—the *Borassus sundai-cus*, sometimes called the palmyra but known in Indonesia as the *lontar* palm.

Unlike the lush rainforests of Borneo, Suma-tra and Sulawesi, the landscapes of Nusa Teng-gara are subject to drought. Hot winds blow northward from the deserts of Australia, creat-ing a long dry season between March and Octo-ber; rice and sorghum will not grow then, and famine is ever near. But the drought-resistant *lontar* has proven a tree of life for the Savunese, as for the inhabitants of the larger island of Roti off the southern tip of Timor. Other trees are im-portant to Indonesia's indigenous people—bam-boo, sago, betel and coconut, all of which offer in varying degrees building materials, fruit and rit-ual comfort wherever they are found. But few trees have proven as essential to survival as the *lontar*.

Houses, furniture, tobacco pipes and other im-plements are made from its wood; its leaves be-come baskets to carry everything from food to ba-bies; eight different kinds of hats are formed

from its fronds; even the resonating box of a lute-like instrument called the *sasando* is made from the leaves, shaped into a deep bowl. But it is as food that the *lontar* is most important. During the dry months, the sap of the lontar is harvested by men who climb the tree in the morning (using a *lontar*-stalk rope), place a basket (*lontar*, of course) beneath the cut spadix and return in the evening to take home the tree's sap.

Drunk fresh, the juice is sweet and refreshing; allowed to ferment, it becomes palm wine or *tuak*. (The word originates in Nusa Tenggara—on Roti and Timor the *lontar* is called *tua*; on Savu it is the *duwe*.) Boiled into a syrup and di-luted with water, it becomes a nutritious soup, a staple of the diet; boiled further still, it is refined into cakes of palm sugar that can be preserved for months. Froth and dregs from refining the liquid are fed to horses, goats and pigs; the animal ma-nure, and leaves from the *lontar*, are spread on gardens as fertilizer and mulch, to retain the earth's moisture during the dry months. Infants at birth are ceremonially fed the juice of the *lon-tar* before their own mother's milk; the dead are buried in coffins hollowed from *lontar* palms. Nearly every aspect of life on Savu (and Roti) is made possible by the productivity of the *lontar*. It has proven an effective economy, with high re-turn on the hours of work involved, so the people have time left over to indulge their talents—the men in warfare (formerly) and trade (today) and the women in weaving and dance.

Taking the landing craft from the *Island Ex-plorer*, we raced across the quiet waters of the harbor to the main port and only "city" on Savu, the town of Seba. (Also known as Seva, of course; but on a watertank on the dock was painted "Seba" in large letters, so that's that.) It was quiet in Seba, still in the hours of morning; perhaps the port is never very busy. Even from the water we spied a yellow truck with an open bed—the kind used for transporting cows and goats—ready to take us on the twenty-two-kilometer journey across the island to the town of Bolou.

After the previous day's agonizingly long and bumpy drive on Flores, no one looked forward to the hour-long trip across Savu; from the first, however, it was clearly going to be different. The town was clean, quiet, its streets shaded by decid-

The Greater and Lesser Blossom motifs of Savu's distinctive ikat *adorn the sarongs of these young women, who harmonize to the mystical drone of the native lute, the* sasando. *(Christian Kallen)*

uous trees that formed leafy green tunnels; the people were curious but not intrusive. When we broke into open country outside of Seba, we saw that Savu was almost idyllic—the fields were green, streams flush with the season's rains, water buffalo cool in deep pools. Several small vales supported sawah cultivation, and corn was growing in circular pens fenced by bushes planted close together, of the kind of fast-growing tree the Jamaicans call "quick-stick."

The road led past several schools, where burgundy-shorted schoolchildren waved and cheered our passage; we passed what looked like the crumbled core of an ancient volcano, though these islands on the southern margin of Nusa Tenggara are not volcanic in origin; extraordinarily clear air afforded virtually limitless views

across distant green ridges. Aside from the schoolchildren, our companions on the road were goats, pigs, bicycles and the occasional horse-drawn carts. The bays pulling the carts were the smart-stepping sandalwood pony bred primarily on Sumba and Savu. The goats and pigs had sticks tied about their necks, to prevent them from slipping between the branches of the fences into the corn fields. Everywhere the tall, thin *lontar* palms clustered, reaching toward the clear skies, baskets nestled in their crowns.

Three huge banyan trees arched over the village square of Bolou, where hundreds of Savunese had gathered in anticipation of our arrival. Happy schoolchildren, festive families, smiling old men with red gums toothless from the betel habit and beautiful young men and women dressed in gorgeous *ikat* cloth—all surrounded the square eager to share a holiday with us, the holiday of the calling of a cruise ship.

The celebration started with a call from a conch horn, blown somewhat inexpertly by a giggling boy of about sixteen. He and his half-dozen or so companions were wearing dark woven *selimut*, a panel of *ikat* cloth about two-by-one-plus meters worn wrapped around the waist. Narrow, fringed shawls called *selindang* were tossed over their shoulders, and they all wore "headkerchiefs," scarves folded and worn like hats. About eight young women were also arrayed in *ikat* finery, wearing long tube sarongs bunched under their arms, folded over their breasts, and held by silver belts around their narrow waists. Red vests and bead necklaces completed the costumes, though most also wore silver brooches, bracelets and earrings.

The quality of the *ikat* was extraordinary—simply by being worn it rendered the already handsome men mythically powerful and the beautiful women alluring. Broad black panels were offset by maroon bars filled with white geometric shapes, animistic symbols, detailed flower patterns. The flowers delineate the two major female moieties found on Savu, known as Greater Blossom and Lesser Blossom (*Hubi Ae* and *Hubi Iki* respectively), corresponding to the mythical clan founders of sixteen generations ago, the sisters Majibado and Lobado. Each moiety is further broken down into "seeds," or *wini*, and the *ikat* pattern details exact information about the wearer that places him or her within the specific context of the entire culture. Most surprising of all, this information is imparted on a plane beyond language—it is never spoken of, revealed only through *ikat*; men, who have no role in the weaving, are said to be in ignorance of much of this nonlinguistic female symbology.

A local man armed with a bullhorn introduced the day's four dances and made an attempt to explain their cultural meanings. It was then up to Alex to translate our host's Bahasa Indonesia into English, a language that most of us could more or less easily understand. Visitors to different lands sometimes have the experience that explanations of myths and clans take on the cloying taste of artifice, hollow stories trotted out to make tourists feel like they are getting the inside dope on the locals. But beneath the banyan's shade in Bolou, as we sipped cool juice from the coconuts we were offered and watched the presentation, we all entered the time of legend.

For the first dance, eight young women swayed into the arena and, to the accompaniment of a small gamelan orchestra, enacted a description of the harvest and uses of the *lontar* palm. Their long bare arms waved, their feet stamped and slid on the sand, their downcast eyes took furtive looks at the audience. Meanwhile their hands formed signs, mudras, stories, as they split into files of four, then couples, then regrouped in an elegant cycle of planting, of harvest, of tapping, of weaving.

The women left the sandy area to the applause of the villagers and guests and were followed by six men with roosters, who staged a "mock" cockfight—real cocks, real fighting, but no spurs and no blood. Encouraged by their masters, the cocks bent their heads and raised their feathers in threat, dodging and faking; then in a flurry of feathers and claw they leaped into each other. The demonstration was greeted with enthusiastic applause, and its sudden truncation with the shadows of disappointment; I couldn't help but doubt what our Savunese host had told us, that the people of Savu no longer indulge in the manly sport of cockfighting.

Until the Dutch solidified their control of Nusa Tenggara, warfare was a major preoccupation of Savunese men; when that was taken away, ceremonial cockfighting was elevated to replace it. Since the missionaries have decreed that improper, the expression of masculinity finds its ritual outlet in dance. From a male expression to surrogacy in an animal to a female's domain, the avenues for a man to show his pride have been altered, qualified, deflected. The next dance showed this sublimation in an unintentionally humorous way.

Three couples came out, and while the women

mimed the harvest the men pranced about waving swords in "defense" of the working women. At certain points in the music, however, the men and women faced off, and the swords were presented aggressively to the women—who lightly fended them off with an elegantly poised hand. One of the male dancers kept missing his steps and almost fell over when he had to swing the sword; the crowd laughed uproariously at his gaffes, and he himself could barely contain his own self-conscious giggles.

However, another of the three men—older, leaner, harder—looked and danced like a warrior. His movements were precise and abrupt, proud and strong, like the staccato prance of a rooster in display. Authority infused his every step, and when he swung the sword the gesture contained very real elements of both dominance and protection. During the dance the couples shared companions, and when each of the three women danced with him in turn their own movements seemed to become more evocative, and provocative, as if in his studied aloofness he dictated their physical responsiveness, compelling them beyond themselves.

Then a tall, thin, sad-faced man seated himself on a small chair. He brought with him a *sasando*, the native lute with its *lontar*-basket sounding box. Carefully he picked out a dronelike melody with his thumb and two fingers, four repeating notes; the haunting simple rhythm formed the basis for the six women who stood behind him, and they began to sing a lilting melody that evolved into a complicated round with surprising harmonies. When the first song was over, the man patiently waited until another series of repeating notes came to his fingers, and then another song embellished its quiet foundation. They sang four songs in all, all in the Savunese dialect. There was no one to translate them for us, but sad melodies of loss, spry syncopated tunes of happiness and warm rich songs of love need no glossary.

The last dance was a true dance of welcome—a harvest dance, as evidenced by the baskets of dried rice tied to the ankles of the dancers. A large ring of all the traditionally dressed Savunese gathered with arms interlocked on each other's shoulders, and to the rhythm of the percussive orchestra they moved in a great circle around a singing leader, shuffling their sibilant feet in unison. Then the women broke out of the circle to invite the men among our own group to dance, and the men offered their hands to our women.

I put down my camera and threw myself into this spinning universe; the brown shoulders of the man to my right and the woman to my left were slick with sweat. Fixing my eyes on the steps of the man next to me, I tried to keep pace with the complicated dance, and to a measure I succeeded—I could hear the crowd behind me clap and cheer as I stayed in step with the dance for longer than I thought possible. Finally I lost it, the crowd laughed and we all continued the frenzied, sweaty, accelerating circle dance of friendship.

It was not without a little breathlessness on everyone's part that the dance finally ended, and the cheering crowd began to break up. Now the market was opened, where *ikat* cloth was displayed on racks and tables—sarongs and shawls in a riot of color, symbol and texture. Each piece was marked with the name of the weaver and what we would call a "suggested retail price," though a degree of bargaining was expected. Brenda strode about, offering advice to timid buyers and finding a piece or two for herself; Judi and Kurt Dimter methodically draped every piece they found attractive over their arms, then bartered for them one by one until they had spent their limit. I found a beautiful sarong, then after buying it saw an even more beautiful one and traded the first for it: black background bands with narrow deep-blue lines buried in them, both broad and narrow brick-red bands decorated with geometric designs of ancient meaning.

It was late afternoon by the time we returned to the *Island Explorer*—eyes still dazzled with images of *ikat*-clad dancers, the music of the *sasando* haunting our ears and newly purchased weavings held close to our chests. Too soon, the anchor chain howled in complaint as it was dragged aboard, and our single working engine erupted wearily into life. A spell seemed to lift; the itinerary again became the motivation—we were under way around five o'clock, forced to leave in order to make the next port of call some

Still on a backstrap loom, this weaving shows the animal motifs of whales, turtles and dragons typical of Sumba's ikat *designs. (Christian Kallen)*

sixteen hours away on the island of Sumba. I had the feeling of being that particularly distasteful kind of traveler, the hit-and-run culture vulture: we were guerrilla tourists, leaving with the setting sun, another island paradise in our wake.

When we docked at Sumba's busy port of Waingapu the next morning, a cargo ship was being loaded with water buffalo and horses. The buffalo had harnesses tied around their horns and were being winched up one by one over the dock to the middle of the boat; then the enormous squirming bulk was lowered into the hold. The horses had it easier—they were just mounted and ridden up the plank onto the ship. Sumba is the center of sandalwood horse breeding, since stock husbandry is made practical by the extensive grasslands of its dry climate. The sandalwood

tree itself was another major source of revenue for Sumba in past years, and in fact Sumba was known for some time as Sandalwood Island.

But the dry climate is also ideal for growing cotton, and it is Sumbanese *ikat* that remains the island's main source of attention. Although the weavings we had seen on Flores and Savu featured largely geometric, animistic symbols, Sumba's longer history of trade has rendered its textile arts more catholic. Even as we stepped onto the dock, several men converged with armloads of *ikat*, displaying a dizzying array of animal, human and geometric motifs. Horses are common, as are lions (derived from Dutch coins) and dragons (from Chinese influences). So are deer, snakes and turtles, and shrimp, roosters and dogs. One of the most common motifs is the skull tree, a relic of the past age of head-hunting when the skulls of slain enemies were prominently displayed on a tree or post at village center.

There are usually eight heads on a skull tree, symbolizing the eight stages of the afterlife in Sumbanese belief, though more may be found on some cloth. East Sumba—culturally the richer half of the island—was also divided into eight traditional kingdoms, each one of which used to have its own distinctive motifs. In recent times, however, the division between the kingdoms has become less significant, and such royal symbols as crocodiles and deer are now found on the same cloth. Large sarongs with red, black and white motifs that were worn by royalty are called *hinggi kombu*, while the simpler blue and white ones are called *hinggi kaworu*.

Kombu, I know thanks to Mrs. Sweeney, is the Sumbanese word for *Morinda citrofolia*, the tree whose roots are used for the red dye (the plant is known as *mengkudu* elsewhere in Indonesia); *kaworu* is the word for *Indigofera tinctoria*, the indigo plant common throughout much of Asia as a blue dye. In former times, red was worn only by royalty, and the finest examples of the cloth were used for burials. Fifty or more *ikat hinggi* could be buried with the king of a Sumbanese clan, each one of enormous value as determined by its complexity, colors and the amount of time that went into its weaving. To weave even the simplest *ikat* piece takes almost a year—spinning the cotton during the wet season (November to February), binding and dyeing the designs during the spring when indigo and *mengkudu* are most prevalent; and weaving during the dry summer months. Finer cloth takes longer to spin; more complex designs take multiple dyeings.

Time, effort and social significance all contribute to the magical quality that some *ikat* is said to possess. Certain pieces are held to bring good luck and protect their owners against illness and evil. In many areas, specific stages of the preparation are tabooed, as in Savu, where burial cloths are woven in the burial grounds, and the sacrifice of a pig is necessary to make the weaving process complete. In Sumba, the enclosure where thread is dyed is traditionally forbidden to men. And on Flores a jealous woman can use magic to ruin a rival's weaving while it is on the loom.

Ikat cloth is also one of the most significant parts of a wedding. While girls are allowed to do the spinning of cotton, and later the binding, they cannot begin actual weaving until they are of age. The completion of the first *hinggi* is a sign of womanhood, and a prerequisite to marriage. Since a weaver's character is said to be evident in the cloth she creates, the prospective mother-in-law will examine the *ikat* to read the true nature of the woman who would marry her son.

Much of the symbolic, ritualistic and cosmological significance of *ikat* cloth is being lost in the modern age. The old kingdoms are all but gone, Christian burials are replacing Neolithic rites, marriages now take place between men and women of different islands if not different nations. We visited the weaving village of Prailiu, a twenty-minute drive from Waingapu, where several women wove beautiful blankets and sarongs on traditional backstrap looms, while the binding and dyeing of the thread took place in different parts of the houses. But men were doing the tying, and not only men but tourists were allowed to witness the dyeing. Always, ghosting our every step that hot morning in Sumba, hoards of blanket-bearing entrepreneurs offered their "antique" weavings, which bore bizarre combinations of flying horses, prancing roosters and bloodthirsty warriors.

Between Waingapu and Prailiu we stopped at a local market in Lambanapu, where our arrival was clearly a surprise to the villagers. None were dressed in the ceremonial clothes we had seen on Savu; they wore instead stained and torn Western-style shirts and pants. Few *ikat* blankets were to be seen at all, as the merchants had only food, tobacco and betel nut to sell. Betel, in fact, drooled out of almost every mouth in the marketplace, red spittle stained the earth, nearly everyone's gums seemed to be eroding and teeth in the mouth of anyone over forty were unusual.

One has to wonder about the long-term effects of betel use among Indonesians. Clearly it destroys the gums; possibly it affects the will. I wondered what lay behind the bright unwavering stare of habitual users, and had my own curiosity been greater I might have welcomed their offered samples. But what if I couldn't stop at just a taste—would I spend the truncated rest of my earthly life in a tattered daze, privy to secret and unspeakable alkaloid revelations?

Further research helped ease my mind. The

active ingredient in betel, the alkaloid arecoline (C_8-H_{13}-NO_2), has been shown to stimulate the parasympathetic nervous system, resulting in a state of alertness and improved serial memory while also affecting the somatic motor nerves. So betel chewers may be happily alert and loose limbed, though their brick-red drool is less than flattering. In medicinal use, arecoline has promise as a short-lived but effective treatment for symptoms of Alzheimer's disease, particularly in combatting depression and memory loss. All is not roses, however: betel taken orally is carcinogenic, and mouth and lip lesions are common in Indonesia among betel users.

In the afternoon, after duck à l'orange aboard the *Island Explorer*, we visited a family *ikat* "factory" at the Sandlewood Hotel. We were surrounded, of course, by an army of cloth merchants, for word had by now spread throughout East Sumba that the *Island Explorer* had called at Waingapu. They advanced on us like angels from hell, their spread wings draped with blood-red blankets and skull trees, reeking of clove and mold. The slightest glance of interest was rewarded with an almost obscene spread and display, which Alex likened to the raincoated skulker of inner-city subways.

Nonetheless, I bought a lovely black, maroon and yellow shawl from the hotel manager, a shawl that had in fact come from Savu. Alex and Nikki entered into a lengthy negotiation with one of the salesmen over a blanket, for despite the superabundance of goods and the crass atmosphere, there were some truly remarkable pieces available. The asking price was unusually exorbitant; when the initial three-hundred-thousand-rupiah tag (almost two hundred dollars) failed to drop as rapidly as expected, Alex exclaimed in Bahasa, "I thought Sumba was a Christian island—clearly you men are Moslems, trying to earn money for the Haj!" The laughter was strained, and the joke produced only a slight reduction in price.

When we returned to the ship, the captain and crew had finally decided that their options for continuing the cruise were limited. In order for the boat to make it back to Bali and repair in time

for its next charter it would have to travel directly from Sumba to Benoa Harbor with no stops, a journey of about three days. Three unrelieved days at sea seemed a bit much for all, so Alex made arrangements for us to fly from Waingapu to Denpasar the next morning for a full extra day, and a half of sightseeing and relaxation in Bali. Some people would give anything for a day and a night in Bali, yet we found ourselves only reluctantly accepting this inevitable end of our cruise.

On our last night on the *Island Explorer* a special dinner was served on the deck, an array of barbecued meats including lamb chops, shrimp, chicken and lobster, as well as *babi gulung*—roast suckling pig, the Indonesian equivalent of Thanksgiving turkey. The wine came out, and we busily exchanged addresses, vowed to send each other photographs, asked about future travel plans. We were taking leave of friends with whom we had shared experiences and insights over a thousand miles of travel, a week of sailing the seas of Indonesia into its cultural past. Then, for the first time on the cruise, rain pelted the deck, and we moved inside to the lounge, and the bar, for a long evening of goodbyes.

Slides, journal entries and random recollections are often all that one retains of any journey, but it is the last named that seem the most permanent. The next morning after breakfast, when I went down to my cabin to pack my bags, I took down the wooden monkey hanging from the air conditioner, the frog mask from over the bedlamp and the batik off the bed. I emptied the closet, cleaned off the desk and filled the suitcase with all I had brought with me, moving out of cabin number nine. Last to be packed, one by one, were the panel of *ikat* from Flores, the Savunese shawl I bought in Sumba and the large traditional sarong from the village of Bolou.

All else packed, I gathered up this last from its place over the back of the pastel sofa and on impulse buried my face in it. Taking a long deep breath, I filled my lungs with the rich scent of *lontar*, of thatch and soil, of Savu; and warm sunlight seemed to spread out from my lungs to fill my eyes and heart. After a long moment I folded the sarong carefully, laid it on top of the rest and locked my bag for the long trip home.

SULAWESI

Traveling through Torajaland

It sometimes seems today's traveler moves too easily between air-conditioned hotels, tour buses, memorial plazas and native markets, as if the world has been reduced to a series of theme parks. Much of adventure travel may be an effort to find the unknown, to leave behind the all-too-familiar world and reveal instead the raw, unaffected reality of an earlier, more elemental planet. Tana Toraja—known also as Torajaland, a translation that, indeed, makes this beautiful landscape of limestone cliffs, rice fields and palm forest sound like a quadrant of Disneyland—is one such discovery. Its people, born into a resilient kinship network as deep as the roots of a sturdy forest giant, are centered in their ancient world, and the seductions of the modern age seem to pass over them like dry wind. The Toraja people may not have the familiarity of the Balinese nor the exotic appearance of the Grand Valley Dani of Irian Jaya, but from the valleys of their homeland rise the mists of timeless sanctuary.

Part of a wave of immigrants known as the Proto-Malay, which reached Indonesia from Indochina around 2500 B.C., the Toraja remember their arrival in the shape of every house they build. The double-prowed *tongkonan* houses, their bamboo roofs sweeping up from the center to two great peaks at either end, not only look like boats but are similar to the houses of the Batak of Sumatra, another group of Proto-Malay descendants. Once you've seen a *tongkonan*, however, you can never mistake any other tribal long house, granary or family dwelling for it, for it is more than just a shelter: it is a work of art.

Every flat surface is carved and painted in three or four colors—black, red, white and sometimes yellow; the most obvious cultural export of the Toraja is this folk-art style of carving. The geometries of knots, mazes and stars, and elegant arches like interlinked buffalo horns, thickly cover all available space with color and pattern. In their density they resemble the wood carvings of the Haida of the Pacific Northwest. Some designs appear similar to the work of the Hopi; many have an Arabic air. The style is uniquely Torajan, however: the shapes and animal representations all have meanings, rooted in the centuries-old culture of the Toraja.

Early in 1987, I received a telex from Dr. Halim Indrakasuma, the director of the Indonesian tour group PACTO. "IMPORTANT FUNERAL TANA TORAJA 29 JAN," it read. "STRONGLY ADVISE U ATTEND." The name was unfamiliar to me: where in the world was Tana Toraja? A few answered questions later, the essence of the message came clear. It was enough to make me decide to fly from California halfway around the world to Sulawesi and Tana Toraja—the mountain homeland of one of the oldest cultures in Indonesia, which has been almost completely isolated in the central highlands of Sulawesi for close to five thousand years. For the Toraja are known best for their elaborate burial ceremonies, a time of dancing, song and celebration, which culminates with the slaughter of dozens of water buffalo to assure that the wealth of the deceased is carried into the afterlife.

If one's first impression of Indonesia is, like mine was, through Jakarta, one is bound to be somewhat intimidated. It is a huge city, some seven million strong—not enormous by modern standards, but just forty years ago it was home to only two hundred thousand; and it shows the stresses and wrinkles of that rapid growth. Sprawling, uncoordinated, poorly sanitized and clotted with traffic, trash and people, Jakarta in many of its quarters is all that is wrong with the modern world. But elsewhere it is clean, well run and hospitable, for Jakarta is the administrative, business and intellectual center of the world's fifth largest nation (in both area and people). For better or worse, no quaint colonial relic would do.

One of the islands of civility in this wilderness is the Hotel Borobudur, a five-star, eighteen-story minicity with its famous hundred-hectare garden of tennis courts, pools, jogging track, trees and shaded walkways. Shortly after I arrived in Indonesia for the first time, in late January 1987, I looked out on the garden from my room at the Borobudur. In the disconnected swirl of associations that can plague the jet-age traveler, the first thing I thought of was the cinema of John Ford. I recalled an analysis of Ford's classic Westerns—*Fort Apache, She Wore a Yellow Ribbon, The Man Who Shot Liberty Valance* and *The Searchers*—as pitting the uncivilized, untamed, savage and inhospitable Wilderness against the Garden, with its cultivation of manners as well as plants, situated snugly within the

borders of the settlement. So this is the Garden, I thought: squash courts and swimming pools. And the Wilderness outside is one of swerving traffic, polluted canals, overcrowding. The irony was in the civilization that fought back the Wilderness now becoming the very thing it once battled. And the security from danger was now found in a carefully planned and planted synthesis of a lost Eden, the Garden itself.

Still, there does reside within some of us the hard-to-kill kernel of romanticism that keeps us believing in a better world, a world closer to the way it has always been than the way it is too rapidly becoming. Perhaps that is what I hoped to find on Sulawesi, an island draped across the equator where the buffalo are said to look like deer and the deer to look like pigs, and where the mountain people slaughter buffalo as well as pigs by the score upon the death of a nobleman. I would be going to such a funeral, having crossed the Pacific to attend the burial of a man I'd never met.

Sulawesi was known for centuries as Celebes. That name may have been applied by Portuguese who simply mispronounced the native name. (*Borneo*, for instance, appears to be a corruption of *Brunei*, itself the name of a native fruit.) Or it may have been derived from the Portuguese map name for the northern peninsula of the island, Ponto dos Celebres (Cape of the Infamous). *Sulawesi* is officially held to be the traditional name of the island, though until the Dutch came there was little perception among the people of the island that they lived on an island—they knew their homelands simply as Tana, as in Tana Towa, Tana Mandar, Tana Toraja. In Bahasa Indonesia—a national tongue created with independence in 1949, based on a Malay dialect spoken on the island of Madura off Sumatra's north coast—*tanah* means "earth"; the country is lovingly referred to by its inhabitants as *Tanah Air Kita*, "Our Land, Our Water."

"Curiously sprawling," "sprawled like a starfish *in excelsis*," and "a spider, a scorpion, a pair of pajamas drying on a clothes line": these are all descriptions of the appearance of Sulawesi. By far the most popular is "the orchid-shaped island," a term virtually epidemic in travel literature. All of these similes strive to assist the reader in visualizing the shape of the island, an effort that only delays the inevitable duty of any traveler: look at a map.

You'll find Sulawesi to the east of Borneo, north of the string of small islands known as Nusa Tenggara or the Lesser Sundas. Sulawesi is, in fact, one of the Greater Sundas, along with Java, Sumatra and Kalimantan (Borneo). Unlike many of Indonesia's other islands, however, vulcanism had but little to do with its uplifting. Nor is it a part of either the Sunda continental shelf, which extends out from Southeast Asia and includes Java, Sumatra and Kalimantan, or of the Sahul Shelf that links New Guinea and the Aru Islands with Australia.

As such, Sulawesi may be the largest of the islands of "Wallacea," the transition zone between Asia and Australia. The nineteenth-century English naturalist Alfred Russel Wallace—who spent eight extremely productive years in these waters and whose book *The Malay Archipelago* (1869) is an informative resource for the Indonesian traveler—was fascinated by the natural history of the island, which he saw as filled with "anomalies and eccentricities."

> . . . Celebes must be one of the oldest parts of the Archipelago. It probably dates from a period not only anterior to that when Borneo, Java and Sumatra were separated from the continent, but from that still more remote epoch when the land that now constitutes these islands had not risen above the ocean. Such an antiquity is necessary to account for the number of animal forms it possesses, which show no relation to those of India or Australia, but rather with those of Africa. . . .

Among the unique forms of life that Wallace found on Sulawesi, and which led to this curious linkage with Africa, are the *babirusa*, or "pig-deer," the *anoa*, or "dwarf buffalo," and the black macaque, or "Celebes baboon." The *babirusa*, which somewhat resembles the warthog of Africa, has upper canines that grow upward dramatically, curling over the eyes. The *anoa* actually appears closer to the antelopes of Africa than to the water buffalo of Southeast Asia; and the black macaque looks so much like a small baboon that it's uncanny, despite the macaque's significant evolutionary distance from the African primate. Several unusual bird species and even insects (Wallace's particular area of expertise) also display curious relations with African life forms, further underscoring Wallace's contention that "this island is really one of the most isolated portions of the Archipelago, although situated in its very centre."

Today, Sulawesi is divided into four provinces, named somewhat unimaginatively North, South, Central and Southeast. The most populous is Sulawesi Selatan, or "Sul-Sel" (Sulawesi South), whose capital is a squat city of nine hundred thousand called Ujung Pandang. The name means "farthest point of sight," or perhaps "the farthest point of the pandan tree" (better known as the screw pine). More poetic, and briefer, translations such as "Horizon" and "Land's End" have been suggested, but even these fail to mask what Australian travel writer Colin Simpson called "the ugly mouthful" of the name Ujung Pandang, formerly known as Makassar.

Wallace's investigation of southern Sulawesi never took him far from Makassar, a city he found "prettier and cleaner than any I had yet seen in the East." Joseph Conrad, too, was favorably struck by Makassar, though in a slightly different way, and he began his first novel, *Almayer's Folly*, with a golden-hued evocation of its glory days:

> At that time Macassar was teeming with life and commerce. It was the point in the islands where tended all those bold spirits who, fitting out schooners on the Australian coast, invaded the Malay Archipelago in

search of money and adventure. Bold, reckless, keen in business, not disinclined for a brush with the pirates that were to be found on many a coast as yet, making money fast, they used to have a general "rendezvous" in the bay for the purposes of trade and dissipation.

All of which could lead the unwary traveler to expect a great deal of historical charm, tropical ambience and swashbuckling grace from Ujung Pandang. The unwary would soon be set aright. A wind-whipped rain lacerated the windows of the Viscount as we landed at Hasanuddin Airport, some twenty-five cluttered kilometers from downtown Ujung Pandang. New rice sprouted in the overflowing fields, which surrounded compounds of houses stilted above the extensive floodplain; traffic flowed in the random style of Indonesia, from lane to lane with blithe disregard for the lines in the street and the rules of the road, accompanied by the irregular yet constant bleating of horns by Mitsubishi and Toyota. We drove past the Graveyard of the Heroes, where the bodies of those who fought in Indonesia's 1945–49 war of independence lay; and past the Islamic and Christian cemeteries, a mismatched pair divided by the road. The Chinese cemetery, however, is being dug up: Ujung Pandang needs room to grow, and the Chinese communists have been blamed for the uprising against Soekarno in 1965. (There is in fact a general national paranoia against things Chinese: in Jakarta the papers were full of the storm of controversy over the popularity of the Chinese martial arts. President Soeharto himself finally decreed that *t'ai chi* could stay, but it must now be called "Indonesian Therapeutic Exercise.")

The Makassar people and their close neighbors in Sul-Sel, the Bugi, have long been noted for their expertise in boat building. Their craft—known collectively as *praus* (or *prahus* or *pirahus*) and ranging in size from small 2.4-meter canoes to 38-meter seaworthy craft known as *pinisi*—have plied the waters of Southeast Asia for perhaps fifteen hundred years. There is evidence that via these ships Indonesians settled islands as far away as Madagascar and brought northern

Australia, Polynesia and China into their trade network long before Europeans came to Indonesia. Their goods included palm oil, copra and especially fish; their ships also serviced the trade of Maluku (formerly the Moluccas) to the east in nutmeg, cloves and other spices. The Bugi and Makassar have been among the most mobile of Indonesians, settling in far-off fishing communities on Java, Sumatra and Malaysia.

Although the official modern history of Indonesia gives the primary role in ship building, commerce and settlement to the Bugi, many people believe it was the Makassar who were the more creative and commercial of the two groups. The sultanate of Gowa was one of the strongest kingdoms in the Malay Archipelago at the time of the coming of the Dutch; it was a Makassar kingdom, with its center in the port of Makassar. Between 1530 and 1611, Gowa's influence spread throughout not only Sulawesi—it dominated the Minahasa region of northern Sulawesi, and it subjugated the Bugi kingdom of Bone in 1611—but to Nusa Tenggara and southern Maluku as well. Only the sultanates of Ternate and Tidore in the heart of the Maluku's lucrative spice islands rivaled Gowa for dominance in the post-Majapahit period of Indonesia's precolonial history.

The dominance of Gowa was broken only by an alliance between the Dutch and the disenfranchised Bugi. In 1660, the Bugi prince Arung Palakka led an unsuccessful rebellion against the Gowa sultan, Hasanuddin. After sheltering Palakka in Jakarta (then known as Batavia), the Dutch—with a large fleet, European troops, Ambonese mercenaries, and Palakka's Bugi warriors—moved against the Makassarese in 1666. After a year of bitter fighting, Hasanuddin was finally forced to sign the Treaty of Bungaya. As was a standard clause in Dutch peace treaties of the time, Hasanuddin lost all his royal status and the Makassarese their independence. The economic boom that followed, under the watchful guardianship of the Dutch East Indies Company, led to Makassar's greatest success in its traditional role: that of a trading center for the Malay Archipelago and beyond.

It may be one of those curiosities of national

self-perception to emphasize the Bugi role and deemphasize that of the Makassar. The nation of Indonesia, after all, would not exist without the unifying influence of the Dutch, who were aided in their efforts by the Bugi. (Although, in fairness, the Bugi and Makassar both continued to chafe under Dutch rule into the 1930s.) But some think that neither group is the most significant of Sulawesi traders, that the honor should go to the virtually unknown Mandar, tucked under the lip of Sulawesi's west coast to the north of the Makassar kingdom. Whatever the true patterns of commerce and settlement were, they have been adjusted over the centuries to fit contemporary readings of history. Still, when in Indonesia you come across a "Bugi village" on the coasts of Borneo, Lombok, Sumbawa or Ambon, whether its

origin was Bugi, Makassar or Mandar, it was surely Sulawesian.

I had been in Indonesia for a full week, having spent several days in Jakarta before coming to Ujung Pandang. Most people in Indonesia couldn't believe that I lived in an American town smaller than Ujung Pandang—they didn't realize there was such a thing. If I were to believe my guidebooks, I lived in a town about the same size as Rantepao, the cultural center of the Sa'dang Toraja people I was going to visit. So I was used to seeing the lay of the land instead of gridlock and enjoyed the sounds of a waking forest more than the amplified predawn call of the muezzin, interrupted as it was by the first of many honks from the day's traffic.

Sweeping rooftops of Toraja houses and granaries ride the terrain amid the rice fields of Torajaland. (Christian Kallen)

Finally my companions in travel arrived, by an afternoon flight from Bali: Sobek travel agent Karen Bridges and photographer Pam Roberson, who immediately headed for bed to sleep off the effects of jet lag. The next morning we left for the hills, with our PACTO guide Rauf Nyarrang and an earnest, silent driver named Abdullah.

Almost as soon as one leaves Ujung Pandang, the land again asserts itself. To the east, Gunung Lompobatang rises to nearly 2800 meters, like the sky anchor for the peninsula to the north. This ancient volcano has been uplifted over the eons, pulling up a ridge of limestone buttes in its wake. The steady erosive action of rice cultivation in sawahs—the small terraced pools with their irregular walls that are so typical of the Asian landscape—has further lowered the level of the surrounding sedimentary floor. As a consequence, these bulging buttes with their sheer white walls seem to balance on narrow stumps; even stands of trees have their bases 2 to 3 meters above surrounding rice fields.

These limestone buttes are the advance guard of the central knot of mountains, crowned by Gandadiwata (3074 meters) and Rantemario (3440 meters). In the midst of these uplifted ridges of limestone and granite are said still to live a few of Indonesia's oldest inhabitants, the Toala. These nomads were living on Sulawesi uncounted thousands of years ago; their artifacts are still being unearthed and the dates of their arrival on the island being pushed ever further back. Most significant of their traces are the monoliths of the Gintu region, west of Lake Poso (and north of Tana Toraja)—rounded blocks of stone carved into statues of fertility gods. Imaginative investigators compare them to the *moai* of Easter Island or the Olmec heads of Mexico and draw elaborate conclusions. Whatever the Toala's origins, their destiny was to be largely absorbed into the blood and traditions of their successors on Sulawesi, the Toraja.

The weather had been cloudy and wet for the past month on Sulawesi. Rain followed us up the long, winding mountain road from Pare Pare, the last coastal town on the route. Heavy clouds obscured the bulk of Rantemario, the towering peak that stands sentinel to Torajaland. As dusk fell, however, we passed beneath the model *tong-konan* that is the gate to the regency of Tana Toraja, and the rain ceased. The road twisted and rose and dropped and rose again, and in the darkening light we caught glimpses of small villages of the twin-prowed *tongkonan*, tiny rice sawahs and thick stands of lean bamboo and tall, slender palms. Something about the atmosphere itself seemed different: a permanence, a peacefulness—shattered only when Abdullah, tired from the nine-hour drive from Ujung Pandang, leaned on the horn to scatter the boys leading their water buffalo through the twilight.

It had indeed been a long drive from Ujung Pandang, and Abdullah was not the only one frustrated by it. As soon as we checked into the Hotel Misiliana I left my room and walked along the road in the night. Here were the sounds of the Sa'dang River rushing by, the bleating of frogs and the rhythmic buzzing and rattling of insects. Two kilometers down the road I came to Rantepao, a town lively by comparison to its mountain surround yet a relaxing contrast to the earnest rush of Ujung Pandang. For the first time since my arrival in Indonesia I heard music, real music played by living souls, issuing from the balconies and porches of the simple wood-frame houses along the road. Later, Rauf would state categorically that all music in Tana Toraja was religious, due to the deeply spiritual nature of the people; but that night I swear I heard the slow-strumming guitar chords of familiar ballads, the sad wisdom of country singers of heartache, Jim Reeves and Ferlin Husky and Lefty Frizzell, drifting softly into the black night of Torajaland.

Dawn had yet to break when I woke the next morning, and in the quiet hour before sunrise I could hear the waking village near the hotel, the water being run for washing and the steady beating of the wooden mallets that pulverized the coffee beans. I dressed and went out to watch the village come to life. The women carried loads on their backs with a headstrap support as they pounded betel in small portable grinders. While some of the men led water buffalo down the road or over the sawah walls to the far terraces, others just stood smoking as the mist rose from the rice fields, sarongs draped over their shoulders to cover more modern shirts and trousers.

Tana Toraja in the full light of day proved to

The mortuary wall at Lemo, with its cave crypts and balconies of tau-taus, *effigies of the dead. Today, even fewer effigies remain, a result of continuing artifact theft in Torajaland. (Christian Kallen)*

be no less magical than augured thus far. The funeral ceremony we had come for had not yet begun, so we had time to see some of the traditional graves and houses for which the Toraja are famous. First stop was Lemo, an elaborate series of crypts and caves chiseled out of a limestone cliff. On shelves among these hanging graves, supported by bannisters, stand dozens of *tau-tau*, effigies of the deceased—their hands outstretched, their wide painted eyes staring vacantly across the rice fields. When a Toraja dies—especially a nobleman, for the Toraja have a heavily structured social order—a statue of him is carved to keep his presence visible to coming generations. Men and women *tau-tau*, about half life-size, line the rock wall of Lemo, the men distinguished by the *sambu* draped crosswise over their chests. Their hands are held out in an established ges-

ture: the right with palm up to accept the benefits of the afterlife, the left with palm in to ward off bad luck for the coming generations.

The walls of Lemo no longer hold as many effigies as they did a few years ago—postcards sold in town show twice as many *tau-tau* on these balconies, crowded shoulder to shoulder. Some say that souvenir hunters have stolen them, though the polite Toraja carefully blame no particular group. In any case it's a cultural tragedy, a crime that affects not only the sensibilities of the living but, according to Aluk Todolo—the animistic, ancestor-worshiping religion of traditional Toraja—the afterlife of the deceased.

In Indonesia, all the rituals and beliefs of a people compose what is known as the *adat*. The word means custom, belief system or behavior, and many Indonesians are quite conscious of liv-

During the week-long funeral ceremonies of Torajaland, guests are housed in elaborate but temporary shelters like these at Kete Kesu. (Christian Kallen)

ing in harmony with their *adat*. While most Indonesians are Moslem (although the Toraja are nominally Christian), the *adat* is something much deeper and older than these religions. To live without *adat* is to live without rules, without purpose; even a Moslem or Christian, should he ignore the customary law of his people, is felt to be lost. The tribal chief of one traditional people of southern Sulawesi, the Towa, put it succinctly to writer Robin Handbury-Tenison: "Here the *adat* is both the rule we follow and the message for the way ahead."

Closer to the morbid caves, I climbed into the stillness of death, a passive quiet in these morning hours. I found myself thinking how powerful it is to be in the presence of worked stone: Mayan temples, Inca walls, carved Buddhist lintels or cliffside necropolises. It is the most elemental and enduring of humanity's communication with the world. A record of belief and cultural perception more durable than words or wood, stonework is a link with a time frame greater than any other scale we can know, a first tentative reach toward immortality—and perhaps still the most near.

Before the seventeenth century, the Toraja placed their dead in wooden coffins and sealed them in natural caves; some feel that the site at Lemo is the first of the new style of burial, the manmade crypts dug into the cliffside. Every family member is placed in the same cave, the wrapped bodies of the newly dead joining the bones of their ancestors. But burial in stone is only for those who have had the privilege to live: infants, babies who have yet to cut their first teeth, have had no chance to grow in the world they have been born into. Their bodies are placed inside holes cut in large breadfruit trees, so at least in death they can know life, and growth.

That afternoon we went to Kete Kesu, the traditional village where the funeral was to be held. Though we had passed through several villages that morning on our Cook's Tour of Torajaland, nothing we had seen prepared us for Kete Kesu: surrounding a broad rice field were literally dozens of traditional-style houses, many of them rice barns and living structures but many more being temporary buildings erected to house the gathering clan. When a Toraja nobleman dies, all members of his clan are expected to return for the funeral, no matter where they live, whether in a small mountain village or in Ujung Pandang or Jakarta. Not to return for the funeral is to forsake one's position in the clan, one's family membership. For a people as committed to their *adat* as the Toraja are—especially when that *adat* includes a powerful belief in the afterlife—to miss a funeral is virtually unthinkable.

Each temporary structure sported the double-prowed roof of the *tongkonan*; each was covered with the red, black and white carvings of Torajan art. While the living quarters of the village were pointed to the north—the home of Puang Matua, the creator—the temporary structures were arrayed to the east and west, facing in toward the rice fields. This elaborate cluster of colorful buildings gave the village an almost cosmopolitan air: literally hundreds of people milled about in anticipation, most of them of Torajan heritage greeting long-missed friends and relations. A few tourists, their height and light hair even more conspicuous than their cameras, circulated in the crowds, while the immediate family of the deceased pasted his red coffin with silver and gold designs.

In the middle of the town stood the *tau-tau*, the effigy of the deceased. "Ne' Reba, 1912–1986," read the inscription over the statue's small shelter. So this was the man we had come to see buried—a straight-backed old man with a stubborn yet kindly expression on his face, smokey glasses perched on his nose, garbed in this form in the clothes he had worn in life. The effect was

incredibly lifelike: Rauf drew his breath in shock at seeing the *tau-tau*. "That is just like him! That is just what he looked like!" Just then Pam Roberson, who had missed Rauf's explanation of the function of the statue while she had been off taking photographs, came back to take some establishing shots of the town square. "How long is that old man going to stand there?" she asked.

Some say the effigies are not supposed to look like the deceased, being merely symbolic representations. In fact, the older *tau-tau* at places like Lemo can hardly be called representative, with their globelike heads and cartoon eyes. But in recent years the artistic representation of the dead is becoming more and more realistic, and the effect of having the spitting image of the deceased watching over the extensive ceremonies of his own burial is more than a bit eerie. Possibly the sculptor's art has improved in Tana Toraja; possibly the actual procedure of burial itself, a ritual that has changed in this century with the introduction of embalming, has helped preserve the physical remains of the body long enough to permit more exact artistic mimicry.

Ne' Reba had died in early November, but the three-month delay between death and burial is not long by Toraja standards. If anything, it's quite prompt. Delays of six months or even a year are not uncommon, time during which the disparate clan families must all agree to meet in Tana Toraja to pay their final respects. During this interval, the deceased is believed not to be dead—he is regarded merely as "the sick one," temporarily indisposed but still living. He is placed on a bed in the southernmost room of the *tongkonan*, the traditional room of the parents in the family dwelling and the symbolic seat of the soul. Food and drink are placed before the body, which in former times was decomposing. The final elaborate burial ceremonies, known as the Rambu Solo, were marked not only by processions and buffalo sacrifices but by a ritual cleansing of the remains.

Among the changes wrought by the Dutch and their missionaries since the Christianization of Tana Toraja in 1907 was the elimination of some of the cruder aspects of native practices, including this washing of the remains of the de-

ceased. Today, entirely Christian burials are often held, and the colorful ceremonies of the Rambu Solo that we had come to see are becoming increasingly rare. Ne' Reba was a Christian, and a cross was prominent on the small shelter for his effigy. He was, in fact, a founder of the regional interdenominational council, as well as being a founder of a financial cooperative and a strong advocate of Torajan rights in the difficult years following Indonesian independence. But he was first and foremost an influential and wealthy Toraja nobleman, and as such he was due to receive the largest traditional funeral ceremony in eight years.

There are two main rituals in Tana Toraja: Rambu Tuka is held in the morning, usually for the raising of a new house; its purpose is to safeguard human lives. Rambu Solo, on the other hand, is a ritual of the afternoon, the time of the sun's descent, and it is designed for the burial of the dead and the passage of the soul into the world of night. Meaning literally "smoke descending" or "an offering going down," the entire ceremony is a display of respect and offer of material possessions to the departed spirit, to assure his wealth and comfort in the afterlife (in the *puya*, the soul's world).

The next day the public part of Rambu Solo began. The entire funeral ceremony is actually a long and complex series of rituals, including the wrapping of the body, elaborate village preparations and fasting among the family. But with Ma'Palao the Torajan funeral enters the phase of celebration, without leaving mourning behind. This is the day the body is moved from its temporary resting place on the floor of the main rice barn, lifted into a special bier and paraded through the village and around the rice fields en route to its ritual position above the *rante* (field of ceremony). Here the final rituals take place, including the sacrifice of buffalo and pigs, the number of which is determined by the importance of the deceased.

Although the funeral was being held in the middle of the rainy season, the family of the deceased clearly hoped that the elements would cooperate. Indeed they seemed to be in luck: the morning of Ma'Palao dawned cool but clear, and the crowd filling the road from Rantepao to Kete Kesu was in high spirits. Among everyone, including Torajans, outside Indonesians and a scattering of international tourists, the anticipation was electric. The local Toraja showed their involvement in the ceremony by leading slow-moving, stolid water buffalo down the road to Kete Kesu.

Colorful banners rose into the skies; people milled about waiting with unconcealed excitement for the ceremony to begin; everyone seemed to be dressed in their most elaborate dress, as if a wedding were about to take place instead of a funeral. In my own cultural history, I could only compare the excitement with a huge Fourth of July gathering: the abundance of colorful decorations, the happy anticipation of the crowd. I thought this might be an irrelevant, not to say impious, comparison, but any culture needs ceremony; in America this need is often fulfilled by patriotic parades, held on secular holidays, sponsored by chambers of commerce and choreographed for broadcast to a national flock, the viewing public. It is, in its own way, no less religious than a funeral in harmony with *adat*.

Since Ne' Reba was a highly involved member of his community, the preparatory hours leading up to the actual moving of his coffin were filled with testimonial speeches. A business associate praised his contributions, then a politician delivered a speech about his role in preserving Torajan heritage; finally a preacher—strangely enough, given the traditional nature of society in Indonesia in general and Tana Toraja in particular, a woman—led the community in prayer. The assembled crowd politely listened and amened, then wandered around the village, admiring the most beautiful of the offered buffalo and waiting for the sun to pass the zenith so that Rambu Solo could begin.

As noon approached, a restlessness stirred the

OPPOSITE: *The* tau-tau *of Ne' Reba, high noble of Toraja's Kete Kesu village, at the outset of his final procession.* (Christian Kallen)

crowd. The coffin was placed in its *duba-duba*, the ceremonial bier in the shape of a traditional house that would be paraded through the village. The widow and the To Ma'parandan—the woman who is entrusted with the distribution of the food brought to the dead—took their seats in their own enclosed palanquins, to be borne by members of the clan. Meanwhile the man in charge of the burial ceremony, the To Mebalun, and his assistants—all dressed in colorful red and black woven shirts, similar in style to the native wear from the highlands of Guatemala—retired to a corner of the village to prepare themselves, psychologically, for the rigors of the Ma'Palao.

Palm wine, or *tuak*, here derived from the sap of the sugar palm, is one of Indonesia's favorite and most prevalent native inebriants. In the early morning hours the fruit is removed and a bamboo tube placed in the scar, there to receive the first rush of sweet juice sent to the missing fruit. The skin of the fruit is added, just as the skin of the grape is kept in to supply the necessary yeasts for fermentation; within just a few hours, the resulting liquor has foamed up and reached an alcohol content of around 5 percent, about as strong as an ale. Left to ferment longer, it becomes red in color, the strongest inebriant the Toraja know, and as such its role at ritual ceremonies is assured.

I had been off taking photos of the bier and the black-gowned family of Ne' Reba when a chorus of shouting and what sounded like ridicule rose from a shaded corner of the village. The male funeral officials were drinking down great draughts of *tuak* from the long bamboo trunks, punctuating their ritualistic endeavor with bursts of hilarity and bravado. They broke into hoots, shouts and hollers, waved and pointed and yelled insults at the nearby clan cousins, and drank still more. For the most part I had been content to let Rauf translate the Torajan proceedings, realizing I could never learn enough of this remote Malay dialect in the short time I had on Sulawesi; but now I longed to know the language, to understand these coarse ejaculations of the drunk men,

to join in their hoarse laughter and perhaps to share a draught of that sweet palm wine.

Then the hot sun passed the zenith, the men stumbled back to the *duba-duba* and the crowd was pushed back out of the main road of Kete Kesu. The excitement grew as the black-gowned women of the immediate family unfurled a long bolt of red cloth and held it over their heads. Bursts of chanting and impatient shouts rose from the procession; the *duba-duba*, with its burden of the earthly remains of Ne' Reba supported by a heavy latticed structure of thick bamboo poles, was raised on the shoulders of the strongest men of Kete Kesu.

I had foreseen a ritualistic procession through town, led by the buffalo and dancers, with the gong beaters, palanquins and bier following—like a funeral, of course, orderly and somewhat somber. So despite the palm wine and the awareness that buffalo sacrifice was not likely to be a gentle event, I was not prepared for what happened next: the men carrying the bier suddenly all shouted and, under the direction of a man riding the sacred bier like a train lineman, they raced forward, leaned to the side, shook the bier and ran backward, moving in a huge, wildly precarious circular motion that threatened to topple the roof-heavy *duba-duba* onto the muddy street, there to burst the coffin and spill the earthly remains of the dearly departed.

The effect was catalytic: the crowd surrounding the parade scattered as if at a riot, and the men carrying the bier shouted encouragement to each other; I looked around in vain for a single face with the grim visage of mourning. To no avail: a wide grin creased every face, eyes sparkled with exultation and the heavy press of people seemed as graceful and light as a troupe of Balinese dancers.

Since he is assumed to be still present in spirit, the dead person must be jolted and coaxed to leave his body behind. The procession around his village and the familiar rice fields of his earthly days is his last journey on earth and is designed to satisfy the spirit's wishes to remain with the

OPPOSITE: *The widow and eldest son of Ne' Reba, dressed in mourning attire at his funeral. (Christian Kallen)*

body. Still, the journey is not an easy one, and the wild swaying and shaking of the body—and the sympathetic shaking of the widow and the To Ma'parandan in their palanquins—is the necessary effort of the living to rid their world of ghosts.

Soon the procession itself began—the buffalo and the gong beaters plowing through the crowded street, the red fabric snake of the women in mourning weaving jerkily along, the sedans and bier being shaken without mercy, all led by the sightless *tau-tau* of Ne' Reba. There was a stuffed bird of paradise stuck on the front peak of the *duba-duba*; one episode of shaking knocked it off, and a boy was recruited to stand on another's shoulders to replace it, as the crowd yelled rowdy encouragement and advice. It was hardly the scene of restrained emotion I had expected of a funeral. If there was sadness, it was hidden behind the black veil surrounding the widow's quaking palanquin.

At last the procession left town, reflected in the rice paddy along with the distant peak of Sesean, the 2300-meter mountain that crowns Tana Toraja. The lightest sprinkle of rain began to fall, and it occurred to me later that, since the sun was still shining, a rainbow may have arced over Kete Kesu. The procession was gone for an hour, to give Ne' Reba one last glimpse of the sawahs and scenery of his home; by the time it returned, the sky had clouded over and the day had cooled.

The focus of the ceremony shifted from the main street of Kete Kesu to the temporarily erected *lakkian*, a ceremonial building from which the dead would witness the events of the coming days, including the greeting of guests and the sacrifice of buffalo. The *lakkian* was built on top of a small hillside, the open area known as the *rante*. By itself, *rante* means "field"—*Rantepao* means "field of mangoes," for instance—but *rante* alone usually indicates the area of a village where the sacrifices are made, the killing field.

The heavily decorated bier on its rack of bamboo was carried up the muddy slope of the *rante*; then the bier was removed and the rack of bamboo was leaned against the *lakkian* to serve as a ladder. The tall peaked roof of the *duba-duba* was taken off, and almost a dozen men joined in hauling the coffin up the bamboo rack step by slippery step, as the pace of the rainfall began to increase. At first the coffin seemed to resist entry to the *lakkian*, and I wondered how seriously these people took such signs and portents. Not very seriously at all, I decided as the coffin was hefted and jammed almost rudely into the *lakkian*. At last a dozen strong hands spread over the stern of the red coffin, and with a mighty shout and shove the pallbearers wedged it into its sacred vantage. And then the heavens opened.

The village was deluged by rainfall; the dirt turned to mud, the black buffalo dung ran into the earth, rivulets of brown runoff cascaded into the rice fields. Everyone ran for cover, ceremonial official and bystander, Toraja and tourist alike; sheets of water spilled off the peaked edges of the roofs, limiting visibility behind liquid veils. And what had been a fairly orderly event—despite the wild dance of the pallbearers—descended into chaos.

A man raced from out of shelter onto the *rante* and, pointing at a buffalo, yelled to the crowd. A cheer went up as his challenge was answered, and another man ran into the mud to point to his buffalo. The first raced back and forth between the crowd and the beasts, collecting sodden rupiah notes as bets, and I realized we were about to witness a buffalo fight, another traditional aspect of Torajan funerals. Then the beasts were released, pushed toward each other—and immediately they turned and ran away, down the muddy slope into the thick pools of the rice field.

Enmired, they could hardly fight; but the butting of heads and the clashing of horns is not what a buffalo fight is about. Rather, it is intimidation that determines the victor, and the first to run is held to be the loser. In this case, I certainly couldn't tell which side would keep the kitty. Perhaps no one could, for soon two more buffalo were paired off, then more; few of the matches resulted in actual head butting, however. For the

OPPOSITE: *The funeral procession through the streets of Kete Kesu is almost festive, marked by gong beats, chanting and the enthusiastic cries of the crowd. (Christian Kallen)*

next rain-swept hour, muddy buffalo went barreling across the rice fields, up the hillsides around the sawah, and through the streets of Kete Kesu, scattering celebrants, mourners and photographers without prejudice, pummeling the wet earth of Tana Toraja into a thick, viscid ooze.

Soon we left Kete Kesu and began the long walk back to Rantepao. The rain showed no sign of letting up, and the day's ceremony was over: the body of Ne' Reba had been moved from the family rice barn to his *lakkian* overlooking the killing field. He was now, I was told, officially dead, his spirit at last released from his body, perhaps to hover in the village for the next several days to enjoy the tribute his clan had prepared for him, then to move on to the north and *puya*, the realm of souls.

Yet the ecstasy of the day's events remained: my blood was flushed with adrenalin, my face ached from uncontrollable grinning and a new sunburn blazed in the rain. Suddenly I thought back to the morning's preparation and realized that there was perhaps more to the holiday comparison I had drawn than I had thought. This had not been just a funeral but a cultural festival so grand and unifying that rain and mud became the very stuff of it, a cleansing bath of earth and water; and the motley assortment of near relations, distant cousins and foreign strangers had become united into a nation, all kin and celebrants to the passing of Ne' Reba.

A tedong bonga, *or* piebald water buffalo, *the most highly prized offering in the rituals of Sulawesi's Toraja people.*
(Christian Kallen)

The next morning began the second public phase of Rambu Solo, the greeting of guests. Again Kete Kesu was crowded, though primarily with the friends and relations of Ne' Reba. They were dressed to the teeth: the finest and most colorful dresses, sarongs and hats were on display for a series of parades. Each wound its way into town, between the *tongkonan* and rice barns on the main street and down across the central sawah to a large building called the *bala'kayan*. Here the immediate family of Ne' Reba received the thousands of guests, cataloging and stacking their gifts for future distribution and repayment.

In the traditional Toraja belief structure of Aluk Todolo, you can take it with you: the gifts brought to the funeral and the animals sacrificed are thought to symbolically accompany the dead to *puya* and establish his status in the afterlife. Clan members are eager to show their respect for nobles like Ne' Reba by being lavish with their gifts, not only for the sake of the deceased but for their own eventual status. At the bottom of the scale is rice or maize, with cigarettes and candy a step above. *Kreteks*, or clove cigarettes, are the approved gift for unrelated visitors—we purchased a carton of Bentoel Internationals, wrapped in brown paper and tied with string, for the occasion. Next in order are the traditional betel leaf and nut, exceeded by chickens, then pigs, then buffalo. Not only the number of buffalo but the type is important: not any scrawny old ox will do, though if a family is poor even the scrawniest is appreciated as the sacrifice it is, and will become.

Of the many gifts presented, the most valued is the *tedong bonga*, the "spotted buffalo." These strange-looking beasts are not the usual brown or black of most water buffalo; instead they bear a piebald coat of pink, white and black markings. Their physical oddity is their spiritual strength and hence economic value: a healthy specimen—standing a meter and a half at the shoulder, with horns perfectly shaped and hooves matching his coat—is worth about four thousand dollars. Though these are the most expensive buffalo, if an average value of a thousand dollars is estimated for each of the fifty buffalo brought to a funeral as elaborate as Ne' Reba's, and only fifty dollars for each of the hundreds of pigs offered,

it is clear that these social occasions are economic events of the first magnitude.

While these offerings are generously given, they are not given without purpose: nothing is free, not even in Torajaland. The offerings of each family are recorded carefully; some are paybacks on old debts, perhaps left over from the last funeral, and some are investments against coming ceremonies. The number of buffalo presented by a descendant of the deceased is a deciding factor in his or her share of the inheritance. Coupled with the fact that each generation and family strives to pay off more than they are indebted, it is clear that this expensive ceremony leads to a concentration of wealth among the nobility.

The Toraja have a fairly stratified society. There are now about three hundred thousand Toraja in the geographically central region of Sulawesi, far more than there were a century ago, and they seem to have moved into the twentieth century with ease, adapting to the intensive agricultural techniques of wet rice and coffee cultivation. The noble class, of which Ne' Reba was a member, composes about 5 percent of the populace; the middle class, wealthy enough perhaps to own land and have an extended family clan, another 25 percent. This leaves some 70 percent who can only be classed as workers, or peasants—hired out to nearby landowners, they are themselves too poor to warrant the sacrifice of a single buffalo on a wedding day, or with death.

All this lends a certain practical, even political significance to the greeting of guests and their gifts, which was missing from the more emotional and ecstatic events of Ma'Palao. Yet the day of greeting and gift giving was not without its ceremonial aspects. Each time another family was ready to make its offerings, a new parade was organized to follow the same route through town. The parade was led by a small group of dancing warriors, each with an elaborate headdress symbolic of buffalo horns on his head. Shuffling and twisting their bodies, heads held down in the posture of buffalo, they raised their faces to give irregular cries or screams, then continued their curious dance. From afar they presented an unearthly aspect, as if possessed by the spirits of buffalo; up close I was sure I could de-

tect a bemused smile beneath more than one headdress.

Then came the youngest daughter of Ne' Reba, surrounded by an entourage of protectresses. In her golden gown, this pretty ten-year-old held the role of "crown princess" of the ceremony. While smiles and joking and good-natured role playing seemed to be the mood of many of the participants, I never saw this girl look anything less than totally committed to the funeral, her role in it and the memory of her aged father. There was something almost uncanny about her, as if her dedication and hers alone would endure. The burial tradition of the Toraja might change still more in the coming years, the slaughter of buffalo and expensive exchange of gifts might be foresworn for economic and political reasons; but the sacred wake for Ne' Reba would be carried in her memory into the next century, till she was an old woman confronting her own last procession.

The family and friends of the clan followed, all clothed in bright colors—some women with tight-fitting blue silk blouses, some with conical black bamboo hats, some with green dresses; many of the men wore headkerchiefs. Many carried long hollow tubes of bamboo, either foaming over with *tuak*, stuffed with prepared food or empty and ready to serve as cooking vessels for the fresh meat to come. And of course there were the animals—huge hogs suspended from bamboo logs, presented a dozen or more at a time, their tiny fearful eyes almost hidden by folds of fat; and the buffalo, one after another, plodding with stately pace in the wake of a handler. The doomed buffalo were led across the *rante* to mud-sunk stone stakes, the *simbuangan*, and each was tied to his final hitching post.

With the thousands of clan members in attendance, called from throughout Indonesia to the funeral of Ne' Reba, food became a prime concern. Yet with hundreds of pigs ripe for slaughter no one was to go hungry—once the gifts had been duly recorded, the swine were carried around behind the village to be converted, squealing, to pork. Each family was assigned one of the temporary bamboo houses surrounding Kete Kesu, which were marked with numbers and letters as addresses. Inside these two-story buildings—built on stilts, like so many traditional buildings on Sulawesi, and walled in with woven bamboo mats—the families congregated, conversed and feasted. It was a perfect opportunity for the young to meet equals of the opposite sex, members of other families whose marriage would satisfy the kinship structures of the Toraja. The afternoon became blue with smoke, before the rains came again to cleanse the air, to drip off the bamboo roofs of the houses, to muddy the hoof-plowed fields of Kete Kesu. Then the kerosene lamps and bonfires were lit, and the night was enriched with song and dance and dalliance.

The next day was yet another day of greeting, and as such a good opportunity for us to go elsewhere in Tana Toraja. Not being family members, it was unlikely we would meet a distant cousin to court and wed; and our gift of cigarettes had been duly recorded for eventual redistribution. So Karen, Pam and I joined Rauf in a Toyota Land Cruiser for a four-wheel foray up the muddy mountain roads of Torajaland, toward the foggy flanks of Sesean.

The road headed north out of Rantepao and crossed a flat plain at the base of Sesean to the village of Bori. Here an old *rante* was overgrown with grasses, the stone *simbuangans* rising from the tangled vegetation to reach toward the sky like an ancient Stonehenge. Two of the houses in Bori—which itself was nearly deserted, as this was midmorning in the rice planting season—showed evidence of the Rambu Solo held here in past years. At the front of one of the *tongkonan*, the major support for the peaked north roof was decorated with buffalo horns, rising from the largest at ground level to the smallest high up the post. It sported fifty-four buffalo horns, silent testimony to a riot of tribute.

In these quiet hours of midmorning we had

OPPOSITE: *The coffin is hefted into the* lakkian, *a temporary resting place from which the spirit of the deceased will view the events of his funeral ceremonies. (Christian Kallen)*

the chance to look closely at the *tongkonan*, the most highly visible of Torajan artifacts. Every flat surface of the large rectangular houses, which can be up to eighteen meters long, is carved and painted in traditional black, red, white and yellow. These carvings are elaborate, detailed and geometric, a densely illustrated screen of Torajan symbols. Some animal representations are common—the interlaced horns of the buffalo, a decoration called *pori-situtu* that signifies unity; and two proud, heroic roosters facing each other over the front of the house, each standing on a circular pattern illustrating the sun and moon. At the crossbeam of the central support many houses have a carved *katik*, a cock's head on a snake's body, symbolic of the supernatural forces that arrange fertility. With *katik* or not, nearly all have a realistic carving of a buffalo head, its white face (symbolizing the color of bones) staring northward.

In a Torajan village all houses are lined up east to west, and all face north toward the place of the creator, Puang Matua; the rice barns parallel them, but they face to the south. The effect is to create a broad avenue lined by opposing structures, whose roofs reach out toward one another over the central passage. Climbing up a steep flight of stairs brings one to the interior of the house, the ground level being left open for sitting. (*Tongkon* means, in fact, "to sit.") There are three rooms on the second floor. The northern room is where the guests are permitted to sleep, but not because they are closest to the creator—the north is also the direction from which hostility comes, and guests represent a potential threat. The children live in the center room, and the parents live in the southernmost room—as mentioned, the "soul" of the house, where the "sick" body is kept before the funeral that confirms death.

The distinctive double-prowed roof is an elaborate bamboo construction, though in more recently built houses corrugated tin is frequently used. On top of a tongue-and-groove frame—no nails are used in traditional Torajan construction—split bamboo shafts are interlaced, alternately facing up and down, so arranged that rainfall is kept out. The roof itself is thatched with fronds, organic material that can sprout grasses and bromeliads under the stimulating influence of rainfall. In spring, I was told, the roofs often come into flower with orchids. Somehow, the story that the roofs are symbolic boats, reminders of the Proto-Malays' arrival from the Asian mainland millennia ago, fails to do these distinctive structures justice. They look more like the inverse of boats, their shape representing the hold rather than the hull. And given the prevalence of buffalo horns on the centerposts and buffalo imagery in their carvings, and the role of buffalo in the daily life and ritual, the double-prowed shape of the houses appears at least as representative of the wide span of a strong bull's horns.

The rice fields lay flat and flooded in this part of Tana Toraja; the inhabitants of Bori were hard at work, transferring the thin green seedlings from the nursery fields to the sawah, where they would reach maturity. For the Toraja, rice is of pivotal symbolic as well as economic importance. Their legends hold that Puang Matua made the first man, the first rice and the first buffalo on the same day; these three are brothers, kin in creation. The planting of rice—the seeding of the fields, the thinning of the shoots—is accompanied by song and prayer. And at harvest, as Harry Wilcox recounted in his 1949 *White Stranger: Six Moons in Celebes*, "Each stem of standing rice was cut separately, the reaper approaching it with the knife concealed in his palm so that his brother rice should not see the blade coming and be afraid."

This morning the rice shoots were new and green, and harvest was several months away. Lines of women, singing and chatting, pulled up handfuls of shoots, washed their roots, then bunched them for transfer to the growing fields. As we stopped to photograph one such group my

OPPOSITE: *Beneath the rain-heavy skies of Sulawesi's highlands, Toraja women stoop to thin young rice shoots for transplanting. (Pamela Roberson)*

attention was caught by a man bearing a full shoulder of *tuak*-filled bamboo tubes down the road, and I became absorbed in taking his photograph. When I looked up, there was Karen—pants rolled up to her knees, her feet sinking to the ankles in mud—wading out to join the women in their work.

Throughout our stay in Torajaland, Karen had seemed fascinated with the agriculture of the people. She investigated their small domestic gardens, naming vegetables and flowers, and she watched the work going on in the rice fields with deep interest. Now she had a chance to join in the fun, and she took it. Naturally, the women of Bori laughed as she came across the sawah wall, but soon she stooped with them and pulled up rice shoots; they laughed when she pulled up too many at a time, but she tried until she got it right. When she followed their example and shook the roots in the water to cleanse them, again they laughed, because the shoots came up too muddy. But she laughed with them, and soon she learned exactly what kind of work goes into transplanting rice seedlings from nursery to growing field. And the Toraja learned that tourists might want more than photographs and could give more than candy.

The road continued on past a series of small settlements and began to climb the slopes of Sesean. Here the rice fields became terraced, and where it was too steep or rugged to cultivate, the trees grew strong and thick. Every now and then a cluster of *tongkonan* roofs could be seen floating in a sea of sugar palm and bamboo; every now and then the forest parted to reveal an ever-higher vista of terraces descending toward the valley floor.

But the road grew more difficult, and our progress slowed to less than five kilometers an hour; several times our wheels spun in mud, and when they finally got traction we bumped and jounced, jumped and bounced into the next muddy pool. Finally it became too much: near the village of Batutumonga I begged to get out and volunteered to walk the last mile to Lokomata, our lunch stop.

We pulled over, I climbed out and the Toyota ground on up the hill. I looked over the edge of the road and was transported. Terraces swept down the hillside almost a thousand meters toward the Sadang River, far below. The irregular shapes of the sawahs combined in an almost cellular structure, like skin, an organic carpet of cultivation dropping in short steps down the wide viridescent valley. Pools of water, reflecting the cloudy sky, alternated with bright green nursery ponds, where new rice sprouted; mud walls isolated each pool from its neighbors, and granite boulders from the core of Sesean, too tough to erode and too huge to move, scattered across the landscape like grazing beasts. Far away, distant ridges were draped by wisps of cloud; in bamboo groves below, the double-prowed roofs rode the motionless waves of the terrain, all pointing northward, bamboo needles in a world compass. Villagers worked the fields in pairs and groups, hoeing and pulling and planting, figures out of Brueghel. Herons and egrets waded and soared; colorful finches clustered and scattered. And finally, with the Toyota gone and the mad celebration of Kete Kesu a dozen miles away, I could hear the sounds of mud, of labor, of wind and the turning of the earth, and the silence behind it all.

I watched, and listened, and breathed in this world for a timeless moment; then I was tugged by a vague sense of recollection, as if déjà vu were about to visit. Suddenly I remembered looking down on another scene not so long ago—the garden at the Hotel Borobudur, with its symmetrical palm groves, its conscientiously curved jogging path, its Olympic-sized pool reflecting the smoggy skies of Jakarta. Here, then, was the real "Garden," the cultivated landscape of people at home in their world, a true island of civilization amidst the truer Wilderness. The Borobudur held out the promise of such a spiritual center, but it was a synthetic substitute, an idle fantasy. This terraced valley was the real thing, the low-humming heart of the human world, the promised land.

Almost as soon as I knew this—just at the instant the warm realization washed through me like the shiver of an answered prayer—the veil began to fall again. The mind, its analytical faculties crying out for exercise and its superfluity of information in ever-rising tide, flooded over and drowned the insights of the heart. Despite myself, I knew that this was no ancient landscape, no timeless Eden. Until this century, the Toraja didn't even cultivate rice in these beautiful sawahs but used instead a swidden agriculture that burned and abused and shifted fields every couple years; then they allowed their buffalo to overgraze them. Until this century, there were no strong ties between the separate villages—none sufficient anyway to support the bloated excesses that characterized the regional celebration at the funeral of Ne' Reba. Until this century, the class stratification was more basic: a strong chief ruled over his clansmen and a large population of slaves, which were captured in war or traded for debt. The Toraja were not "noble savages," idyllic people living in a state of natural grace. Their villages were walled fortresses perched atop small hills; they were warlike, they were fearful and feared and, until the Dutch subdued them in 1907, they were headhunters.

The taking of heads is one of the quaintest of human traditions—quaint in the sense of ancient, singular and archaic. Archaeologists excavating skulls from European peat bogs or African riverbeds are hard pressed to find intact specimens without sizeable manmade holes for the eating of brains. Head-hunting—usually a taking of "trophies" from enemies, as a test of manhood or an expression of vengeance—may have been pandemic throughout Southeast Asia at one time. On the island of New Guinea it survived well into the current century, and cases of *kuru*, a viral disease transmitted by the eating of brains, still appear in the highlands of New Guinea. Elsewhere in Indonesia, at least three distinct and widely separated groups—the Batak on Sumatra, the Dayaks on Borneo and the Toraja on Sulawesi—all continued head-hunting through at least the last century. The practice, abhorrent to our civilized thinking though it may be, can neither be denied nor completely extirpated. Soldiers during recent wars were sometimes asked to prove their kills with the ears of their victims, a shadow of more savage conduct. Although we may think that head-hunting

(and its companion cannibalism) is the single most reprehensible human practice, the one that virtually identifies the savage by its presence and defines the civilized by its absence, this is not the case. Elaborate social structures, sophisticated art and architecture, and even the stirrings of monotheistic religious belief are found among headhunters. Surely the architecture and wood carvings of the Toraja and the similar expressions of the Batak of Sumatra did not spontaneously arise with the arrival of the Dutch. Closer to home, one of North America's most developed cultures, the Kwakiutl of the Pacific Northwest, had a true civilization based on the annual harvest of salmon, with plenty of leisure time for the pursuit of the arts and a wide trading network that ranged from Alaska to California. They also went on periodic forays to attack near or distant enemies and proved their success with souvenir skulls. And, not unlike the Toraja, they advertised their wealth in a feast of conspicuous consumption, the potlatch ceremony that proved the wealth of a chief by the plenty he could squander.

During the many hundreds if not thousands of years that the Toraja lived in isolation in the mountains of Sulawesi, their villages were walled in security against their neighbors; fear, tension and warfare were the normal social conditions. Head-hunting was but one expression of this savage world view: the head of a dead man was considered a source of supernatural power, and to take an enemy's head was not only to capture this power for one's self but to abduct it from the enemy. Heads were necessary to assure the fertility of crops, the success of new houses and temples, the appeasement of ancestral spirits—the entire spiritual well-being of the community. But witchcraft and sorcery were commonplace too, and all sickness and bad luck was thought to be the work of evil spirits who could entice one's soul away from the body. If accused of witchcraft, the suspect had to dip his or her finger into burning pitch; only the unburned hand could prove innocence. Needless to say, to be accused was usually to be proven guilty, and witches were either executed or sold to another village as slaves, for eventual execution.

More than half the inhabitants of Tana Toraja at the outset of the twentieth century were slaves, captives of war or people in debt. While some of the Toraja tribes had a slave class that was bound by heredity, others permitted a slave to earn his or her "freedom," if the word can be applied to release into a society plagued by warfare, witchcraft and internal strife. Then, as now, funeral ceremonies and the dedications of new houses were events at which sacrifices were made; the sacrifice did not end with buffalo, however, but included the offering of at least one human head for any Toraja of influence. Naturally, slaves and recent captives from an enemy village were the ready sources of such sacrifice.

The first Protestant missionaries entered Tana Toraja in 1892; prior to this time, contact with the outside world had been virtually nonexistent, except for marginal trade with the coastal people of Sulawesi. But so rigid was the Torajan belief structure that these first missionaries made no converts. (Similarly, the Toraja were said to have resisted earlier Islamic conversion because they were too fond of palm wine and pork.) In 1905, the Dutch were in the midst of converting their Indonesian trade monopolies to a colonial empire; they invaded Tana Toraja, subdued its scattered villages, outlawed head-hunting and the ritual cleansing of bones and forced the people to move down to the valley floors and give up their hilltop fortresses. Within two years, the millennia-old social fabric of the Toraja had been completely shredded. The last chief to fight against the onslaught of the West, Siambe Pong Tiku, was executed on July 10, 1907, on the banks of the Sa'dang River in Rantepao. The conversion to Christianity could begin.

Even as I stood on the brink of Batutumonga,

Men and women of a Toraja village offer a song at the Rambu Solo *rituals in Kete Kesu. (Christian Kallen)*

transported by the beauty of the rice fields, the floating roofs and the distant ridges, I was seeing only the moment and not the epoch. This is one of the conundrums of travel: to witness a ritual, a family event or a day's work is to snatch only an instant out of context, just as to take a photograph captures only a fraction of an action. The meaning of the funeral of Ne' Reba was on the one hand rich and inspirational, a fertile source of satisfaction for the Toraja and its witnesses; but on the other it was just a distant echo of far more ancient rituals, based on deep traditions of life and death that reach back over the centuries into the dark secrets of the human soul.

Midday had arrived; I continued walking into the nearby village of Lokomata as the clouds accumulated over the valley, blocking out the sunlight. Sitting under the sweeping roof of an old *tongkonan*, Karen and Pam had already begun lunch, a cold boxed meal of fruit, chicken and bread prepared by the hotel, while the household's children giggled and begged for *gula gula* (sweets). Then the day's rains began, slowly in isolated drops at first, then inevitably into a driving wall of water that soon isolated our lunchtime shelter in a sea of sticky, primordial mire. We slogged back to the Land Cruiser and drove down the bumpy road back to Rantepao, barely able to see the dripping villages or the flooding rice fields of Tana Toraja.

When we returned to Kete Kesu the following morning, it was as if an age had passed. We had missed only a day, and not a very active day at that, but the temporary bamboo houses for the relatives and friends of the deceased had markedly deteriorated. Their plaited walls were unraveled, the carved wood decorations falling askew; every surface of the village, flat or vertical, was covered to half a meter high with mud. Most funerals in Tana Toraja take place in the fall, at the end of harvest season and before the onset of the rainiest months; Ne' Reba had died just after the beginning of the rains. Perhaps because of his importance to his clan and to recent Torajan history, many who wanted to attend his funeral were eager to do so, and his funeral was scheduled relatively quickly by traditional standards. The result was to hold it in the rainiest of

months, in the rainiest of years that Sulawesi had seen in a long, long time. That decision was now haunting Tana Toraja more than Ne' Reba's unsettled spirit ever could have done.

You could see it on the faces of those remaining for this fourth day of the funeral, the day of Mantunu. Gone were the ready smiles of camaraderie, gone the bright eyes of celebration. Even the young seemed to drag themselves through the day's activities, as if the ritual were no longer a living process but a hollow remnant of tradition. This despite the fact that the program for today was the most famous of all Toraja rites: the slaughter of the water buffalo to accompany Ne' Reba to the world beyond the grave.

Back in California, when I had told an Indonesian friend that I would be going to a Torajan funeral, he asked me if I knew what that meant. I answered that I understood they would sacrifice a buffalo. He smiled, in that flat and enigmatic smile seen throughout Indonesia, and replied, "At least." To sacrifice one buffalo is to state simply that the deceased was a Toraja; for a member of the nobility, the sacrifice of a single buffalo would be unthinkable, and no fewer than a dozen would be an insult. Ne' Reba was a member of the highest caste, Tana' Bulaan, and the full Aluk Todolo ceremony we were witnessing had passed into the highest tier of ritual: Rapasan Sapu Randanan, for which at least thirty buffalo must be offered.

For agriculturalists in Indonesia, the water buffalo is of tremendous importance. It is the basic beast of burden, its strong back pulling the plows that turn the rice fields; in the former absence of plows, only the heavy tread of a team of buffalo, combined with their waste and water, was needed to convert hard soil into loam. Buffalo also provide meat for the growing population of Tana Toraja, so their value is greater still. In addition, a young child is often given a buffalo to tend, which may be a first initiation into responsibility in adult society and the start of the child's own herd. The tending of buffalo itself is a job that further integrates the animals into human cycles, for in the hot climate of the tropics the buffalo must be watered down daily, as its skin will not retain moisture. Hence, the combination of its values—as labor, as food, as social catalyst, all combined with the constant tending it needs—makes its worth considerable. A water buffalo may not be worth its weight in gold; for a farming family in a marginal economy, it is worth far more.

In Tana Toraja the situation used to be only slightly different, since the old swidden agricultural techniques did not necessitate animal labor, and buffalo served primarily as ritual sacrifices and food for feasts. Now, with the conversion in this century to sawah, wet rice agriculture, the water buffalo is becoming more important; meanwhile, the traditional insistence on large numbers of sacrifices has not changed. As a result, the practice of buffalo slaughter is an even greater drain on the economic stability of the Toraja than it had been in the past, and there is an effort underway (by the less-traditional Toraja as well as influential people outside the community) to limit the number of sacrifices or abolish them altogether. Similarly, cock fighting was a very important part of traditional funeral ceremonies, but government and religious disapproval has led to its virtual elimination. As a consequence of these signs of change, some people feel that funerals on the scale of Ne' Reba's may never be held again.

But change has already come to Tana Toraja, and the funeral of Ne' Raba was a different ceremony than it would have been in the last decade, let alone last century. As the buffalo were being prepared for sacrifice that drizzly morning, the ceremonial chief announced the animal's donating clan and its anticipated dispersal to members of Ne' Reba's family over a loudspeaker system. A television crew from Jakarta had been in attendance all week, recording the events for use on the weekly national tourism program, broadcast in Indonesian and English. And not only were there no cock fights, and no ritual offering of the head of a slave or enemy to the memory of Ne' Reba, but in the end the slaughter of half the fifty-odd buffalo was itself deferred.

Some twenty-four buffalo were killed that day, most of them two at a time in a paired dance of death. Their throats were cut in a single stroke by appointed butchers; they stood in shock or struggled, kicking out their life's last energy as the blood pulsed blackly into the thick muck at their feet. They fell, finally, to breathe their last weak breaths, coats covered with mud, eyes glazing over as they watched the world disappear. Boys then ran out to the expiring beast and shoved empty bamboo tubes into the broad neck wounds, collecting blood for cooking—and in the process becoming as coated with the bull's blood as the dying bull himself. Then over the loudspeaker would come the disembodied voice of the ceremony's chief, reading the names of the next offering's donors and distribution.

In the end, the muddy streets and depressed attendance had their effect on the ceremony, and, in a variation on tradition, only half the buffalo were sacrificed for the funeral of Ne' Reba. The others were distributed by the family of the deceased and allowed to be led away to the separate villages, there to be slaughtered as need arose. Whether or not there was relief among the Toraja at this innovation in tradition, none of us thought to ask; but for the few outsiders in the crowd whose familiarity with animal sacrifice had been limited to written accounts and exotic postcards, two dozen was twice enough.

The ceremony of burial, Ma'Peliang, is the last time the body of the deceased is moved; again, as on the day of Ma'Palao, the coffin is carried in the bier, and again it is shaken to confuse the lingering spirit. The route from the lakkian led across the blood-bathed rante, through the center of town and down a muddy path behind Kete Kesu to the village's graveyard. Pam, Karen and I had visited this graveyard earlier in the ceremonies and found it to be more than slightly eerie. Unlike the well-maintained cliff site at Lemo, the graves of Kete Kesu were in disarray, sepulchers spilled open, the bones of the long dead rearranged in the skull and crossbones by playful if somewhat morbid children. The bones were at the base of a near-vertical limestone cliff, and looking up we had seen the small doors that marked cliff graves and, higher up the wall, the suspended coffins that had been traditional in previous centuries. New to the graveyard, however, was a massive concrete crypt, built to accommodate the bodies of Ne' Reba and, later, of his family. The walls of the crypt were molded into the familiar Torajan designs, with a new brass knob in its wood access door. I wondered if there was a knob on the inside as well, just in case.

But the next day was Sunday and, since Ne' Reba was ostensibly a Christian, it was thought inappropriate to conclude his burial on the Sabbath. There was also discussion of delaying the final procession to the base of the cave-riddled limestone cliff where his ancestors had been interred. The slippery condition of the village paths due to the heavy rains might lead to disaster, should the final procession of the body across the *rante* to the crypt prove too difficult for the bearers. Sunday, Monday—the end of the ceremony receded into a future blurred by rainfall; and the rains showed no sign of letting up.

Saturday evening our party gathered to discuss leaving. We were not related to Ne' Reba, after all, and our absence would not be missed. Besides, we were beginning to become more than a little self-conscious of our role as tourists, especially as every two days another batch would descend in a busload on Rantepao, cameras ablaze and tongues ababble. Our previous week in Torajaland had given us a unique opportunity to explore its traditional villages with their elaborately decorated houses and rice barns, to enjoy the festive dances and processions of the funeral, to see buffalo living, dead and dying, and to investigate enough crypts and caves to last a lifetime. As a final straw, the call of the mythical bird of Hindu mythology, the Garuda, could be heard: our return tickets on Indonesia's national airline were written for the next day's flight back home, and Torajaland is still remote enough to forbid the ready telephone alteration of an international airline ticket. We rose before dawn the next day and roused Rauf and Abdullah for the long drive back to Ujung Pandang. Whether in tribute, irritation or farewell I couldn't say, but Abdullah honked his horn as we left Tana Toraja.

MALUKU

Sampling the Spice Islands

"IF there were no Maluku, there would be no America!" It is a statement heard in more places than just Maluku, though nowhere else in the world is it taken as seriously. Absurd, but not without basis in fact: Columbus persuaded the Spanish royalty to back his trans-Atlantic explorations on the assumption that the Spice Islands lay on the other side of the ocean. He sought not Hispañola, Cuba or Miami Beach but the wealthy sultanates of spice of the Moluccas, the islands now known as the Indonesian provinces of Maluku.

With this heritage, Maluku should be a region of more than passing interest. But to visit any of modern Maluku's three most important islands—Ambon, Ternate and Banda—is to journey less into the past than into a cultural backwater. Most of the indigenous tribal traditions have been forever destroyed by centuries of rivalry over the spice trade. Many of the potential tourist attractions of these tropical islands are completely undeveloped, due to the marginal standard of living in the area. All that remains are footnote historical attractions such as old Dutch and Portuguese forts, a struggling trade in the traditional spices and the hopes for an improved tomorrow.

But sometimes finding the footnotes can provide an adventure of its own. Some of these tropical islands, for instance, boast coral reefs as beautiful and unexplored as any in the world, reefs whose beauty was mentioned only in passing, if at all, by the preoccupied spice merchants. It was a footnote in scientific history, however, that most drew me to Maluku. On one of the tiny volcanic islands off the west coast of Halmahera—Maluku's largest island, a sprawling equatorial land to the east of Sulawesi—was launched perhaps the most significant revolution in modern thought, the cornerstone of evolutionary theory: natural selection. And its discoverer was not the well-known Charles Darwin but the virtually forgotten Alfred Russel Wallace.

Still, it was cloves, nutmeg, mace and the other spices of the islands that drew explorers to Maluku in past centuries and made the region jealously guarded and protected for hundreds of years before the Europeans came in pursuit of these riches. The thousand islands of Maluku (some say 999, some say 1027; it may depend on the tides) scattered between Irian Jaya and Sulawesi derive their name from the Arabic traders' "Jazirat-al-Muluk"—"land of many kings." The most wealthy of these kings were the sultans of

Ternate and Tidore, rulers of what were virtually the only clove-producing islands in the world. It was these clove-producing islands—a total of five small volcanic islets off Halmahera—that were originally called the Moluccas. In the centuries following the Portuguese conquest of these islands and the rest of the East Indies, the name "Moluccas" was erroneously applied to the entire region; "Maluku" is the modern Indonesian name for the region and the three provinces that compose it.

The call of spices, their appeal and attraction for the romantic imagination, has not recently been the stuff of literature (save for that of James Beard and Craig Claiborne). But it has not been overlooked: Joseph Conrad, himself a former habitué of the scented winds of the Malay Archipelago, wrote of the fictional land of Patusan (perhaps Sumatra, perhaps not), where Lord Jim found his princedom.

> You find the name of the country pretty often in collections of old voyages. The seventeenth-century traders went there for pepper, because the passion for pepper seemed to burn like a flame of love in the breast of Dutch and English adventurers about the time of James the First. Where wouldn't they go for pepper? For a bag of pepper they would cut each other's throats without hesitation, and would forswear their souls, of which they were so careful otherwise: the bizarre obstinacy of that desire made them defy death in a thousand shapes; the unknown seas, the loathsome and strange diseases; wounds, captivity, hunger, pestilence, and despair. It made them great! By heavens! it made them heroic. . . . To us, their less tried successors, they appear magnified, not as agents of trade but as instruments of a recorded destiny, pushing out into the unknown in obedience to an inward voice, to an impulse beating in the blood, to a dream of the future.

In ancient Chinese courts, cloves were used to scent the breath in the presence of the emperor; even earlier, they had been an ingredient in the embalming potions of the Egyptians. The Romans used to burn nutmeg along their roadsides as a fragrant incense; its warm taste readily became a favorite in sweet foods and its musky odor a basic one in perfumes. Cinnamon and pepper too were prized, to enliven a meal or render the dull cuisine of Europe more worldly. The wealth of the Arabian states was to a large extent due to their trade in these spices, a trade they developed by sailing over the Indian Ocean to the Malay Archipelago. Remember that spices and incense were also the gifts of the Magi to the Christ child, two millennia ago. In today's Indonesia, cloves, the prized spice of the "land of many kings," are mixed with tobacco to make the characteristic *kretek* cigarette, onomatopoetically named from the crackling sound of the burning spice. The smell of Indonesia is the smell of cloves, an incenselike cloud that virtually defines the atmosphere of the country.

The Moluccas were not the only "Spice Islands"—cinnamon from Ceylon attracted the attention of Roman traders in the sixth century, and Indian ginger and cardamon made many a trader wealthy. In fact, the rise of Venice as a power in Europe was due largely to its control of the spice trade from India, Ceylon, the East Indies and China, a trade that developed in part as a result of Marco Polo's politic peregrinations in the thirteenth century. It was to break the hold of Venice on the spice trade that the rival courts of Spain, Portugal, England and later Holland financed a series of voyages into uncharted waters, an economic gambit that turned into a geographic and cultural assault on the world. For every early voyage, the first destination was always the East Indies, and the rationale for launching was the promised wealth of the islands today known as Maluku.

Ambon is located almost dead center in Maluku, a situation that certainly influenced the Dutch in

PAGE 164: *The nutmeg, surrounded by its crimson mace, magnet spice for the Age of Discovery. (Christian Kallen)*

Colorful "water taxis" ferry Ambonese across the inner harbor from their villages on the Leihitu Peninsula to the capital city of Kota Ambon. (Christian Kallen)

making it their major port. The island is snuggled beneath the larger curved body of "Ceram" (old style), or "Seram" (new). Ambon itself resembles a whale and its nursing calf, the two unequal halves separated by large gulfs but linked by a narrow isthmus at Passo (like many of the place names in this part of Indonesia, a word of Portuguese origin). The larger, northern half, Leihitu, is by far the less inhabited; smaller Leitimur has a population density rivaling that of Java, a quarter of a million jammed into noisy and dirty Ambon City, or Kota Ambon.

My own reason for going to Ambon was exactly that of most travelers—it is a necessary stop between the former clove sultanate Ternate, to the north, and Banda, the former center of the nutmeg trade. Still, since my visit to Maluku was

in some ways prompted by my interest in Alfred Russel Wallace, I took note in his book *The Malay Archipelago* of his descriptions of Ambon, which he found to be one of the most attractive of his many stops within that span of islands. He wrote: "There is perhaps no spot in the world richer in marine productions, corals, shells and fishes, than the harbour of Amboyna [as it was then known]." In addition, after spending several months there over the course of his three visits, he declared that it "will always remain as a bright spot in the review of my Eastern travels, since it was there that I first made the acquaintance of those glorious birds and insects, which rendered the Moluccas classic ground in the eyes of the naturalist, and characterize its fauna as one of the most remarkable and beautiful upon the globe."

While some things have changed in the intervening 130 years, some remain the same—among them the reliance by large numbers of Ambonese on the sago. This thick, relatively short palm, which superficially at least resembles a coco palm, grows in the swampy coastal zones of many tropical Asian islands, but on Ambon and Seram it has become elevated to a tree of life. The middle ribs of its leaves are used in building, supplanting bamboo; the leaves themselves are used as roof thatch, and many native houses are built entirely of sago. Baskets and tools are also made of sago, but most remarkable is the use of the palm as a staple food. After a thorough process of cleaning and filtering, the tree's pith is reduced to a starchy flour, which is baked into cakes that have long been the prime sustenance for hundreds of thousands of people.

During my brief stay in Ambon, I witnessed the cooking stage of the sago process. With my guide Boet Nanlohy, an energetic tour agent in Kota Ambon, I stopped at a small house on the west end of town to watch an old woman cook the paste into cakes. Passing through the living quarters of the house we reached a long kitchen, where a wood stove was hot with fire in a sooty corner. Over the past three days, the woman had been treating the sago—pulverizing and sifting it, and leaving it to air to reduce its bitterness. This morning she was engaged in the final stage—mixing it with shredded coconut into a dry dough, spooning the mixture by hand into cast-iron molds shaped somewhat like an egg crate to form six uniform cakes, then dropping a dollop of brown sugar into the center of each cake. The result of her efforts was already accumulating on a long table in the corner—a veritable mountain of sago cakes, warm and fragrant.

The proof of any recipe, of course, is not in the cooking but the consumption. I took a healthy bite of one of the warm cakes: it was excellent, with an honest chewy texture and a natural sweetness in both coconut-laced dough and syrupy center. Sometimes the cakes are mixed with chilies, sometimes with other available nuts and spices; these variations might make its role as a staple quite tolerable, I thought, as long as there was always a supply of these desert sago cakes on hand.

The flour from one sago tree can feed a family for up to three months—from small barrels of dried reddish paste to large bowls of white powder to mounds of browned cakes, the process converts one tree into a considerable stock. Considering the amount of work that goes into harvesting and cooking this food source—a week or so to prepare, a couple of days to cook—sago is a remarkably inexpensive and abundant food source.

Another local product caught my eye during the three days I spent in Ambon—model galleons, frigates and schooners made entirely of clove buds, with fragrant sails spreading stiffly from rigid masts. Clove and nutmeg trees are almost as prevalent as sago in Ambon—ironically, for until the Dutch came to the island in the seventeenth century, neither cloves nor nutmeg grew on Ambon.

It has always been Ambon's fortune, both for good and ill, to be located on the trade routes between Ternate and Banda. In the fourteenth century, the sultan of Ternate invaded Ambon and replaced its animistic head-hunting cults with Islam; the interlopers drove the tall, bearded, curly-headed natives into the island's mountains, where they became known as Alfuros. In the sixteenth century, the Portuguese drove out the sultan's men and instituted the practice of Catholicism. By early the next century, the Ambonese—by now a mix of Alfuro, Malay and Portuguese blood—allied themselves with the latest wave of conquerors, the Dutch. It was an alliance that was to prove beneficial to both parties, for not only did the Dutch bring some measure of wealth to Ambon by planting clove and nutmeg on the island, but the Ambonese repaid the favor by eventually providing

OPPOSITE: *A young man hammers loose the pith from a felled sago tree, which will be processed into the starchy flour that forms the staple of the Ambonese diet. (Christian Kallen)*

the major share of native soldiers for Dutch military endeavors, including the subjugation of Banda.

Properly speaking, Banda should be the Bandas, a tiny cluster of six islands overrepresented on any map that shows them. From the west end of Palau Run (Run Island) to the eastern shores of Rozengain is only some thirty-two kilometers; the largest island, Palau Lonthor, can be walked around in one day, and only about a hundred kilometers of dry land remain at high tide upon all these islands. In addition to Lonthor, the major islands are Palau Neira (or Bandaneira, now the site of the main city of the same name), Palau Ai and Gunung Api, the conical volcano in the heart of the small archipelago.

From all appearances, this is a tropical paradise: "a gem-like cluster of idyllic tropical islets ornamented by crystal waters, brilliant coral gardens, aromatic spice trees in which feasted flocks of red parrots and green pigeons . . . set against the immediate backdrop of a Fuji-like volcano," as Banda's historian Willard Hanna describes it in his *Indonesian Banda*. Banda's blessing, and its curse, was the *Myristica fragrans*, whose apricot-like fruit holds the fragrant nutmeg that is in turn surrounded by a red aril—mace, itself a piquant spice. It is uncertain whether the nutmeg is historically indigenous only to Banda; but only the Bandanese developed the tree for trade, and they reaped the rewards—and suffered the consequences. The tale, as Hanna relates, is filled with incidents of cultural misunderstanding, intentional duplicity and appalling acts of massacre and destruction.

The Dutch set their sights on Banda because of its nutmeg productivity, coupled with its geographical isolation—an ideal situation for monopoly. Irritated by the existence of an English outpost on Palau Run, the Dutch pressured the Bandanese of Lonthor and Palau Neira to grant them exclusive rights to purchase Banda's nutmeg and mace. The *orang kaya* (literally "rich men"—the Bandanese village chiefs), who had been trading for centuries with the highest bidder, were confused by this unorthodox request, but they politely signed the document, in May 1602.

For the next several years, relations between the two peoples were strained; the Dutch believed the agreement of 1602 gave them the right to buy nutmeg at whatever price they chose, while the Bandanese simply tried to ignore the demands of the Dutch, trading with them to appease their tempers but carrying on open trade with other partners, including the English. In April of 1609, the Dutch East Indies Company—Vereenigde Oostindische Compagnie, or V.O.C.—weary of Banda's dismissal of the contract, sent a fleet of ships and 750 men to build a fortress on Palau Neira to preserve Dutch hegemony over the islands. Awed by this display of power, the Bandanese retreated into the hills, there to watch in apparent stunned submission as Fort Nassau took shape.

After about a month the *orang kaya* invited the Dutch leaders to discuss a new contract, taking into account their obvious superior strength. Confident, Adm. Pieterszoon Verhoeven agreed to meet without guards in a tranquil glen, and with some thirty of his staff he marched into an ambush. Nearly all were killed, the admiral outright; Dutch scouts who searched the island the next day found only the headless bodies of their compatriots. The shocking massacre led to attacks and counterattacks, and although a new contract was indeed drawn up in favor of the Dutch later that year, it was not until 1621 that the Dutch finally achieved their revenge, through a man who had been a junior merchant under Verhoeven—Vice Adm. Jan Pieterszoon Coen.

Under Coen the V.O.C. undertook a policy of unremitting cruelty, in the name of economic efficacy. With a fleet of thirteen ships and a huge army of nearly two thousand men, Coen seized the large island of Lonthor, built Fort Hollandia and once again drew up a new contract with the

OPPOSITE: *On the outskirts of Kota Ambon, houses line the river as the growing population reaches deeper into the island's forested interior. (Christian Kallen)*

Bandanese *orang kaya*. When they failed to live up to its broad terms, as Coen fully anticipated, he embarked on a merciless campaign of burning and razing villages, cruelly executing forty-four *orang kaya* and conscripting the population into slavery. In addition, Coen instituted the Dutch policy of "extirpation"—denuding most of the Bandanese islands of their nutmeg trees, leaving groves only on Lonthor and Palau Neira under the guns of the Dutch fortresses of Nassau and Hollandia.

The next stage—once genocide and herbicide had been accomplished—was to offer land grants to Dutchmen willing to settle in the Bandanese islands to oversee production of spices for the V.O.C, using slave labor as a workforce. The grants were called *perken*, or parcels; their settlers became known as *perkeniers*. Prices and quotas were established, and tithes to the company instituted—a system that should have given each *perkenier* a healthy income. However, the V.O.C. reserved for itself a markup between what it paid for nutmeg in Banda and what it received in Amsterdam of 1220 percent.

For the first few years of this system there remained the nagging matter of the English. They had never completely given up their trade with the Bandanese, and since they were often more civil and paid better prices than the Dutch, their presence was particularly galling to the monopolists. In 1664, to finally rid themselves of British traders, the Dutch signed away in trade for Palau Run their only North American possession. In exchange for the loss of this minute nutmeg island, the English flag was raised over a small town on the island of Manhattan, and its name was changed from New Amsterdam to New York.

Over the next three hundred years, the effects of Dutch monopoly on Banda's harvest of nutmeg, off to such a firm start under the policies of Jan Coen, were ultimately debilitating. Even the V.O.C.'s generous profit margin could not pay for its monopoly strategy—the cost of protection afforded by the forts, forces and fleets—and the V.O.C. went bankrupt in 1795. Even more important for the Dutch companies that followed it, a monopoly built around an organic product can-

not long survive—seeds can be smuggled to other equally hospitable climates, and the whims of public taste can shift. So it was with nutmeg: soon the plants were growing in the West Indies, and the Spanish colony of Grenada began to undercut the Dutch monopoly. Eventually, in the nineteenth century, one of the major uses for flavoring agents such as nutmeg and cloves—to retard the spoilage of meat by preventing oxidation—was circumvented by the invention of refrigeration. And the value of the spices collapsed worldwide.

Today, Banda is home to about sixteen thousand people, roughly the same as four hundred years ago. Bandaneira, the major town of the islands, is a quiet settlement of a few thousand people, with a small port, a rarely visited airport and a few modest hotels. People on the islands still travel largely by horsecart, motorboat and foot, comfortable in their simplicity; automobiles are almost nonexistent. The nutmeg islands of Banda float in a sea of obscurity, abandoned by the tides of history.

Ambon and Banda have their role in the history of the Spice Islands, but after months of researching and traveling in Indonesia, I found myself drawn to the minute island of Ternate. Birthplace of the clove trade, seat of East India's most powerful sultan, Ternate was also Alfred Russel Wallace's home base for three of the eight years he spent in the Malay Archipelago. His book had become my constant companion, his insights the touchstones by which I judged my own. And now at last I found myself descending the narrow staircase of the Merpati Airlines plane onto the tarmac of the modest Ternate airport, inhaling the warm, spicy atmosphere of the original Moluccas.

I was met at the baggage counter by a short, smiling, dark-skinned older man who introduced himself as Mr. Westplat; Boet Nanlohy in Ambon had apparently telexed forward to him about my arrival. First he helped me clear the police checkpoint. (What was an American doing in Ternate anyway? It was apparently not a common destination.) Then Westplat led me out to a small blue van to meet his wife and two

Fresh nutmeg is separated from its mace, then both are set out to dry in the sun before being sold in Ternate's market.
(Christian Kallen)

children. They were not, it turned out, his own children, but students at the school for the handicapped where Mrs. Westplat worked and Mr. Westplat donated his time in his retirement. I shook the fingerless hand of one of the girls and smiled into her eyes; the other just giggled at me and blushed.

Not sure exactly what I expected of Ternate, in spite of my anticipations, I kept my eyes wide during the brief ride into town from the airport. Despite the simplicity of the wood frame houses and the narrow streets, the stately white palace of the sultan and the gray stone walls of the Dutch bastion Benteng Oranye (Fort Orange), the tiny island was permeated by a sense of antiquity, as if the years had merely passed by, with little of the sound and fury that history would suggest.

Ternate was the most celebrated of the five tiny islands called the Moluccas in antiquity. Though both it and Tidore were homes to influential sultans during the centuries before Europeans came to the East Indies, Ternate was always the more powerful of the two—its military strength was felt eastward to Irian Jaya, northward to Mindanao, west to Sulawesi and south to Ambon and Flores. Even so, the competition between the two Islamic sultanates was not settled until 1814, when the Dutch finally managed to bring their own brand of peace to the region.

Considering the pivotal role these two islands have played in history, their size always comes as a revelation. The nearly circular Ternate is about nine kilometers in diameter, some hundred square kilometers in area; the more oblong Tidore measures twelve kilometers at its longest. Ternate can be driven around in an afternoon—

The volcano Gamalama, pivot and anchor of the island of Ternate, in northern Maluku. (Christian Kallen)

or preferably in a morning, when it's cooler and the central volcano is not hidden in cloud. These are classic volcanic islands, the near-perfect cone of Gamalama at the very center of Ternate and a string of three volcanoes linking slopes to form Tidore.

Of course, it is the clove—the nail-shaped fragrant bud of the evergreen *Syzygium aromaticum*—around which the history and fate of these islands have been woven. The Portuguese were the first Europeans to reach the Spice Islands, in 1512; almost at once they set up forts on Ternate and, with the sultan's approval, attempted to monopolize the clove trade in order to gain the upper hand against Tidore. After a few decades, however, the sultan of Ternate began to chafe under increasing Portuguese dominance, so the Europeans had him poisoned. This assertive action

prompted the inhabitants to rebellion, and in 1575 the Portuguese were kicked off the island. They simply moved across the narrow strait, set up a similar arrangement with the sultan of Tidore and continued their efforts to control the regional spice trade. Ultimately, however, the Portuguese were not able to consolidate their power in the East Indies to the degree the Dutch were later able to, and by the beginning of the 1600s their influence had all but evaporated.

This rich colonial history has left its obvious traces—there are at least a half-dozen forts on this tiny island, including Benteng Oranye in the middle of the town of Ternate itself, about a kilometer from the palace of the sultan. Most are reverting to the soil, overgrown by vines and riddled with the thick roots of trees; a couple are fairly well preserved, and Benteng Oranye was still housing Dutch soldiers into this century. Still, it was not for the forts that I had come to Ternate, nor for the historic groves of clove nor the mile-high summit of Gamalama, nor to trace the evolution of a once-thriving capital of trade into a quiet equatorial outpost. I had come because Wallace had lived here, and I hoped to find not a ruined fortress but perhaps the simple house where he developed and wrote his theory.

It is impossible to travel in Indonesia in educated company and not encounter the name Wallace. A retired clinical psychologist at the funeral in Tana Toraja, a batik importer from Los Angeles, an expatriate from Minnesota living in Jakarta, a French sailor with his own hand-built yacht berthed in Bali: each of them admitted to a fascination with this little-known figure of nineteenth-century science. In fact, were it not for the eponymous Wallace Line—the demarcation between the westernmost limit of Australian life forms that runs between Bali and Lombok, Borneo and Sulawesi and, beyond, south of the Philippines—the name itself might have faded into obscurity. Then again, any traveler in Indonesia is doing himself a disservice if he remains unfamiliar with Wallace's own account of his eight years of travel and research here, *The Malay Archipelago* (first published in 1869, six years after his return to England). The book is currently in print in a Dover facsimile edition. But in general Wallace's work is difficult to find, and this is a curious fate for one whose name was once linked with those of Francis Galton and Charles Darwin as among the most influential scientists of their century.

Alfred Russel Wallace was born the eighth of nine children in 1823; his father was a tutor and librarian who never made enough money to support all the children his wife bore him. The Wallaces were not of the landed gentry that produced the Charles Lyells, Thomas Huxleys and Charles Darwins, leading lights of science in the nineteenth century. At the age of fourteen, Alfred had to abandon his formal education to earn his living in the early years of the Industrial Revolution, when the entire society was undergoing abrupt change. That he ever developed an inter-

est in botany was surprising; that it evolved into a passionate study of coleoptera, or beetles, was more than a bit unusual. It was to prove, however, fateful.

At the age of twenty-two, at the then-considerable height of six feet, two inches, Wallace took a job as an English teacher in Leicester. The relative ease of rural life let him develop his interest in botany, and here Wallace met another enthusiastic amateur scientist, Henry Walter Bates. Bates had been studying beetles for years, and it was he who introduced Wallace to this specialized discipline—one that had earlier provided the open door to scientific inquiry for Charles Darwin. Wallace and Bates struck up a fast friendship based on their common scientific interests, among them the question of the origin of species—a question sure to occur to victims of beetlemania, who encounter dozens of closely related species. How did all these species, so similar in appearance and structure, differentiate—and why?

After returning to more lucrative work as a land surveyor for two years, Wallace had saved several hundred pounds, enough for him to propose to Bates that they undertake their own scientific expedition to the terra incognita of South America's Amazon Basin. In the spring of 1848 they pooled their resources and set out for the Amazon—without official sanction, royal sponsorship or the corporate financing that even today's "expeditions" are crippled without. For four years, Wallace and Bates traveled thousands of miles in the Amazon Basin, sometimes together and sometimes apart. They sent their finds—beetles, butterflies and other insects, lizards, birds and small mammals—back to London, where an agent sold their discoveries to collectors, schools and museums. Bates remained in South America for six more years after Wallace left, becoming one of the most respected and important naturalists to work the fertile field of the Amazon. He was also the developer of the theory of mimicry, which outlines the evolutionary facility of certain species to mime the appearance of another.

As Wallace was returning to England in the summer of 1852 aboard the square-rigged trading ship *Helen*, the vessel caught fire and sank; all hands spent ten days on the open seas in long boats. They were finally picked up more than three hundred kilometers from the nearest landfall, Bermuda. However, Wallace's scientifically invaluable collections, journals and drawings were lost, except for a single notebook and a handful of sketches. Cruelly disappointed but undaunted, upon his return to England Wallace turned the sketches into the small book *Palms of the Amazon* and milked his notes and mined his memory to produce *A Narrative of Travels on the Amazon and Rio Negro*, both of which were well received among the established scientific community. His unfortunate lack of substantiating material had its effect, however. None other than Charles Darwin expressed some disappointment in the works: "Not enough facts," he complained.

Wallace's financial situation was again precarious; the loss of his valuable specimens aboard the *Helen* meant that he still had a living to earn. So after less than two years in England he was ready once more to leave his homeland for a tropical wilderness. After briefly considering the Philippines as an area of study, Wallace decided upon a detailed investigation of the East Indies. The Malay Archipelago had been studied from a scientific viewpoint by only two men since its "discovery" by the Portuguese adventurers of the sixteenth century—one of whom was the noted English statesman Sir Thomas Stamford Raffles, who wrote almost exclusively of Java's flora and fauna (and whose collection, coincidentally, also was lost at sea, off the coast of Sumatra). For a working naturalist such as Wallace, whose continued livelihood depended on collecting unusual specimens for study in the parlors and laboratories of the civilized world, these virtually unknown islands were ideal places to continue his labors. He was hopeful, too, of further developing his own scientific interests in geology, anthropology, botany and biology, as well as in the question that continued to intrigue him—evolution.

Ambitiously, Wallace envisioned a project taking him from Singapore to Borneo, Sulawesi (then Celebes), Timor, the Moluccas, New Guinea and even the Philippines, and lasting

some six years. Only the Philippines eluded his landfall during what became eight years that he spent in the Malay Archipelago, from April 1854 to February 1862. The results of his travels included an astounding collection of 125,660 specimens, including 310 mammals, 100 reptiles, more than 8000 birds, 7500 shells, 13,000 butterflies, 83,000 beetles, and 13,000 other insects. He traveled more than 22,400 kilometers and visited virtually every island of interest in the archipelago, many of them several times—Timor, Ambon, Sulawesi, Seram, Banda and New Guinea, as well as the remote Kei, Matabello and Aru island groups.

As a result of his extensive collections and observations, Wallace developed ideas he and Bates had first discussed on their South American journey—namely, that geography was influential in zoology. Their self-hewn scientific rigor led them to note the places of collection of species, and from these notes they were able to relate the distribution of birds, mammals and insects not only to their habitat but to geographical features such as rivers, mountain ranges and other obstacles. In the Malay Archipelago, Wallace almost at once perceived the differences between life forms on Bali, where Asian species predominated to the exclusion of any other, and on Lombok across the narrow Lombok Strait, where species common to New Guinea and Australia were found. Further study of the island groups to the east of Bali led Wallace to conclude that there was a break between the Asian species—including monkeys, elephants, tigers and wild cattle—and the Australian species, such as cockatoos and parrots, monitor lizards and marsupials.

In other words, although the island chain of the Sundas from Sumatra to Timor appears of a continuum, there is a historical break between Bali and Lombok, and Borneo and Sulawesi, that represents a barrier between the two life zones. This barrier, the Wallace Line, represents the westernmost limit of Australian species. The easternmost limit of Asian species, on the other hand, later became known as the Lydekker Line, isolating Irian Jaya and its offshore islands such as the Aru group from the rest of the Malay Archipelago. Over a century of scientific research has neither failed to completely substantiate these demarcations nor to disprove them. In general, today's biologist regards the region between the Wallace Line and the Lydekker Line—including Sulawesi, Nusa Tenggara and Maluku—as the Celebesian Transition, more popularly known as Wallacea.

Wallace eventually detailed his theories on zoogeography, as the discipline came to be known, in his 1876 book *The Geographical Distribution of Animals*. But decades earlier his interest in these manifestations of historical influences on evolution was a further goad to his passionate curiosity about the larger question: what caused the differentiation of species? Shortly after his arrival in the East Indies, in 1855, he wrote a paper in Sarawak (on Borneo) entitled "On the Law Which has Regulated the Introduction of New Species." In this he argued that new species arise from varieties of closely allied species; that geographically isolated regions are literally the breeding ground for new species, which lead to the succession of species over time. He recognized it as an incomplete theory, however, for it failed to provide a mechanism by which one of the many varieties of a species eventually differentiates into a new species. And that, to paraphrase Shakespeare, was the question.

At that point in European intellectual history, evolution was what we would call a hot topic. While many men of science were content with the Biblical version of history, and regarded the identification of species as a cataloging of the passengers aboard the Ark, many more were frankly skeptical of the limits imposed by such scriptural explanations. Foremost among these limits was time: if the world was in fact created in 4004 B.C. as Bishop Ussher had calculated, what then to make of fossils of strange creatures, seashells in high mountains and the other anomalies of the real world? The first major light on the subject was shed by Charles Lyell, a land surveyor (like Wallace after him) whose examinations of English topography had led to his 1833 *Principles of Geology*. Lyell suggested that the age of the earth was to be measured in the millions of years, not the thousands. This not only gave the necessarily slow development of species a

time frame in which to take place, it indirectly supported the notion that cataclysmic change (earthquakes, ice ages, flooding and mountain building) could affect the survival of species.

At the outset of the nineteenth century, Lamarck had proposed that species develop out of need for their circumstances—as per the famous example of the giraffe stretching his neck for higher branches, which suggested that faculties developed in one life could be passed on to progeny. Other scientists in horticulture, philosophy and anthropology had suggested that new species develop over time. But the greatest stir was caused by a popular book called *Vestiges of the Natural History of Creation*, by journalist Robert Chambers (though published anonymously, in 1844). *Vestiges* boldly asserted that species evolve into higher species following not the specific instructions of God (or Lamarckian principles) but rather the general tendency of development. However, *Vestiges* provided no mechanism for this developmental law, and it was criticized not only by the clergy but by scientists as well.

At about this time Charles Darwin was assembling his own thoughts on the subject and writing up his notes from his pigeon breeding experiments, beetle collecting and observations as the *Beagle*'s onboard naturalist. According to his notes and the recollections of his associates, he had begun work on a "big book" on the theory of the origin of species about the same time *Vestiges* appeared. But by the time Wallace's Sarawak paper was mailed from Borneo and found its way into the pages of *The Annals and Magazine of Natural History* in September of 1855, Darwin had not published a single word of his ruminations or researches. With the publication of Wallace's paper, Sir Charles Lyell perceived that Darwin's own claim to priority in the field was about to be usurped by the distant amateur, and he urged his reticent friend Darwin to begin at once to prepare his notes for publication.

While Darwin undertook that operation, Wallace continued to travel in the Malay Archipelago. Just after the New Year in 1858 he arrived at Ternate, which he chose to make the base of his researches in northern Maluku. Over the years he had endured his share of adventures: a three-meter python shared his roof in Ambon; leeches and biting insects infected his limbs; head-hunting alarms gave him pause in Lombok; he suffered almost continuously from dysentery and that bane of nearly all tropical travelers, malaria. But he had also continued to write up his notes and had published twenty-three monographs and lesser contributions in English scientific journals, all submitted from the most remote of fields. And he was coming ever closer to unraveling the knot at the heart of evolutionary theory.

Shortly after his arrival in Ternate, Wallace found a house to use as a regional base of operations with the assistance of the Dutch governor-general Duivenboden; then he set off to explore the nearby island of Halmahera. His investigations were cut short by a severe malarial attack, and at the end of February he returned to his house in Ternate. There the fevers continued, and often he entered that state of lucid excitability that can make a fever almost entertaining. During one such attack Wallace again became caught up in pondering—if the feverish jumble of impressions and memories that fever begets can be called "pondering"—the reason behind the origin of species. He already had established, in his Sarawak paper, that new species must arise from varieties of old species. But what creates the break between an old species and a successful variety? This was the question that had puzzled biologists throughout the nineteenth century, the question wrestled with by Darwin for more than fifteen years and by Wallace ever since his first obsessions with beetle collection, in 1847.

Then, in the grip of the fever, Wallace recollected the works of Malthus on population dynamics, which he had read some thirteen years earlier. Humans can reproduce faster than food sources; therefore, argued Malthus, there must be a check upon the survival rate to keep a balance. Accidents, predation, disease and warfare among them all kept human populations in check and prevented the overrunning of the world. Wallace abruptly recognized that this dynamic must also affect animal populations—that it was, in other words, part of the puzzle of the origin of the species.

As he recounted forty years later in his *The Wonderful Century*, this is how the crucial insight came:

> While vaguely thinking how this would affect any species, there suddenly flashed upon me the idea of the survival of the fittest—that the individuals removed by these checks must be, on the whole, inferior to those that survived. Then, considering the variations continually occurring in every fresh generation of animals or plants, and the changes of climate, of food, of enemies always in progress, the whole method of specific modification became clear to me, and in the two hours of my fit I had thought the main points of the theory.

Upon his recovery from the fever he quickly wrote down the theory, and a couple of days later he sent it off by trade steamer to Charles Darwin. His choice of Darwin was a curious twist of fate, for it was not Darwin but the geologist Lyell, at the time the leading scientist in Victorian England, whom Wallace hoped to impress with the work, and Wallace included a note asking Darwin to forward the paper to Lyell. Unbeknownst to Wallace, however, Darwin was at work on exactly the same puzzle, the origin of species; and his receipt of Wallace's Ternate paper—titled "On the Tendency of Varieties to Depart Indefinitely from the Original Type"—was described by Darwin's confidant Sir Joseph Dalton Hooker as "a bolt from the blue." For here was the missing piece of the puzzle, the very mechanism by which species could diverge and evolution could proceed: the process of natural selection.

Although the term "natural selection" does not appear in Wallace's Ternate paper, here the term "struggle for existence" was introduced; the phrase reappears a year and a half later with the publication of Darwin's own work on the subject, *On the Origin of Species by Means of Natural Selection, or the Preservation of Favored Races in the Struggle for Life*. Darwin's book was an instant cause célèbre and led to a radical reevaluation of scientific thought; so rapid was its effect that by the time Wallace returned from the Malay Archipelago in 1862 Darwin's evolutionary

A quiet back street in Ternate, lined with papaya and banana palms, in the neighborhood where Alfred Russel Wallace developed the theory of natural selection. (Christian Kallen)

theories were influencing not only the sciences but politics, economics and the arts, and of course theology.

The question that too few historians have asked themselves is whether Darwin appropriated the insights of Wallace's Ternate paper for his own ends. After all, Darwin had been working on the theory of evolution for nearly fifteen years; his so-called big book on the subject was said to be some five hundred thousand words long by 1858. To have the upstart Wallace—an uneducated commoner, a self-employed bug collector without formal recognition, and fourteen years Darwin's junior—usurp priority in the matter was a bitter pill to swallow; history shows that Darwin didn't. At the urging of his friends and fellow scientific illuminati Sir Charles Lyell

and botanist Sir Joseph Dalton Hooker, Darwin forged a "joint announcement" at the July 1, 1858, Linnaean Society meeting, when the reading of a single paper—Wallace's—would have been ethically the more responsible act. Darwin, after all his work, still had no paper to present. And Wallace was halfway around the world; could he very well question Darwin's unsubstantiated claim that he himself had, coincidentally, written out the exact same solution just a few days earlier, while having thought of it—unfortunately never committing to paper, let alone print—more than fifteen years before?

Darwin, in fact, never published his "big book." He describes the *Origin of Species* as "an abstract," its publication motivated by the "many more years" necessary to complete his researches, and the "far from strong" condition of his health. (Ironically, he only lived another twenty-three years.) Still, he does fully elaborate the theory of natural selection, as well as the complementary theory of sexual selection. And history has perpetuated the version that Darwin, Lyell and Hooker endeavored to create: that Wallace quite by coincidence rediscovered Darwin's well-worked theories, and a benevolent Darwin graciously allowed Wallace's paper to be read to the prestigious Linnaean Society, along with Darwin's own outline of the theory, to establish their joint priority as codiscoverers.

The truth of the matter may never be revealed; popular historian Arnold C. Brackman puts forth Wallace's case in *A Delicate Arrangement*. Brackman points out that the only "paper" read at the Linnaean Society was Wallace's; Darwin's contribution consisted of excerpts from a letter written to American botanist Asa Gray in 1857 and related extracts from an unpublished 1844 essay by Darwin (which contains no mention of the principle of divergence). Then there's the matter of substantiating correspondence: there is none. Missing is virtually every letter of Darwin's, or letters from others to him—including those of Lyell, Hooker, Asa Gray and even Wallace himself—during the period from the publication of Wallace's Sarawak paper, in 1855, to 1861, two years following the publication of Darwin's *Origin of Species*. "It is as if," overstates Brackman, "*Rheingold* were missing from Wagner's Ring cycle." Darwin, otherwise organized and fastidious to the point of neurosis (he suffered throughout his life from mysterious ailments that kept him bedridden for long periods of time), seems to have misplaced this significant body of correspondence.

After his return to England, Wallace threw himself into the controversy over the publication of *Origin of Species*. He steadfastly gave Darwin all credit for the breakthrough theory of evolution, going so far as to dedicate *The Malay Archipelago* to Darwin "as a token of personal esteem and friendship, but also to express my deep admiration for his genius and his work." Although he never openly doubted the official version of events, he was apparently surprised to find out, in 1887 (five years after Darwin's death), that

Darwin had been deeply disturbed by the arrival of Wallace's Ternate paper. Even though he may have suspected that he had been used unfairly by his friend, Wallace remained loyal if not servile: he eventually proved to be even more of a Darwinian than Darwin, as many observers noted. This may be because the firmest foundation of "Darwinism" (a phrase coined by Wallace himself and the title of his 1889 popular book interpreting the first thirty years of modern evolutionary theory) was natural selection, most forcefully presented and argued by Wallace himself.

In later editions of *Origin of Species*, Darwin began to downplay natural selection as the prime mechanism of evolution and to emphasize the role of sexual selection—the choice by the female of a species of a suitable mate, as shown by the colorful displays of dance and feather in several bird species. Modern biologists acknowledge that sexual selection does play a role in reproduction, but its role in evolution is minor at best. The principle of natural selection is still almost universally regarded as the prime component in evolutionary theory; and Alfred Russel Wallace, historically the first to provide a coherent portrait of its effect, never backed away from espousing it as such.

Over the remaining years of his life, Wallace refused to confine himself to the topic of evolution alone, as Darwin had. His writings in the following decades covered such diverse topics as the origin of human races, zoogeography, mimicry, climatology, glaciation and government aid to science; in addition, he wrote extensively on spiritualism and the supernatural, to the consternation of his more literal-minded contemporaries. He published more than twenty books and innumerable articles; he was married in 1866 to a woman twenty years his junior, with whom he had three children; and he continued to pursue his diverse interests and to write until the year of his death—1913, two months shy of his ninety-first birthday. Despite his illustrious career in science and letters he remained a common man to his grave: the knighthood that Queen Victoria bestowed on men of science such as Sir James Galton, Sir Charles Lyell, Sir Thomas Huxley, Sir Joseph Hooker and Sir Charles Darwin forever eluded Mr. Alfred Wallace.

What has survived the cosmetic effects of coincidence and conspiracy is Wallace's luminous vision. And whatever the judgment of history in the matter, there is the minor victory that reflects on Indonesia. For all the fame that the Galapagos Islands off the coast of Ecuador have gained over the years as the "birthplace of evolution," due to the several weeks Charles Darwin watched the finches of those igneous motes, it is clear that the tiny Moluccas, the green volcanic cones scented by clove off the dark coast of Halmahera, equally deserve this title. As much as they are Spice Islands they are also the islands where Alfred Russel Wallace saw into the spinning machinery of life's most fundamental process, the origin of species.

After picking me up at the airport, Mr. Westplat brought me to the Hotel Nirwana in the center of Kota Ternate. Then he left to take his charges back to the school, promising to visit me after lunch to see how he could help me survey the island of Ternate.

I settled into the modest room on the ground floor of the hotel, then asked for a cup of coffee and sat in the shaded garden wondering what to do next. My interest in Wallace had brought me here, but the guidebooks listed little to see besides the forts and palace (and related nothing about Wallace). There was, however, a brief note in one book about the oldest clove tree on the island, a morning's hike up the flanks of Gamalama. I decided to ask Mr. Westplat about that; then I began to wonder what to call my local contact.

The proper term of address for a superior or associate in Indonesia is "Bapak," meaning "Father," or "Ibu," for "Mother." Jan Westplat had introduced himself as Mr. Westplat. I would be spending some time with him over the next several days, and I thought it might prove overly stilted to call him "Mr. Westplat" all the time. Something less formal would have to do, I decided. Finally I settled on the familiar form of Bapak, combined with his family name—'Pak Westplat. It meant roughly "Dad Westplat," and in fact the terminal k is silent in Indonesian pronunciation. To come this far to find a surrogate father struck me as wry; still, its combination of affection and formality seemed appropriate to the

genial elderly man who had met me at the airport.

'Pak Westplat arrived before I finished my coffee, so I invited him to join me, and he sat down in one of the wicker chairs. Cautiously, he cleared his throat and said, "I am not a travel agent. You understand? I work in community service." His voice was both rich and rough, like brass beautifully tarnished by decades of clove cigarettes. "I do not know if I can show you everything you wish."

Briefly, I told him that whatever time he had to spare would be fine, and I could make do on my own. Then I asked him if he had ever heard of Alfred Russel Wallace.

His face showed the struggle of memory, then he nodded. "Yes, a scientist, yes? He lived in Ternate."

"Right. And I would like to find where he lived. His book gives a description of his house, and its location, and perhaps with your help we can find the place. He is not very well known now, but he was an important scientist, and it would be interesting to find out where he lived."

'Pak Westplat listened to this carefully, then smiled and nodded his head. "Yes, I think maybe I know someone who can help you. We go there now."

Outside the hotel we climbed into the blue van from the school, then drove slowly through the afternoon streets. They were filled with children in either blue or maroon uniforms, with pressed white shirts or blouses, on their way home from the state-run schools. I tried to orient myself to the picture of Ternate that Wallace had portrayed, and it was surprisingly easy—the town has not grown as rapidly as Jakarta or even Ambon; its importance in the world has decreased as its population has risen slowly, through improved health care rather than economic and commercial incentive.

I didn't really expect to find what I was beginning to call the "Wallace House." It had been, after all, 130 years. Still, in the 458 pages of *The Malay Archipelago* Wallace gives a detailed description of only one house and its location, the "rather ruinous" structure he used as a base in Ternate. In Ambon, Nanlohy told me I would find the Wallace House opposite the main mosque, on the drive in from the airport—"the one with the pillars." But that house was a huge, rambling stone edifice, the kind where an important Dutch merchant might have lived; and the humble house Wallace described was one of sago-palm walls and thatch roof, albeit with a stone foundation. There is even a diagram of the floor plan of the house, which may strike the reader as a bit odd. In the years following Darwin's publication of *Origin of Species*, Wallace brushed aside all claim to priority in the question of the theory of natural selection; yet it is almost as if this precise description of the house and its location is included as a hedge against history. Perhaps he left these accurate notes on the place where he wrote his Ternate paper in case it ever became significant—if not to all of his readers, perhaps to a handful of scholars, or to a writer on the scent of a story.

We pulled up in front of a large wood-frame house, its crumbling eaves decorated with antique Dutch filigree. The old man that Westplat was looking for was a former teacher, a man who had lived all his life in Ternate and who might have known something about Wallace. Westplat left me briefly and entered the house from the back, to return a few minutes later; meanwhile schoolchildren shyly peered into the van's front seat, where I studied my Indonesian phrasebook.

"He is here; come in." Westplat led me across the dusty front yard and up the front steps onto a broad verandah, where an ancient thin man in pajamas rose to greet us. He was beyond being thin, he was skeletal; his neck was leathered, and dessicated skin hung from frail jawbones. Despite Westplat's own formality, "Juan" was all I ever learned of this man's name: a name clearly of Portuguese origin, though what could be read in the man's wrinkled features was uncertain.

Westplat told the man who I was and what I was looking for, casting his eyes at me every now and then as if for confirmation. I could understand only occasional words—"travel agent," "American" and "Wallace," but Juan nodded vigorously at this last and led us slowly into the house's parlor. Stately bamboo furniture was arranged in one corner of the large room, but with its bare floors and high ceiling the room still seemed empty. Another old man shuffled to the

doorway as we took our seats; a hot breeze came through the glassless windows and out the open door.

Juan returned with a manila folder full of papers. His hands shook as he opened it and brought out newspaper clippings, a *Reader's Digest* article on the *Homo habilis* find called Lucy, a child's textbook on the origin of the earth and a sheet of yellowed foolscap with the writings of a young man, hurried and inspired. For a moment I wondered if these scribblings might be some lost letters of Wallace; then I realized that they too, like everything else in this folder, were written in Dutch. They were probably Juan's own notes on evolution, written in the language that educated men used in the country well into the 1950s.

As Westplat and I looked over these papers, we made satisfactory sounds of interest; then Westplat again asked whether or not Juan knew where Wallace might have lived. Struggling with a lost vocabulary, Juan stammered, "My mother's grandfather was Wallace's friend. He was chief of Chinese village." He repeated this statement several times, in Dutch and Indonesian as well as English, so his meaning was clear.

Eventually we managed to determine that Juan's great-grandfather was the chief of the Chinese settlement in Ternate, and Wallace was a friend of the Chinese while he stayed here. In fact, Wallace may have lived in the Chinese quarter, a neighborhood behind Benteng Oranye—which jibes with his description in *The Malay Archipelago*: "Just below my house is the fort, built by the Portuguese, below which is an open space to the beach, and beyond this the native town extends for about a mile to the north-east."

But learning more from Juan was beginning to seem unlikely; Westplat at one point politely asked his age, and when he answered Westplat turned to me with his hands spread in sympathy. "Eighty-one. So you see—he is not the same now." Still, I was elated at this contact with the previous century: at least this aged, skeletal man knew who Wallace was, as his papers on evolution showed; and his family's friendship with the scientist had been considered important at some point in the past.

"I am sorry. He is very old, you see," Westplat

apologized as we began to drive away. "But he has lived all his life here in Ternate." I had assumed that nearly everyone here had lived all his life in Ternate; when I asked 'Pak Westplat, I was surprised to learn that he was from Ambon and had come to Ternate as a soldier after World War II. That would mean he was a Dutch soldier, I thought to myself; I was eager to learn more, but meanwhile he had begun to drive up to a village in the hills, where the trail to the old clove tree began. And 'Pak Westplat does not talk while he drives.

Back at the hotel, I had asked Westplat about the old clove tree, and he agreed to show me where the trail to it began. We followed a road leading south out of town, past a number of round-domed mosques, then turned toward the west and the sloping flanks of Gamalama. As we drove past modest houses, I noticed a series of crudely stenciled signs urging participation in the upcoming election; then the houses were replaced by irregular groves of clove trees. Soon we came to a village, marked at its outset by a sign that read "Marekurubu." The paved road wound between the houses and finally turned back on itself, where an overgrown dirt track disappeared into the shaded forest.

To stretch our legs, we began to stroll up this track; the old clove tree known as *cengkih afu* was something more than an hour's hike up the mountainside, though we had no intention of going that far on this first day. Then a small, bright-eyed woman appeared from one of the houses and clutched Westplat's arm. "Jan," she cried out, then a flurry of words I couldn't understand. It seemed a long time had passed since they had seen each other, for clearly there was emotion here, and a warmth between my aging companion and this woman, herself no longer young. With evident embarrassment, Westplat introduced her to me as Siri, and she eagerly invited us into her home.

Over hot, sweet tea and cookies in the simple stucco house, I learned that Siri remembered well the good work that Westplat had performed for Marekurubu when he had been the *burgemeester*, or mayor, of Ternate. I was only a little surprised; sipping my *teh manis* in the humid afternoon, I took advantage of Siri's eagerness to reminisce

and asked 'Pak Westplat to tell me more about himself. He smiled reflectively when I asked him to tell me when he came to Ternate, as if it were all so long ago the recollection had become sweetened by time. And Siri too, though her command of English was on a par with mine of Bahasa Indonesia, listened attentively to his story, as though the memories of aged people are their own comfort, and the language is almost irrelevant.

Jan A. Westplat came to Ternate in 1947 at the age of twenty-four, conscripted into the Dutch East Indies army. An educated and bright young man, he was put in charge of intelligence on Ternate. After two years he was transferred to Makassar on the island of Celebes, as Sulawesi was then known, but in 1952, when Maluku became one of the last provinces to establish its independence from the Dutch, Westplat had returned to Ternate and adopted it as his home. He married and in 1954 became mayor of Ternate, to supervise the reconstruction of the city that had been abused for hundreds of years by sultanate, colonial forces and warfare. He urged the people to be self-sufficient, to return to growing and consuming their own goods; he laid out new streets in straight lines, on the pattern of European cities, unlike the chaos of Ambon's growth; he planted clove plantations on the outskirts of town and came up to Marekurubu several times a week to oversee the clove planting and, by working the soil himself, to rejuvenate himself from the pressures of his office.

By 1961, however, he was in trouble with the government in Jakarta. He was, he told me, "hard on the communists," and he uncharacteristically slammed his fist into the opposite palm, and screwed it in. Soekarno was at the time growing ever more attracted to communism, and Westplat was replaced. For the past quarter of a century he had devoted himself instead to civil service, helping his Ternate-born wife with her handicapped children's school and enjoying his adopted homeland.

"You pictures?" Siri had noticed my camera. I raised my camera to focus on her, but she shamefacedly hid her mouth, which had the red lips and raw gums of a betel habit. Rather, she urged me to take photographs of her house, and

The bride and groom, with friends and relatives, stand before the marriage bed following their Moslem wedding.
(Christian Kallen)

showed me the system of bamboo pipes that caught rainwater from the roof and drained it into a holding tank; the coconut shredder being used by her son in the kitchen; and last, in a curtained-off room, the elaborately decorated bed of her nephew, with its colorful silk awning and adornment of flowers. It was a groom's bed, for the next day he was to be married.

It had begun to cool off by the time Westplat dropped me back at the hotel; after a shower I spent some time writing in my journal and reviewing Wallace's account of his time in Ternate. Scanning his report of his years in Indonesia, I realized that he had little scientific reason to spend so much time in Ternate, as he had virtually nothing to say about the natural history of

either Ternate or its neighbors Tidore and Halmahera. I concluded that he must have been attracted to Ternate for its own charms: clean air, sea breezes, a dramatic landscape and congenial company—charms not altogether relevant to science but quite compelling for the professional traveler.

When Westplat came to the hotel the next morning, he wore a quiet, secret smile, as if he had a surprise up his sleeve. Indeed he did: although the climb to the old clove tree was what I had planned for the day, Westplat pulled his van over short of the town of Marekurubu, closer to the village of Tongoli. I looked at him quizzically, and he answered in his deep burnished voice, "The wedding is here. We stay?"

Even though I realized that the marriage of Siri's nephew was this day, I was taken aback. My understanding was that weddings are usually family matters, and unexpected outsiders might not be appreciated. Besides, I didn't really feel dressed for the occasion, since I had planned on climbing up the steep slopes of Gamalama. Then there was the matter of religion: it was to be a Moslem wedding, in the traditional style, a binding of two close-knit families into a larger whole. As a victim of history's present dilemma—as are we all—which pits East against West over the battlegrounds of the Middle East, I was not sure that someone bearing my name would be welcome at a Moslem wedding.

Still, I was certain I'd never have a chance like this again, so I agreed to stay if the families would allow it. 'Pak Westplat must have already asked for me, for he just smiled and invited me in. "You will take the pictures," he said as he led the way to the porch of a nearby house. I smirked to myself: wedding pictures, every photographer's dream job.

A dozen men sat on the porch, talking among themselves and waiting. These were the relations of the bride, whose name I learned was Hadija Arsala; the family of the groom would march down the road from Marekurubu to her house, where the ceremony would take place. The men greeted me with some caution, until Westplat pointed out my camera—then they smiled and extended their arms, inviting me to look around.

At the back of the house, rice steamed in huge black pots, while shirt-sleeved men stirred the grains to keep them separated. Within the house itself, dozens of plates were being arrayed with small samplings of food—meats, fish, stews, goat soup and roast goat, and bamboo leaves filled with meat paste and folded into festive boxes. On the porch of the house next door, rice spiced to a yellow color was shaped into cone-shaped domes that would take center stage on the long tables where the wedding feast would be held.

Finally the groom's procession was heard, arriving to the steady beat of gongs and tambourines, singing in monotone. The grim-looking groom, Faruk Fane, was bedecked in heavy robes, jewelry and a crown, sweat breaking through his pancake makeup despite the large parasol that shaded him. Excitement rose as the procession turned into the bride's yard, preceded by a dozen prancing children; then the groom was escorted to the front porch by his male relations, where they joined the men of the bride's family.

I suddenly realized that I had not yet seen the bride and asked Westplat in a whisper where she was. He pointed with his chin toward a room off the porch, its door draped with a heavy curtain: the bride, apparently, was not to be seen until after the wedding itself took place. The service— a long ceremony in which the *imam* read from the Koran a list of admonitions and instructions—was concluded when the bride's father and the groom joined hands beneath a handkerchief, like two men in a wrist-wrestling championship. Finally the *imam* made a pronouncement in Arabic, the hands clenched, the handkerchief was removed and the families were conjoined.

After handshakes and congratulations all around, the groom made his way to the draped door and pulled aside the curtain. From within the chamber, a surprisingly large group of women exited one by one, crone to child, like a scene from a Marx Brothers movie. Then the groom stepped inside. The bride sat demurely on her decorated bed, eyes cast down; Faruk walked over to her and, placing his hand on his new wife's head, claimed her as his own.

I spent the next fifteen minutes taking pictures of husband and wife, with various combinations of friends, relations, near relations and village illuminati, until everyone grew too hungry to be intrigued by the newlyweds or an American photographer. The men sat at the long, decorated tables, and the women served them a surfeit of foods, while the bride and groom stayed behind in their wedding chamber, isolated behind the curtain.

After a lengthy prayer in both Arabic and Indonesian, everyone fell to the feast, Westplat and I joining in. I am pleased to report that the meat paste was very like what we would call liverwurst; the roast goat was no worse than cheap tough beef, and no better. After more food, ceremonial photography of the assembled male relatives and good-natured congratulations, Westplat and I left the ceremony to continue on up to Marekurubu.

It was still relatively early when Westplat dropped me off in Marekurubu, leaving me in the company of a lean man who promised to lead me to the old tree. Ali was about forty, dressed in dark slacks, a loose-buttoned shirt and blue flip-flops. A few horny teeth were still standing in his betel-ruined gums. Over one shoulder he carried a long, thick bamboo staff, which I at first took to be a walking stick; but as we rose ever steeper up the slopes, penetrating ever deeper into the forest, he continued to carry the staff over his shoulder, and I began to wonder what purpose it served.

He spoke no English and I the merest Indonesian. We climbed silently up the trail, occasionally passing the rustic huts built in the nutmeg-and-clove groves that served as temporary shelters for the harvesters. In the deepest part of the forest, bamboo bridges spanned steep stony creekbeds, and the narrow footpath climbed down, then up the muddy ravines. Sometimes the vegetation became thick and low, where the older trees had fallen or been cut down; in these areas areca palms poked up through the brush, and their stringy flowers were outlined against the sky. In the distance, the slopes declined to the spreading town of Ternate and its harbors, fronting the wind-creased sea; the great sweeping volcanic cone of Tidore defined the southern horizon. Above us the summit of Gamalama rose, alternately wreathed and revealed by cloud.

After almost an hour, we came to a house built on the steep slope of the volcano. It must have been harvest time: a young man and his wife were stacking dozens of the large, spiny durian fruit on a rough-hewn table, while a young child marched around the yard, singing a tuneless song. Ali greeted them familiarly and stopped to smoke a cigarette. The tree was nearby, he indicated; time to take a rest. Then the young man offered me a durian, and after a moment's doubt I remembered the advice of a friend who told me

that durian was a fruit best eaten in the out-of-doors. Halfway up the flanks of a tropical volcano atop the wind-whipped equatorial seas was about as out-of-doors as I could get. I accepted.

Durian must be one of the world's most unusual fruits. It grows on tall elmlike trees from Borneo to New Guinea and throughout that span is considered one of nature's most prized creations. In flavor it is unique; in scent it is unappealing, almost repellant. But in physical characteristics it is certifiably dangerous: it can weigh up to five and a half kilos, and its husk is spiked with hundreds of thorns, so when it is ripe enough to fall from the tree it can kill anyone foolish enough to nap in its shade. Had Newton lived in Indonesia, he might never have recovered from his discovery of gravity.

Ali took a knife from the nearby table, selected a hefty fruit and carefully examined its hideous hide; then, finding what he was looking for—a thin seam, barely discernible among the spines—he brought down the knife once, twice, and the fruit split. The opened section held four large white masses, gelatinous kidney-shaped seeds spooning in the pod. I reached for one and almost involuntarily recoiled from its slimy texture. But I finally got a grip on it and brought it gingerly to my mouth.

Describing the taste of durian is not unlike the five blind men describing the appearance of the elephant: for my own part, I detected the flavor of onions, cream cheese and brown sherry—all once cited by Wallace, all disguised by more than a hint of rancidity. It put me in mind suddenly of Lewis Carroll and Alice's reaction to the "Drink Me" potion—"It had, in fact, a sort of mixed flavour of cherry-tart, custard, pine-apple, roast turkey, toffy, and hot buttered toast"—though the delicious elements of durian were in a battle royal with the repulsive. I held my breath and wondered if I would shrink or grow.

Politely, I sucked on the slippery meat until the slimy nut was fully exposed, then waited a few minutes before I expelled it. I hoped the conversation would drift away from this stranger's first taste of durian; then I realized that nobody knew it was my first taste, for I could not explain it to them. Rather pleased with this anonymity, I boldly sampled another piece. While I cannot say I enjoyed it, neither did it bring my gorge up quite as far as the first. Its taste, I decided, also had elements of banana, garlic, egg—it was simply unlike anything else, hence strange and queer indeed.

Soon Ali and his friends concluded their conversation, and he gestured that we should be going. Leaving his bamboo pole leaning against the hut, he began to scamper up the hillside. I hefted my camera bag and began to follow, then returned to the table to take another of the flavorsome seeds. I sucked it slowly as I climbed up after him; this time it tasted like durian.

The tree was but five minutes away; I had wondered how we would know an "old clove" in this old forest of cloves, but recognition was immediate. A high cyclone fence topped with barbed wire surrounded the thick-trunked tree, either to keep vandals from defacing it or to clearly isolate the tree from the woodcutter's axe. The gate was unlocked; Ali stood beside the tree so I could take his picture, but the full height of the ancient clove, *cengkih afu*, rose out of the frame. While young cultivated cloves are conical in shape, their bright green leaves easily spotted from afar, this stone-old specimen grew from a gnarled trunk seven meters in diameter into a multitude of branches, some up to thirty meters high, some leaning drunkenly over the surrounding fence.

The clove spice had been the primary resource for Ternate's trade for as long as a thousand years before the coming of the Dutch, but by the seventeenth century, finding it easier to concentrate their harvests on Ambon, they had destroyed

The durian, a rich-tasting and odoriferous fruit, is among the most highly regarded foods of Indonesians. (Christian Kallen)

The ruins of Benteng Tolucco Hollandia, an old Portuguese fort on the northern coast of Ternate. (Christian Kallen)

thousands of clove trees on Ternate. The huge specimen we stood beneath was said to be some three hundred fifty years old, which means it began to grow around 1630; perhaps a few isolated trees in the rugged interior of the island were too remote to be reached in the extirpation, and this venerable plant had become the father of most of today's conical saplings. I've heard that it still produces a hundred fifty kilos of cloves each year—worth about 1.05 million rupiahs, or $700 on the market in Kota Ternate, and at least four times that in overseas markets. Not bad for one old tree.

We rested then, and it seemed only appropriate to have a clove cigarette. I am not a smoker at home but here in Indonesia it seemed more pleasurable. The scent and taste of *kreteks* is certainly one factor; one observer says it's like "smoking dessert." Nowhere else in the world is clove used in cigarettes, so either you enjoy them in Indonesia or not at all (unless you frequent specialty smoking shops and pay the price). Finally, beneath the considerable shade of this historic tree, a *kretek* was an offering, a tribute. It's a part of the economy, the heritage, the mystique of Indonesia and of Ternate.

When we returned to the house down the hill, the couple had braced Ali's staff on a stand and was loading it with durian, tied together in pairs and draped over the notched ends of the bamboo. There was also a large conical basket filled with durian, the cruel-looking oblong fruit brimming over the lip of the woven barrel. The young man hefted the staff on his shoulder, grimaced and directed his wife to add more durian to one end to balance the weight. Ali took off his flip-flops and laced them to the basket, then bent down to slip its leather strap onto his forehead and slowly stood to bear the weight on his back. The three of us headed down the mountain, each of the other two carrying at least sixty kilograms of durian to the village of Marekurubu.

Over the next few days, 'Pak Westplat and I toured the island of Ternate. His greeting in Marekurubu had been typical—everywhere he was met with smiles of fondness. In the village of Kulaba on the north coast, he stopped to give gentle advice to a young mother whose first child had died of malnutrition and whose current babe was ill. Once we stopped in the middle of the road for a good ten minutes while an old man carrying two heavy baskets over his shoulders filled in Westplat on his family's life. Grins, waves, the friendly nodding of heads—and occasionally the "Hello Mister" one hears all over Indonesia. Travel with Westplat was a pleasure, and it was a tour for more than just me alone: Westplat admitted he had not left Kota Ternate for the past twelve years, so the journey around the island must have been for him one of rediscovery and reminiscence.

One day began near the settlement of Dufa-Dufa, just to the north of Kota Ternate. Here is Benteng Tolucco Hollandia, built not by the Dutch as its name would suggest but by the Portuguese, early in the sixteenth century. The fort is well preserved: the royal seal of Portugal is still discernable, carved in the stone just inside the main portal. It is a simple structure, a circular tower on a hillside designed to survey the broad sweep of sea between the island and Halmahera. Immediately below it the tin roofs and earthen streets of Dufa-Dufa spread out peacefully, as if their security were still assured by Tolucco. Westplat and I rested on the fort's walls, surrounded by a series of tall palms, feeling the comfort of the fort's durability. A small group of school-age children from Dufa-Dufa joined us in the fort's small square, frolicking on the ancient walls, looking down on their village and laughing shyly when I pointed my camera their way. Behind a young girl with a paper flower pinned in her black hair and cleansing rice-paste tincture on her cheekbones, the gunmetal sea shimmered in the wind.

Farther up the coast, a ravaged landscape of razor-sharp black stones sweeps down from the crater of Gamalama to the ocean. This is Burnt Corner, Batu Hangus, the result of an eruption in the mid-1700s that sent lava streaming into the sea. Although much of this well-cultivated island disguises its volcanic origin, the violent truth breaks through in jagged ridges, black strata and midnight tremors. The islands of Maluku are among the most explosive in the world, with some seventy major eruptions recorded in the past four hundred years. Geologically as well as zoographically, this is a transition zone, neither Asia nor Australia; projections of plate tectonic movements suggest that this entire region between New Guinea and China will disappear in another fifty million years, victimized by the same global convection currents that have brought it into being.

I took a few photographs at Batu Hangus, then we drove on. Contemplation of such large-scale temporal matters is difficult under even intellectually rarefied conditions, but touring the north shore of a tropical island, where the blue sea's surface disguises coral and pillow lava and coco palms wave in the warm breeze, was far from suitable for such speculation. It was instead an indulgence of sensory pleasures.

It was siesta time; fathers curled up with sons on the cool stones of shaded porches, sleeping through the day's heat. Every settlement seemed to be dominated by a mosque, usually a large, low-lying square building crowned by a broad dome, in turn topped by the crescent moon and star. As we drove, I noticed the mosques seemed to be on the left, toward the mountain; behind them rose the volcano Gamalama, pivot and anchor of Ternate.

The road grew rough; the pavement disappeared altogether for one stretch of about a thousand meters, swept away by flooding, and we slowly bounced over dried mud potholes and a wide stony creekbed. The surrounding forest seemed to press in upon us, not cultivated as clove plantation, insensitive to humanity's preferences. We entered a clearing where a few families at the very northwest edge of the island have carved out the town of Takome. Here Westplat asked for directions, and upon hearing *"Bisa, bisa"* repeated by a thin mother and her two thin daughters, all three speaking in a unified singsong voice, we drove on: "You can, you can go." The road, so they testified, continued.

Soon Westplat made a left turn up a side track, and almost at once the van's wheels spun in sand. "We walk," announced Westplat, and willingly we did, following the rough road until it turned by degrees into a trail. It was not a long walk, but it was steep and hot; not more than halfway to the top I could hear Westplat breathing heavily and beginning to falter. I slowed my already easy pace but still found myself some distance ahead when he stopped in the thin shade of a papaya to catch his breath. "Sixty-five!" he exclaimed. "I am sixty-five!"

Turning, I tried to smile encouragement, but it felt awkward. I had just been contemplating the weight of my own years, which suddenly seemed self-indulgent. I gazed down the trail at the man, dark-skinned and portly, dressed in white shirt, slacks and black oxfords; I wore shorts, a T-shirt and California flip-flops. He took a few deep breaths and finally asked, "How old are you?"

I thought for a moment before I answered. "Thirty-six."

He laughed, not happily, then shook his head. "I am sixty-five," he repeated.

"Then you must have walked many miles," I said.

He shook his head. "These last few years, only drive."

"We'll take it easy," I said, and continued more slowly still up the last fifty meters of the trail.

The path rose to a clearing, and there the earth opened up and time stopped. Deep, deep down in a crater a dark-green lake lay, surrounded by sheer walls of jungle. A large red parrot rose up through the canopies on the other side of the chasm; black diving ducks swam together on the distant surface; a sulfur-crested cockatoo flew overhead, cursing my intrusion. From far off, almost below the threshold of hearing, a low breathy roar like the call of a guardian demon

swept over the lake. Then a grunt and a large splash: crocodile. I was amazed—on the rim where I stood there were coconut and papaya shoots, with boastful graffiti on bare boulders, the misused landscape of old habitation; down in that pit, the forest primeval.

I had read of this lake, Toliri, but was unprepared for the spectacle. It was as if a lost world had come to life, a secret pocket of the Mesozoic preserved on a tropical island. The low roar, I later deduced, was probably the booming call of a fruit pigeon, but the mystery of the moment remained undiluted. At last Westplat arrived at the rim of the lake, breathing heavily; he could find only a shaded rock to rest upon, where after a few minutes he lit a cigarette and watched the clove-scented smoke drift over the crater's rim. Then we trekked back to the van and drove slowly back to Kota Ternate.

In between forays into the far villages of the island, we had continued to keep the goal of finding the Wallace House in mind. To my surprise, Westplat had remained quite curious about the house; he had taken me to see, among other people, the town notary, who told us that Wallace, as a visiting European, had probably lived inside Benteng Oranye itself. This didn't agree with the description in *The Malay Archipelago*, and neither did it agree with the independent personality of the scientist.

The afternoon after my climb to *cengkih afu*, 'Pak Westplat and I stopped to see a friend of Westplat's named Mr. Chin. His house was not far from the palace of the sultan; it pressed close against the main road that ran through Kota Ternate to the airport and on around the island. Chin proved to be a robust, well-dressed man of middle years and mixed blood, a retired army officer interested in civil affairs, like Westplat. But whereas Westplat rarely let his strong feelings show, his friend was quite the opposite.

The slightest question could set Chin off on a finger-waving, eyebrow-wriggling discourse, in the fastest Indonesian speech imaginable; even Westplat seemed to have difficulty following him. I wasn't privy to the details of either Westplat's questions or Chin's arguments, but I

The palace of the sultan of Ternate stands an empty watch at the base of Gamalama. (Christian Kallen)

strongly suspect that it was an innocent remark on the weather that first caused his passions to erupt. When the subject of Wallace came up, Chin espoused complete knowledge of the subject, but I wondered if he knew as much as he led us to believe. He was helpful in telling us the location of the only two houses that had survived the earthquake of 1840, and he seemed to intimate that Wallace (as a distinguished Englishman, no doubt) must have taken up residence in one of them.

Recalling a detail from Wallace's description, I asked Chin if he knew whether either of these two houses had an old well nearby. I am still not sure what his answer might have been, for suddenly he launched into a tirade against Duivenboden, the Dutch governor of the mid-1800s, and

his plan to move the colonial capital from Ternate to Halmahera. Meanwhile, in the street outside, there was a parade underway: the national elections were less than a month away, and to kick off the campaign in Maluku Utara (the northern province), the Jakarta government had sent the Minister of Youth and Sports to Ternate. While Chin raved about Duivenboden, colorful soccer squads and basketball teams of both boys and girls marched through the streets waving banners, filling the air with cheers and their own cadence. Westplat and Chin ignored them and continued to excavate their island's past, searching for its place in history.

Following Chin's lead, we returned to the neighborhood of the fort. We had come here a couple of days earlier to walk through the garrisons of Benteng Oranye. Behind the fort, we had found an old cobbled street too narrow for cars that was lined with simple houses, on whose porches quiet families sat watching us, as still as if sitting for a portrait. This, I had thought to myself, must have been what Ternate was like for Wallace; I had imagined then that one of these plain thatched houses could have been the goal I was seeking.

This time, Westplat drove us to a solid old house on a corner. "I think this is the one," he told me as we stopped, sporting a look of satisfaction and pride. Boldly he walked to the door and introduced himself to the Aquil family. They were of indeterminate number; sons and cousins kept appearing and disappearing, poking their heads into the front room to listen and watch. Mr. Aquil was a well-spoken and curious man who had not heard of Wallace but was more than willing to show us the house and let us examine its architecture.

Gradually, Westplat dug up the story of the house. The back kitchen had been added by Aquil; the front parlor was also added, by converting a verandah. The basic structure itself had been built some seventy years earlier by a Chinese man who lived here; he had used, perhaps, the same stone foundation—or much of the same foundation, at any rate—as an earlier house that had stood on the same site. One outer wall was rough uncut stone, plastered over many years earlier; the remnant of another wall rose just above ground level next to the road. And just across the street, no more than twelve meters from the house, was an old deep well, a circular relic only recently removed from use by sewage pollution.

Aquil and Westplat grew more excited with each architectural anomaly, disused wall and forgotten foundation. Wallace's description inspired them, and from their own inspiration they drew the verdict of confirmation. And although this house was most assuredly Not It, there was the slightest possibility that whatever Chinese had built it or its predecessor on the ruins of an earlier house might have used the same, or roughly the same, or some of the same, materials and design. All of which was enough for Westplat to feel we

had made an important discovery, enough for Aquil to become elevated in the esteem of his neighbors and enough for me to become more than a little bit weary of the whole search at last. It was a Piltdown of a house, half-home and half-hoax, a parody of archaeology in action.

Dutifully I took a few photos, until my flash went dead; then we all congratulated each other on our good fortune, and Westplat and I left. I insisted on walking back to the hotel alone, to have time to be alone with my own thoughts. I realized that finding the Wallace House had become secondary among my pursuits in Ternate—it was possibly unimportant, probably impossible and ultimately irrelevant. What I stood to gain from Ternate was what I had found by default: a sense of its spirit, its *genius loci*, a connection with this igneous rock in the Indonesian seas where fragrant spices grew, sultans ruled, invaders rose and fell and genius came into flower. And four walls, ruined and rebuilt over time, held no secrets.

Westplat came for me about nine o'clock the next morning to take me to the airport for my flight back to Ambon, from where I would fly to Bali and then home. But since my flight was not until eleven, I prevailed upon him to stop off at the one highlight of Ternate I had not yet explored, the palace of the sultan. The palace, which stood white in the morning sun against the huge bulk of Gamalama, dressed up for the day in its ever-changing robe of cloud. We arrived to find the front pavilion filled with people, painting signs for the upcoming national election. They sprayed black paint through stencils, leaving the party's name, "Golongan Karya," and the crude drawing of an eagle, symbol of the government, on large sheets of white cardboard. It was an ironic sight to greet a pilgrim to the seat of the ancient sultanate.

On the other side of the pavilion, offerings were being prepared for a thrice-weekly holy ceremony in the palace; rice, water, candles and incense. Sultans ruled Ternate from the fourteenth century on, though this grand if somewhat undisciplined keep of their rule was built early in the nineteenth century. Despite its wild mixture of native, Dutch, Islamic and French architectural styles, it is a palace indeed, with a commanding view from its columniated portico across the soccer fields to the sea and, beyond that, to the vast dark silhouette of Halmahera.

The forty-seventh sultan, Iskander Muhamad Djabir Syah, by accepting a post in 1950 with the new Indonesian government, gave up the sultanate that had been one of the world's oldest monarchies; thus the monarch suffered by the English, Portuguese and Dutch for nearly four hundred years was assimilated by independence. Djabir Syah moved to Jakarta, and he died in the early 1970s; there was no successor. The palace itself was ceded to the government, which turned it into a museum.

For the caretakers at the palace, the sultan lives still: in the center of the throne room, dishes of food and water had been set out on clean linen scattered with flowers. Right practice was still observed, *adat* preserved. At the entrance to the palace we had taken off our shoes—my red sandals and Westplat's black oxfords. And as we toured the rooms with their spare exhibits—a cabinet of royal walking sticks, a gold-leaf ceremonial ship, a small stiff-backed throne, a display of serving dishes and a collection of chubby dolls dressed in the costumes of the diverse islands of Maluku—I noticed for the first time that 'Pak Westplat wore no socks. His brown feet whispered across the cool tile floor of the palace, at home in Ternate.

IRIAN JAYA

Stepping Back through Time

IT is the kind of tale only the Age of Aviation could produce. On June 23, 1938, a twin-engine Consolidated 28 "flying boat," the *Guba*, flew from the north coast of Dutch New Guinea into the cloud-shrouded central highlands. The *Guba*'s commander, Richard Archbold, was on his third New Guinea expedition, but he was also endeavoring to become the first to fly around the world at the equator—a feat he was indeed to accomplish but which would be overshadowed by the discovery he made that day.

Climbing from sea level to almost 3700 meters, the *Guba* worked its way into the uncharted heart of the Snow Mountains, looking for little-known Lake Habbema to use as a high-altitude base. Between the Idenberg River and the lake, the plane flew over an unmapped, mile-high valley of the Baliem River. As Archbold reported in the *National Geographic* three years later:

> From the number of gardens and stockaded villages composed of groups of round houses roofed with domes of grass thatch, we estimated the population to be at least 60,000. . . . From the air the gardens and ditches and native built walls appeared like the farming country of Central Europe. Never in all my experience in New Guinea

have I seen anything to compare with it. . . . Subsequent meetings with many of the people convinced us that we were the first white men ever to penetrate their isolated domain.

Aerial photography taken by the Archbold expedition showed not only the gardens and houses but a series of tall watchtowers positioned along the village frontiers. From these, guards surveyed the gentle agricultural terrain to warn of attack from enemy tribes. One photo showed a small group of near-naked men, Stone Age warriors, shooting arrows at the huge invading bird. The twentieth century had arrived in the Grand Valley of the Baliem.

Fifty years later, there is still only one way into the Grand Valley—by air. When George Fuller and I boarded the daily Merpati Airlines flight from Sentani, the lakeside airport near Irian Jaya's capital of Jayapura, I turned to the red-bearded adventurer and said kiddingly, "Well, here we go—back to the Stone Age." Time travel may be a fantasy or a joke, but when the prop-driven Fokker, weaving between the steep walls of forested mountains, finally broke into the skies above the Grand Valley, the spectacle below was timeless.

The huge valley—some sixty kilometers long and sixteen kilometers wide, following the leisurely amble of the Baliem—appeared flat enough to be an old lake bed, ideal for the agriculturalists whose signs were everywhere. Small clusters of grass-domed houses; the straight lines of fences, barely perceptible at a plane's altitude; acre upon acre of sweet potato fields divided by irrigation ditches into complex mazes of soft geometry: these could have been the same houses, fences and fields first seen by Archbold half a century earlier. White smoke rose from burning slash, narrow footpaths crossed the fields and spanned the ditches via simple bridges, and every sign of humanity was peaceful and gentle, like the pastoral European analogy Archbold had drawn. There was something new down there, however, something neither of us had expected—a straight and raw road cutting across the landscape, and upon it a red minivan racing itself, a contrail of dust rising behind.

When we landed at the airport in Wamena, the commercial center of the valley, a small cluster of people was pressed against the cyclone fence on the edge of the landing strip. This is common at airports in Indonesia; what was uncommon was their dress. Some wore the international garb of shirt and trousers, but more than half appeared to be naked. Their black skin shone in the morning light, and several of the men had set off their kinky black hair with a single white feather. Rising from the crotch to chest level was a long and narrow gourd, the distinctive *hourim,* or penis sheath, of the Dani. The women wore almost as little—older women had a slight sling skirt draped at hip level, and young girls sported long skirts of arse grass.

After only a few moments I grew used to the near-nakedness of humanity and looked beyond the people to the landscape. As impressive as the Grand Valley was from the air, with its complicated drainage systems and kilometers of cultivated land, from ground level it was stunning. To the west, rolling hills piled up like advancing surf, the farthest and highest set frothed with

cloud—the Jayawijaya Range, at the outset of its two-hundred-kilometer sweep to the border and across into Papua New Guinea. The east was a vision of barren beauty that climbers and prose stylists grow weak kneed and soft penciled over: a tough escarpment of igneous rock, a monolithic screen of sheer stone thrusting into the high cirrus yonder. It was furrowed and creased by fold and crevice, and at its sharp, fence-post summit was a hint of snow yet hidden in secret textured places. This was the mountain wall of the Sudirman Range, formerly called the Snow Mountains, a cordillera averaging more than three thousand meters high on the Grand Valley's sunset flank, in whose depths lurk at least six snow-capped peaks just a few degrees south of the equator.

The Baliem River flows southward, beneath the Sudirman's dramatic face, disappearing into a canyon of broad pyramid peaks and steep terraced gardens. As it divides the Sudirman Range from the Jayawijaya, it drops out of the Grand Valley to plummet with ungauged ferocity to the southern swamplands of Irian, where the cannibalistic Asmat live. Existing as it does in a temperate basin between the snowy peaks and the humid lowlands, the Grand Valley is indeed a lost world, a Shangri-La where time returns to its original slow turning in cycles of day, of night, of birth and death.

Nonetheless, the Grand Valley does intersect with the all-too-common world of Indonesia proper, and visitors to the Baliem area must have in hand a *surat jalan*—travel pass—from Jayapura to show to police in Wamena upon arrival. So our first stop in Wamena, an undistinguished Indonesian-style town of cheap prefabricated housing plunked down in the midst of Shangri-La, was the police station. The ostensible reason for all this caution was that the highlands are a sensitive area, with a threatened native culture and large tracts of unsurveyed terrain where a traveler can get lost. Unspoken is governmental concern over the political security of the region; since Indonesia took over the western half of the

The high walls of the Sudirman Range, on the western flank of the Grand Valley of the Baliem. (Christian Kallen)

island of New Guinea from the Dutch in 1963, the indigenous "Free Papua Movement" (the Operasi Papua Merdeka, or OPM) has been a constant cause of tension, both within Irian Jaya and between Indonesia and its neighbor, Papua New Guinea.

While securing our *surat jalan* in Jayapura, we had gathered some tantalizing information about the Dani tribes of the highlands from an American working on a forestry project in Cyclopes National Park, a rainforest region near the airport at Lake Sentani. What he told us about the Dani suggested a very primitive people indeed—their material culture lacks, for example, the wheel. Unlike most of the world's people of whatever level of cultural sophistication, they completely lack intoxicants. No palm wine or grain beer, no plants to smoke or chew—not even

the betel nut so common throughout Indonesia. In fact, the Indonesians do not even allow alcohol into the highlands, and luggage was searched at the airport in Jayapura and water bottles upon arrival in Wamena to prevent the Dani from ever gaining a taste for liquor.

Our original plans had been to visit the Grand Valley, then fly to the mission station at Ilaga, at the western edge of the Dani cultural area, for a trek across the mountains of the Sudirman Range to Puncak Jaya (formerly the Carstenz Pyramid), at 4884 meters the highest peak in Oceania. However, at the police station the rumors we had been hearing for weeks were finally confirmed: the Sudirman was closed to travel, as were all the mountains of Irian Jaya and many of its remoter tribal areas as well.

Over the next few days we pieced together the

reason for this closure, from both the official sources and the much more reliable unofficial ones. A few months earlier, a group of four mountaineers from Java had been killed on the approach to Puncak Jaya from Ilaga. There had been some confusion over how they died—did they fall in a climbing accident? Did they inadvertently get caught in the cross fire between Indonesian police and native OPM rebels? The true story was more gruesome than we had suspected: the four had been approached by natives of the area who demanded payment from them for money owed by an earlier climbing expedition. The Javanese, not part of the previous team, refused. Tempers rose, exacerbated no doubt by language barriers and cultural pride; too late the climbers realized the trouble they were in. When their bodies were recovered, hands and feet bound with vines, multiple spear wounds were determined to be the cause of death.

George and I decided not to try for the summit of Puncak Jaya after all. There would be plenty to see and do in the mysterious Grand Valley of the Baliem.

The Grand Valley is, despite its occasional lapses into violence and revenge, a particularly benevolent place to live: the temperature in the valley is mild, rarely above 80 degrees Farenheit, rarely below 40; the soil is fertile; the rainfall, moderate; and flooding of the Baliem River is rare and actually beneficial to the croplands. There is no—or no longer—dangerous wildlife such as wild boar to threaten the inhabitants; fatal diseases are almost unheard of, the worst communicable ailments being yaws and pneumonia. In this climate, sweet potatoes can be grown year-round, and if they do not strike Westerners as a particularly engaging diet, they do provide exceptional nutritional value. The proof is in the population: clear eyed, strong, content, able to withstand the passage of the years and, perhaps, able to confront civilization without fear.

The concept of a people hidden from civilization may be as old as Homer; the modern fantasy, the secret valley discovered from the air, found its most famous expression in James Hilton's *Lost Horizon*. Hilton imagined a valley of eternal life amidst the snowy Himalaya, and *Shangri-La* has since become synonymous with longevity and isolation. That name is just one of those given to the Grand Valley of the Baliem in the decades following its discovery, others being Hidden Valley, the Valley that Time Forgot and the Valley of Mystery. More lurid nomenclature reflects the Stone Age habits of its denizens—Valley of the Headhunters and Cannibal Valley. It is almost as if, had there been no Baliem Valley, the mythmakers and missionaries would have had to invent one.

Christian missionaries came to the Grand Valley in 1955 and set up their first camps near the present-day town of Wamena. They found all their worst projections of godless heathens surrounding them: the Dani were polygamous, the men measuring their wealth in wives and beating them into subservience; they were warriors, who were reputed to sometimes eat their captured enemies; and they were essentially unclothed. In addition, they practiced mutilation—severing the fingers of young girls to show mourning and sometimes slicing their own ears when shamed. Although their efforts were slow to gain converts, by 1961 the Christianization of the Grand Valley gained momentum when a native Dani became a charismatic preacher and successfully urged many of his own to give up and burn their weapons and practice war no more. Today, despite the presence of large numbers of missions and churches in the Grand Valley and its surroundings, Christianity remains very much a surface phenomenon, while polygamy, self-mutilation and even warfare are still features of Dani life, albeit much less common.

Warfare, in fact, was the single most significant aspect of Dani culture, both in terms of its role in maintaining the society and in the amount of attention it has received. For warfare among the Dani usually was not to gain land and impose political strictures, as it has become in more "civilized" cultures. Instead, the Dani commonly practiced "ritual warfare"—battles launched, spears thrown and men killed for little purpose other than to reinforce the social fabric of the society. The Grand Valley was among the last places on earth where this distinctive behavior was still practiced. It was a fabulous milieu, a cultural time capsule that in many of its aspects has leaped the centuries from the Stone Age into modern times.

If there is any place on earth where such a culture could survive into the present, it is New Guinea. The world's second largest island is the largest in the tropics, and as such it hosts a bursting diversity of life forms—tropical rainforests dripping with orchids and tree frogs, bats as big as dogs, the Australian marsupial called the cuscus and more than twenty species of the colorful bird of paradise. Much of the terrain of the island is an impossible "broken-bottle" landscape of sharp limestone ridges and sudden sinkholes, with networks of caves so vast they have yet to be fully surveyed and appreciated. It's little wonder: although a new issue of maps has been promised for some years, even the best currently available topographic charts have vast areas described as "Uncharted—Obscured by Clouds."

In this land of geological and biological wonders, it is the cultural plenitude that is most impressive. From the stilted houses of the sea-level Micronesians to the thatched domes of the highlands habitants, the people of New Guinea have provided a wealth of information for generations of anthropologists. For example, there are more then seven hundred languages on the island—about half of the number originally found in the entire continent of North America. In fact the Dani properly speaking are simply a language group, one of twelve main divisions found among the highlands people of Irian Jaya. The very ruggedness of the terrain accounts for this abundance of languages; although linguistic research has shown root relationships between many of the tongues of the highlands tribes— the people collectively known as Papuans—it is nonetheless true that a Dani from the north end of the Grand Valley cannot fully understand a Dani from the canyons to the south.

The first maps showing the entire shape of New Guinea revealed an island that looked curiously like a bird. "Sprawled like a dead turkey" is one of the less poetic descriptions of the island, though many Papuans prefer to compare it to the cassowary. This huge flightless bird of Australasia, distantly related to the ostrich, provides the beautiful long white feathers that Dani warriors covet for their headdresses. Other famous avian inhabitants of the island include the twenty-odd species of the family Paradisaeidae—birds of paradise, whose elaborate plumage and frenzied courting dances seem to provide the extreme case for male decoration as the basis for natural selection. The feathers of the birds of paradise, as well as those of parrots, egrets and herons, also provide color for Papuan headdresses, and the Dani use parrot feathers to cleanse the hands of those who have done magical work. In fact, the Dani linkage between humans and birds is one of the strongest, and strangest, in the world of anthropology.

In 1961, one of the best-known anthropological expeditions in modern times took place in the Grand Valley. This was the Harvard-Peabody New Guinea Expedition, under the direction of anthropologists Robert Gardner and Karl G. Heider. Other members of the group included nature writer and novelist Peter Matthiessen, Dutch anthropologist Jan Broekhuijse, photographer Eliot Elisofon and film sound technician Michael Rockefeller. Among the documents that resulted from this project were Matthiessen's *Under the Mountain Wall*, a detailed chronicle of "two seasons in the Stone Age," several anthropological monographs by Heider and one by Broekhuijse, and the classic anthropological film *Dead Birds*, an eighty-minute documentary on the Dani. These works have helped make the Grand Valley Dani among the most familiar of the world's so-called primitive people.

Dead Birds gets its title from one of the Dani origin myths. In ancient times, the snake and the bird had a contest over whether humans should, like the snake, be born again after they "shed their skin" or should remain dead, like the bird. The bird won, and human mortality was the result. The film takes a close look at Dani ritual warfare, as practiced between the villagers of Wuperainma and their allies against their enemies in the adjacent alliance. Several characters are examined in detail, including the warrior Weaklekek and the young swineherd Tukum (both also profiled in Matthiessen's *Under the Mountain Wall*). There is a pig feast, a funeral and a victory celebration, as well as quieter moments of weaving, gardening and a visit to the

The greased hair, parrot and egret feathers and shoulder paint of this happy man evoke the man-as-bird symbolism of the Dani world view. (Marshall L. Smith)

salt springs. But it is the scenes of ritual warfare—racing men decorated with feathers and pig tusks, spears raised in threat and display and arrows flying through the air—that dominate the film. The scenes of war are real, filmed from nearby rises with telephoto lenses or from the floor of battle itself.

Gardner's narration for the film suggests that the explicit reason for ritual warfare was to placate the ghosts of those who died in battle; these spirits "demand" the death of an enemy in payback. "Unavenged ghosts bring sickness, unhappiness and disaster. It is for this reason they go to war. And because they like to." Thus, the system of ritual warfare was self-perpetuating: the motivation was revenge—to kill an enemy—whose

tribe must then kill in return. The Dani seemed to place great stock in ghosts and the supernatural—special places were marked off where ghosts lived, the spirit of the dead was appeased with pig flesh at funeral feasts and the ground where a mortally wounded combatant had lain was burned to remove all trace of blood. "The ghosts, which more than anything else rule the lives of these people, come out at night. . . . Not even the bravest warrior likes to go out at night, unless there is a full moon and he can see, and not be tripped or injured by the ghosts."

Still, to read Matthiessen's book or to view *Dead Birds* is not to perceive a society of wraith-terrorized savages or grief-crazed warriors bent on revenge. The Dani are seen as generally calm and relaxed, even in the midst of battle, even in the face of death. Heider goes so far as to call them "peaceful warriors": while they did take warfare seriously, they took it lightly too, taunting and joking with each other over the field of battle much like football linemen will hurl insults across the scrimmage just before the ball is snapped. Their arrows were not fletched, so they were inherently inaccurate; they were not shot in volleys, so they were easily avoided; although the Dani were familiar with the power of firearms, they never used guns in battle. Clearly warfare had other purposes than simply killing; clearly it was as much ritualistic as vengeful.

When the expedition members set up camp in the Dugum neighborhood of the central Grand Valley in April 1961, ritual warfare was openly practiced: they recorded some twenty incidents of war between April and September. In general, "ritual warfare" might be defined as a continued state of conflict between two adjacent alliances, a mutual antagonism that is to some degree a stabilizing, rather than disruptive, feature of society. The Dani called it *wim*—an alternating series of killings, motivated and lent momentum by group vengeance, in an established battlefield between two antagonistic alliances.

The point of such warfare was seldom carnage, or the possession of land; instead it was an almost sportive competition marked by bold but generally harmless displays of force and bravery. While these displays sometimes led to fighting and injury, they seldom led to death. The Harvard Expedition saw no deaths on the battlefield, only two that resulted from wounds received during battle, and six effected in raids or ambushes—just eight deaths over six months of "warfare."

Just as the Harvard Expedition was finishing its work, in early September 1961, the district police officer from Wamena led a patrol into the midst of the Gutelu (or Kurelu) alliance that was being studied. The Dutch were at the time coming under international attention for their administration of West New Guinea, which the Indonesians were contesting; to have active tribal warfare in the colony—especially warfare that was being filmed and written about by anthropologists—was deemed inappropriate. The patrol demanded an end to warfare and established a police post at nearby Jawika, then known as Jibiga, to enforce it.

Surprisingly, pacification proved to be a relatively easy matter. In some areas the incidence of suicide increased following pacification, and some Dani were reported to blame a wide variety of ailments on the cessation of warfare, including drought, flood and blindness. For the most part, however, the Dani accepted the new order of things: after all, it meant they could work their fields, walk their pigs and sleep without fear of ambush from their neighbors. Their long-standing tradition of *wim*—once thought to be a cornerstone of their social universe—evaporated literally overnight.

One might suppose that a tradition so central would have been harder to extirpate from Dani culture, especially since it was said to be based on supernatural demands. But perhaps ritual warfare was not a deeply set system of behavior and was instead a fairly recent expression of the hunter-gatherer economy the Dani had followed previously, possibly until several hundred years ago. *Wim* may actually have been closer to ritual hunting than ritual warfare. Karl Heider notes other evidence for this theory in the initiation ritual for adolescent boys, which concludes with a feast of mice, birds, bees, crayfish, grasshoppers, wild greens and pork from a wild pig, all food from a hunting and foraging lifestyle. "It looks like an ancient memory, preserved in ritual, of the pre-Dani past."

Still, there is warfare, and there is war: at dawn on June 4, 1966—almost five years after pacification—hundreds of men from the northern Gutelu alliance attacked their neighbors across the Elogeta River, a small tributary of the Baliem. Within an hour they had killed 125 men, women and children and burned many of the houses, cookhouses and pigsties of the compounds. The raid was led by a new leader of the alliance, Mabel, who chose a moment when the police post at Jawika was deserted and the priest away in Wamena. It was a raid performed not for ritualistic purposes but to right smoldering secular antagonisms between members of the same alliance. The result was a realignment of alliances, the northern Gutelu splitting off from the southern, who then turned to their neighbors to the south, the Widaia.

While the daily cycle of bluster and battle had been broken, the source of social antagonisms had not been touched. Despite the apparently successful missionary presence, and the increasing role of Indonesian police and social influences in the Grand Valley—or perhaps in part because of these factors—the conflict near the Eligota (and several subsequent battles) showed that the Dani, however peaceful they were as warriors, were warriors still.

George Fuller and I awoke at dawn on Sunday, for it was market day in Jawika, and almost everywhere markets begin early. It had rained the night before, and a mist still rose from the flat landscape when we stepped outside to watch the villagers come in for the market. To our surprise, there were only a few people to be seen—a lone man loping quietly down the footpaths between the ditches with his arms folded over his chest and fingers linked behind his neck, to conserve warmth, and the distant, bent figures of three women on the main road. The town itself was almost deserted, but it was not silent—the faraway sound of a hymn floated across the damp fields. I stopped breathing and lifted my head to hear: the melody was "We Shall Overcome."

We had come from Wamena, our base, to Jawika, against the eastern mountains of the Grand Valley, because it was a center for many of the places we wanted to visit—the salt springs, the traditional villages and the native market—and because of the region's fame from the Harvard Expedition. It was also at the end of the road, the new dusty scar across the flat face of the Grand Valley that we had seen from the air. Although missionaries and police had cleared tracks for four-wheel-drive vehicles over the previous thirty years, it had been only six months earlier that "commuter" travel had begun. It was now possible to ride a Mitsubishi minibus—the Colt model so popular as public transport throughout Indonesia—from Wamena to either Hetagima, ten kilometers to the south, or Jawika, thirty kilometers north. Furthermore, plans were underway to extend the road through the rugged mountains north of the Grand Valley and to con-

nect with the paved road being built from Jayapura. When I heard this news, the Sam Cooke song came to me: "A Change Is Gonna Come." If airplanes, Christianity, anthropologists and pacification hadn't yet done the job, a highway surely would.

The fare from Wamena to Jawika had been 1000 rupiahs, about 70 cents. The route crosses the Baliem over a new bridge, passes miles of traditional sweet potato fields and cuts around the base of the large anomalous wedge of land that appears in *Dead Birds* as the contested battlefield, as no-man's land. Sharing the minibus with us had been three schoolgirls, a couple of blacks in Western dress and a half-dozen men replete in *hourim* and hairnets. I had looked again at the clothed black closest to me and seen daylight shining through his pierced nasal septum; he, too, was Dani. For two adventurers in search of the Stone Age, it had proved a little disconcerting to see a robust Dani warrior pull a thin wad of rupiah bills out of his arm band upon arrival in Jawika and peel off a thousand-note to pay the driver.

The market square was up a straight path from the *losmen* (guest house) where we were staying; immediately behind the square a long fence bordered the settlement, behind which there extended a narrow valley that grew sharply narrower before it disappeared into a densely wooded canyon cutting into the limestone wall. All morning long people came in a steady stream from out of the mountains, the men bearing loads of crudely cut wood or long tendrils of vine for construction, the women with multiple string bags on their backs hanging heavy with produce. After dropping their loads, the men gathered around small grass fires, smoking and talking while they warmed up from the damp morning. The women meanwhile spread their produce on the ground—newly introduced crops such as carrots, garlic, onions and a few Japanese eggplant as well as the traditional bananas and seventy-plus varieties of sweet potatoes. Then the women, too, sat in the dust and lit their hand-rolled cigarettes.

It was a scene of peace and cooperation, and one would never suspect that, in addition to practicing tribal warfare into the 1960s, these people probably used to be cannibals—"probably" because, as with most cases of reported cannibalism, eyewitnesses are almost nonexistent, whereas rumor and accusation are abundant. There were more of the cultural oddities that a traveler discovers about a people—for instance, the men are bearded but have no moustaches: they find moustaches stylistically grotesque and pluck all their hair (including chest, limb and genital growth) except on the head and jaw. The men do pierce their noses and, when they feel particularly dressy, wear curved boar's tusks. Finally, the proximity of the market allowed us to confirm the oft-repeated charge that the Dani have an aversion to bathing. It seemed not unreasonable, I charitably decided—after all, the bacteria that cause body odor grow nowhere more rapidly than in the humid confines of clothing,

and the Dani largely avoid such confinement. But as you might expect, without much bathing they do smell: it's a combination of woodsmoke, sweat and tobacco, not unlike a tribe of backpackers. It was not a rank smell, however, but the complex scent of the living.

In one respect clothing is a simple matter for the Dani—the men wear virtually none, except a penis sheath and perhaps some necklaces, bracelets and feather decoration. But the *hourim* is a very strange feature of dress indeed, a narrow gourd grown in village gardens, where it is elongated by tying weights on its end as it matures. Boys begin wearing them at about four to six years of age, well before puberty or any initiation rites. Most men have several *hourim*, including ones curled at the end, which several wore to the market apparently as their Sunday best; some-

Two men enjoy a quiet smoke away from the crowded Sunday market at Jawika, in the heart of the Grand Valley.
(Christian Kallen)

times they dangle the fur tails of the cuscus from the end. The gourds are attached by two thin strings, one at the top that winds around the chest to hold the gourd erect and the other at the bottom, tied around the scrotum. It looks uncomfortable, and George—a physician by trade, photographer by hobby—hypothesized that the relatively low birth rate of the Dani might be explained in part by this tying of the testicles close to the body (thus raising the temperature of the sperm too high for potency). Then again, it might be the several *years* of abstinence expected of a man and his wife who's borne a child, following the baby's birth.

Women's dress is only a little more elaborate. Until marriage, girls and women wear thick skirts of arse grass dyed red and green at the lower ends. Upon marrying, they adopt a skirt of braided cord that is draped over the pubic region like a bead curtain; with marriage, also, they begin to wear the large net bags in which they carry the traditional woman's burden of potatoes, pigs and progeny. A woman's back is almost never bare: I can't recall ever seeing a mature woman without at least three bags hanging down her back, unless she was busily bent over a potato patch in harvest. Even then, a single empty net bag was draped over her, and full bags lay nearby, oftentimes their location defined by the squall of an unseen infant.

This reduction of clothing to the barest minimum had an almost purified quality, as if the entire purpose of clothing had been distilled to its essence: the covering of genitals, a covering that becomes an emphasis. An eighteen-inch gourd rising at a 120-degree angle does not hide the penis, it highlights it. Likewise a string skirt that provides little more coverage than the merest bikini bottom on a French beach. Yet the Dani are not a highly sexual people—premarital intercourse is infrequent, infidelity is rare and their acceptance of the lengthy abstinence of four to six years after childbirth is unusual if not unique in the world. Even the charges of rape that accompanied their direst raids are questioned by many anthropologists and observers familiar with their ways.

Despite this image of an archetypal Stone Age warrior, the Dani are among the friendliest, most hospitable people on earth. Their generosity, commonly in the form of banquets of pigs, potatoes and bananas, is the stuff of legend. Such offerings are not exactly gifts, however, for the Dani are chronic traders whose traditional currency is the cowrie shell, which must make its way up into the highlands from the Micronesian islands in a complex and little-understood network of trade and exchange. Nonetheless, even the all-but-insurmountable barrier of mutual unintelligibility—Bahasa Indonesia was second language to only some of them, and it is far from second to me—failed to discourage the expression of warmth between the Dani and their American visitors.

They are, for example, incurable hand shakers. Richard Archbold reported that even upon his party's first meeting with the Dani, "after a friendly 15-minute chat in sign language, our visitors shook hands all around and departed." They shake hands with anybody—their old friends and clan members as well as a trekker laboring down a dirt path beneath the sweat-inducing burden of an overweight pack. The handshake is what a handshake should be, a sure grip of acceptance and good will: gentle but not soft, comfortable and reassuring. All the while that your hand rests in theirs, they'll look straight into you, their big black eyes smart, clear and confident, emanating a tremendously positive energy; then they'll move on to the next handshake. It's something like being at a wedding reception or a political gathering. Actually, if the Baliem Valley had any connections with some of the more exotic sects of 1970s America I would suspect that I was being "love-bombed"—overwhelmed by good will and concern to the point where my cynicisms and suspicions would disappear and I would embrace the world view of my caring guardians, sign over my inheritance and change my name.

OPPOSITE: *Her string bags spread out before her, a woman adds her produce to the goods sold at the Jawika market.* (*Christian Kallen*)

Years earlier, I had a friend in Seattle who called hippies "Earth People," in a rather derogatory way; he'd point, giggle and otherwise display his disdain for their earnest commitment to dirt farming and the organic lifestyle. The phrase came back to me at the Jawika market: these *were* Earth People, the real thing. They lived, with a parallel clan of rooting pigs, squatting in the dirt, unbathed and wearing only gourds and grass, selling tubers and scraps of wood. A number of women, in mourning, were caked with dried orange mud, and many men wore a black makeup composed of pig fat mixed with ash. Nearly everyone smoked cigarettes, made of strong local tobacco rolled in a rank-smelling spurge leaf. But they weren't living like this on a lark, out of political belief or out of a commitment to voluntary simplicity. This was simply the way it is, how much of humanity has lived for tens of thousands of years, since the dawn of the species.

Stone Age is a rather imprecise term, conjuring low-browed, prognathic, bandy-legged fellows wearing bear skins and wielding clubs with which they bonk their chosen mate before dragging her into the cave for a round of spin the atlatl. Anthropologists prefer to term the Dani Neolithic, which means they have fire, a variety of polished tools, agriculture and animal husbandry even if they lack metallurgy and monumental public architecture, such as temples. At the market and in the potato fields surrounding the settlements one could see that the most significant modern addition to the Dani artifacts is the metal shovel—the wide blade, chopped into a flat edge, has replaced the flattened end of their traditional wooden digging stick; the sharp pick end of the stick, for loosening soil, is maintained. The simple agricultural economy remains for the most part unchanged.

The market itself was primarily a chance to meet and gossip, and the exchange of goods seemed purely secondary. Most Dani grow all the tubers and fruit they need, and the purchase of a few yams or a hand of bananas—for 100 rupiahs, which works out to about 3 cents a pound—was largely left to the visitors, Indonesian or European. While George and I wandered about, taking photographs or just watching, we seemed to

be greeted more warmly and more frequently by the Dani men than were the Indonesians—tourists from elsewhere in the archipelago—or residents of Wamena who had taken a "drive out to the country" for the day. Perhaps it was the attraction of alternate generations, the unfettered fondness of a grandfather for his grandson vaulting over the conflicts inherent in the middle generation. The equation was not condescending on our side; the Dani were clearly the senior generation, with a bemused acceptance of the gadgetry and innocence of these young white children.

Every society has a word for the outsider—"gringo" is one of the better known and least offensive. Since much of George's travels had been elsewhere in Southeast Asia, he kept referring to us as *farang*, a Thai word referring to the French. We never heard it in use, but apparently the Dani call white people *waro*, meaning snake or lizard. The reason seems obscure—is it that newborn chameleons are white? Or is it that the Dani, who consider themselves like birds (and decorate themselves with feathers and paints to underscore the similarity), perceive the natural antipathy between airborne birds and earth-bound snakes? Then there's the matter of mortality: birds are born, fly and die; snakes shed their skins and seemingly live forever, as the Dani origin myth tells. The Christian missionaries who promised immortality played into this dichotomy; in addition, the Dani are quite familiar with the death of their own kind, yet rarely see a white man die.

The robin chat, frequently cited as the bird of the origin myth who races the snake, is a small black bird with white shoulders frequently seen flitting about in the potato fields and along stream margins. The legend continues that the robin chat painted his shoulders with white mud as a sign of sorrow for the mortality of mankind. Today both women and men still cover themselves with mud during mourning and at cremation ceremonies, and we saw several women at the Jawika market with mudded backs, breasts, shoulders and faces. Mudding also used to be frequent as preparation for battle and for victory ceremonies. In all cases the association with mud, birds and death is maintained; the irony—that the airborne bird is for us a symbolic

"Narak!" *Two cultures pass on the new road that is bringing together the isolated villages of the Grand Valley.*
(Christian Kallen)

opposite of the mud-covered "earth people"—is consistent, if mysterious.

The market grew more crowded, with little sign of abating before sundown. In midafternoon I walked back through town, passing on the way a large and unkempt field where two soccer squads were engaged in loud competition. A small crowd was watching, including some older men squatting in the grass. The game moved up the field and down, and at one point a score was made; but the old men watched impassively, perhaps lost in their thoughts. After a few minutes I moved on and returned to the *losmen*. Only weeks later did I fathom the reason for their glumness: in their day, the only "sport" had been ritual warfare, and soccer must seem pointless, both figuratively and literally bloodless next to the real thing.

The *losmen* was a pair of long rectangular buildings of bamboo, each simple room half filled with a raised platform for sleeping. It was called the La'uk Inn, *la'uk* being one of the two common terms of greeting among the Dani. If a group of women is being greeted, one says "*La'uk*"; if men, "*Narak.*" I was proud of my quick retention of these two key words and had used them lavishly at the market. Although I was never able to find out what *la'uk* means, upon returning from Irian Jaya I came across the root for *narak*: it is an abbreviated version of the phrase "*Eyak narak halabok*," which means "Hey friend, I eat your feces." I fervently hope *narak* means friend.

In the small dining room of the La'uk Inn is a guestbook signed by visitors from around the world, and many of them have included com-

ments on their stay. A few content themselves with complaining about the weather or complimenting the *losmen*'s food; most are eager to share their experiences, including trek routes and the names of hospitable villages. Some of the comments are editorial: "A long way away, a long time ago we were like these people. We have changed, they didn't. We can still communicate with a smile. Let's try to have this only influence on them and don't try to spoil their pure, clean and natural way of life," observed an Italian traveler. "I feel very lucky to see the Dani people," noted an artist from the States. "I hope the tourists don't spoil what we cherish about this place."

This was a common theme, the double bind that plagues the visitor to Irian Jaya or any other "unspoiled" area of the world: how to observe without influencing, to visit without being an intruder. It is especially troublesome in the few remaining truly primitive areas, such as the Grand Valley. There is a particular, entrenched problem here that a Swiss tourist noted in the La'uk guestbook: "Please don't spoil the Dani by shooting too much with your camera and distributing all the time '*satu uang merah*!'" The single red bills he refers to are the 100-rupiah notes of Indonesian currency; at some point in the last twenty years visitors began to hand out these notes to the Dani they photographed, and now it is virtually impossible to take someone's picture without being asked for payment.

One doesn't want to play this game, which seems to encourage people to "look weird for the camera." George mentioned that the Masai in Kenya also ask for money when you take their picture; for them, as perhaps for the Dani, the taking of pictures is equivalent to the stealing of souls certain American Indians feared. Perhaps the threat was resolved by a kind of pragmatic primitive capitalism: everything has a price; if our souls are to be stolen, pay up.

Neither the stealing nor the purchase of souls made me comfortable; as a consequence, I found myself trying to sneak shots, which perhaps was more rude than not paying. George was more practical. He refused to speak or understand anything but English, feigned poverty, and instead offered his models cigarettes, a more straightforward gift. Still, the memory of those four Javanese climbers, bound and pierced over a monetary misunderstanding, was never far from mind; and if George's model refused a cigarette, one of those *satu uang merah* could usually be found.

The impressive limestone cliffs that surround the Grand Valley, like the "mountain wall" behind Wuperainma and Jawika, are characteristic of the highlands of New Guinea. They are the result of the slow uplifting of the island around a central cordillera of igneous rock, caused by plate tectonic activity around forty million years ago. Within these limestone territories is an extensive network of caves, due to the permeability to water of the calcite rock. Even the sizeable northern fork of the Baliem disappears into a mountainside cave, only to emerge several miles away at the head of the Grand Valley itself.

Among the features of this limestone terrain are the salt springs. Deposits of oceanic salt from long-ago tidal flats are occasionally pierced by subterranean streams, and when these briny brooks are discovered the spring becomes important as a source of salt. The mineral is useful not only as an essential nutrient but as a tradeable commodity, and a visit to the salt source is one of the most important economic activities of the Dani.

The next day George and I ventured up the canyon behind Jawika to Iluerainma, one of only two salt springs in the Grand Valley area. The well-worn trail rose almost immediately into the dense forest that covered the steep mountain wall. We were not alone: a few women were already on their way down, net bags bulging with dripping fibers. These left purple stains on the limestone rocks that composed the uneven trail, rocks polished smooth by generations of toughened soles. The trail grew steep as a sadist's staircase, each step a minor challenge; overhead the

OPPOSITE: *Spreading banana leaves into the briny waters of the salt pools, traditionally women's work, is now a quiet job shared by both sexes. (Christian Kallen)*

trees were draped with mosses, creating a gloomy atmosphere. At places the density of the forest lifted and we could see the full trunk and crown of the pandanus tree, along with its strange exposed root system of multiple stilts like a life form with more legs than we could conceive a use for. The trail followed the stream that came off the mountainside, but in this stretch even the normally cheerful gurgling of water seemed ominous.

At last the trail leveled, where a small rock pool had been built at streamside. The pool was so old that its human construction was almost invisible; it had become a part of the geomorphology of the stream. Several women were knee deep in the murky water, spreading banana fronds on its surface. A man nearby was pulverizing a banana trunk to loosen its soft, pulpy fiber. Voices were subdued in the morning shadows, beneath the muted pounding of the mallet on the tree's pith. One woman shivered from the water's cold.

The mining of salt from the pools is a matter of breaking down banana fibers by tearing or even chewing them, then soaking them in the saline water. Eventually the cells of the banana trunk are almost completely broken, so that when the material is soaked in the pool the salt is absorbed. The soaked pulp is taken back down to the valley and dried; after it is burned, its salty black ash is used as a seasoning. The ash is also a prized article of trade with tribes farther away from the rare salt wells, such as the Jalemo to the north, from whom the Dani receive cowrie shells in exchange.

After a time a group of three men arrived, one of them a handsome man of about twenty-five with angular features that stood out among the coarse-featured Dani. Relatively tall—almost six feet, well above the Dani average—and well built, he clearly would have been a warrior a generation past. Until pacification, men were seldom seen in the waters of Iluerainma and instead stood by with spears and guarded their wives as they worked. But this morning the young man,

his clear skin unscarred by arrows, stepped down without self-consciousness into the dark cold water and spread out his banana fibers with the women.

After a time George and I, who had been quietly taking photographs, offered cigarettes around. Most were glad for the commercially rolled Gudang Garam, one of Indonesia's most popular brands. Coincidentally, the name means "salt shed." Everyone took a break, and a small fire was started to warm the shivering woman. We stood around quietly in the warmth, smoking, the Dani with a peculiar glottal snap as they inhaled a deep lungful.

We decided on a circuitous route back and followed a little-used trail farther up the mountain canyon. Thin roots and high buttresses rose from the mud of the trail, and we slipped and slid, moving deeper into the forest, before we finally found a wide, well-traveled avenue. This led up another three kilometers to a clearing, where the round thatch roofs of empty Dani huts were linked with each other by long, low wood fences radiating in every direction, like the hubs and spokes of a disassembled wheel. The skeletal appearance of the compound was underscored by its nudity: the region had been clear-cut, the thick trunks of the old araucaria trees torn by axes and burned. The high distant whine of a gasoline saw droned savagely as it rendered more forest into lumber. But the exposed hillside afforded an exceptional view down into the Grand Valley, perhaps three hundred meters below us— flat, cultivated, populous, peaceful, extending in the midmorning distance to the far wall of the Sudirman Range. We could see clear to the polished peak of Puncak (Mount) Trikora, formerly known as Wilhelmina, at 4730 meters the third highest of Irian's mountains.

On our way back down the hill we encountered two middle-aged women, their net bags full and heavy; they were both covered with the yellow-orange mud that signifies mourning. The mud-covered people on the trail and in the villages were women—we saw no mudded men, for

men would only decorate themselves with mud in anticipation of a great battle. The women who were mudded might be of any age, but they did tend to be older, of an age for widowhood, like these two on the trail. I noticed that most of their fingers had been cut off; what remained were short stubs of a single joint each, the ends of which were thick and calloused knobs.

One of the practices the missionaries found most disturbing was the amputation of fingers as a sign of mourning. Most women and many men reached middle age with few of their full digits remaining, for the first two joints of the fingers were chopped off in the funeral ceremonies. Usually a specialist performed the ritual, tying off the circulation above the elbow, hitting the funny bone sharply to numb the arm, then cutting off one or two fingers with a single blow of a stone adze. Young girls related to the deceased were usually chosen for this mutilation, but older men would sometimes voluntarily have their fingers cut off when in shame or in mourning at the loss of a favorite wife. For women, the amputation was a means of placating the ghost of the dead; for the men, however, the act was one of personal grief. In any case, although it is no longer a widespread practice, the short finger stubs are still a common sight around any gathering of Dani; and despite the dominance of the missionaries and police, it is not only the older people who have them.

The casual observer might conclude that Dani women do all the work and suffer the brunt of social obligation, while the men sit around and smoke, adjust their feathers and look important. Truly, most of the garden work and all of the harvesting is done by women, who are usually seen with two or three large string bags hanging from their heads, weighted down by perhaps twenty kilos of produce. But large-scale construction projects are almost entirely the work of the men, including the building of complex and efficient networks of ditches to drain the flatland potato fields as well as the clearing and terracing of the mountainside gardens. The most visible division of labor by sex is in portaging—women do most of the carrying, stooping beneath their string bags; men stride purposeful and unburdened across the fields, a spring in their proud step and a merry gleam in their eye.

Not everyone in the Dani world falls easily into a category considered socially useful; for example, there are the *kepu*, cowards who have done nothing to distinguish themselves—unmarried, unlanded, unproven. In past times these were men who shied from battle, and while they were accepted in Dani society they were never welcomed. Then there are those whose category is universal: at the Jawika market, a man had walked up to me and begun talking a mile a minute, pointing first at me, then the road, finally gesturing to encompass the known world and all the while jabbering away in a rising and falling singsong. It took about three seconds to recognize the type, and I had switched my portable cassette player onto "record." On the tape, his steady muttering is only slightly subdued by the black box I thrust in his direction. Then another voice is heard—that of a helpful onlooker who came up to tell me what I already knew: "Crazy. Crazy man."

To the children falls responsibility for the pigs. This is only natural: as Heider remarks of the Dani baby, "Small pigs are his companions on the floor of the common cooking house and the first creatures with which he can deal as equals." In the morning the pigs are released from the pigsty and are herded by children—usually the boys, though girls also take this responsibility—into the neighborhood to forage. Although a pig may "belong" to a particular child as a favorite, its disposal is always determined by the Dani man, who decides which males are to be castrated, which females bred, which pig to be killed for what occasion and which traded.

Throughout New Guinea, the highlands economy is traditionally one of pigs and potatoes. Archaeologists have uncovered evidence that this

OPPOSITE: *Pigs are the main signature of wealth and source of protein among the Dani and are coddled almost as much as children. (George Fuller)*

lifestyle is perhaps nine thousand years old in some areas of the island, though it is probably more recent in the Grand Valley. In some places, where the forage that's available for pigs must be supplemented by crops, the rearing of pigs is so expensive that they are an uneconomical harvest—it costs more in resources allotted and nutrition returned to have pigs than not to. But their ceremonial importance is enormous: a man's wealth and cultural viability is measured traditionally in wives, warfare and pigs, not necessarily in that order.

Pig festivals are major ceremonial events in Dani life. There is the major "Pig Feast," a mass marriage-cum-initiation ceremony that takes place once every five to eight years when called by the dominant area chief, but in addition there are numerous smaller feasts, called for on any number of occasions from good luck rituals to funerals. In times of ritual warfare feasting followed many engagements, whether in celebration or mourning. When looking for a justification for the cyclical nature of ritual warfare one should not ignore the nutritional motivation—the recurrent need to supplement the carbohydrate of sweet potato with the protein of pork. Even the means of justifying this pork consumption—battle—is a symbolic hunt, another carryover from the preagricultural days when men in bands ventured forth to track down wild boar to provide meat for the family group.

In today's Grand Valley, with its officially imposed pacification, other occasions must be found for pig feasts. One is a performance of the feast sponsored by tourists. It was suggested to us that we "buy" a pig ceremony, a day's revel in a nearby village complete with slaughter, roasting and feasting, and perhaps some dancing thrown in, for a mere hundred dollars. That struck us as the falsest kind of bargain—the illogical extension of the 100-rupiah photograph, a native performance purchased for the sake of a few rolls of film. But just as we had given up on the possibility of seeing a traditional pig feast, upon our return to Wamena we heard of one in the nearby village of Pugima. It was not to be just another traditional pig feast, as it turned out, but an event of some historical significance, to say nothing of irony.

The trail to Pugima from Wamena began at the airport, and we followed a morning scattering of Dani across the broad tarmac to the deep grass lining the Baliem. The day's flight from Jayapura arrived as we reached the river, the heavy roar of the engines sweeping over the valley like an evil wind, a sirocco from the future. We didn't look back but turned to the right and followed the footpath a couple of hundred yards downstream, where a suspension bridge crossed the broad, muddy current. The bridge was built on the traditional model—a wooden step tower at each end, the rough cross planks of the bridge wide enough for two to pass—but the supporting cables were of steel, and as many as twenty people at a time crossed the bridge without pause.

About three kilometers from Wamena the trail was as broad as a highway, a well-traveled road that crested a brief rise and afforded views back into the Grand Valley and, ahead, down into the smaller, more intimate environs of Pugima. Golden fields unlike the viney potato gardens of the Grand Valley surrounded Pugima, and there was an enclosed compound in the center of the valley, from which the harsh metallic sound of a loudspeaker could be heard, blaring out a marching song of false, low-fidelity cheer. A crowd had already gathered there for the day's events.

The occasion for this pig feast was a rice harvest—the first rice harvest in the Baliem region, the result of a project of the Indonesian government to improve the economy of the area. No doubt the project made good national sense: most of Indonesia's rice is grown on Java and the islands of the west, and in the eastern half of the country this staple is relatively expensive. To encourage rice cultivation in Irian Jaya, the easternmost region of Indonesia, would not only bring prices down but might give the Irianese themselves a stake in the national economy. And, as well as exporting the rice, the people of the Baliem could learn to eat it themselves—and become culturally more like the Indonesians they were, legally at least.

Although the sweet potato is evidently quite satisfactory as a staple, it is the food of a primitive culture. The Indonesian government, based on

Java, pays lip service to the diversity of cultures within its borders, but nonetheless it has shown a certain intolerance for alternate lifestyles. In Irian Jaya, where the lifestyle is focused on the sweet potato, the efforts of the government to bring the people into the modern age—or into the Indonesian world view, nutritionally if not politically—may exceed the definition of benevolent government. The anthropologist Karl Heider noted the problem in his book *Grand Valley Dani* in 1979: "I am still surprised at how healthy the sweet potato is, and I anticipate trouble in the future as the Dani get more integrated into Indonesian culture. For most Indonesians, rice is the proper food and the sweet potato has very low status indeed. But since the Dani cannot grow rice, it would be both economically and nutritionally disastrous if they got drawn into a rice diet."

That the Dani *can* grow rice seemed to be the point of the Pugima experiment. When we entered the crowded compound we found rice everywhere, in sheaves beneath the low roof of the market and stacked outside the women's houses, and as hard tiny golden grains newly mixed in the ancient dust of the village floor. At the far end of the compound, beneath the squawking loudspeaker, a temporary tarp roof had been erected over a series of tables. Here dozens of Indonesians sat, their content round, brown faces and bright fabrics in contrast to the dark shapes of the Dani, black women stooped beneath their net bags, black men lean and muscular and erect in the morning sun.

Still, the occasion was a pig feast, and pigs were being slaughtered as we arrived. Two men would hold a pig between them, suspended by its legs and ears, and a third would stand close to it, draw back a long barbed arrow in a crude bow, then shoot at point-blank range into the lungs. The pig's screams were loud and painful, piercing the air like the siren of mortality; one pig got away from the men holding it and ran a terrified and futile race, pulsing blood until it fell. About a dozen pigs were killed, quickly cleaned and prepared for cooking, while the ovens themselves were being readied.

In a large smoldering fire in the middle of the compound, large limestone rocks had been heated amidst the burning coals. Five shallow pits about two meters across had been dug. These pits were quickly and expertly filled with grass, banana leaves, the hot rocks (transferred with split-stick tongs), potatoes and pig, alternately stacked in ever-rising layers until the entire structure was almost shoulder high. About ten women and men worked together on each oven, with much shouting and bossing about, though it was difficult to tell not only who (if anyone) was in charge but whether anyone was paying any attention to anyone else: everyone seemed to know exactly what they were doing, even down to ignoring and working around the red-bearded photographer in their midst. Finally these grass ovens were bound with vines, to hold them upright, and water was poured on top. The hot rocks would steam the damp leaves and water, and the potatoes and pork would cook for the next two hours.

During those hours, the interlopers took over and the procedure of the pig feast deviated from the traditional. A host introduced various officials from Jayapura and Jakarta, who then proceeded to give a series of long speeches, evidently on the great success of the latest five-year economic plan, the increase in productivity and how the new rice harvest at Pugima was symbolic of the continued national progress. At least this is how I interpreted the speeches—I could decipher a series of lists, enumerating quantities of goods, and a few respectful references to Soeharto.

Most of these officials read their speeches, the pages fluttering in the breeze as their voices droned on, drained of feeling and fidelity by the loudspeaker. The Dani surrounding the compound at first stood, respectfully, but soon they dropped to a squat, then a cross-legged sitting position. Eventually the speakers were pretty much ignored, and the Dani greeted each other with their soft broad smiles, their gentle handshakes, their exchange of cigarettes and their own quiet private conversation. Only when the ceremony became surreal did their interest rekindle—a man came out with six elaborate tin insecticide spray tanks, blue-ribbed tubes arching from the backpack-shaped containers, and presented them to young Dani men dressed in trousers and shirts for the occasion. They accepted the tanks eagerly, shiny trophies for initiation into the modern age.

Finally the speeches were over and the feasting began. The steaming grass ovens were quickly torn apart and separated into stacks of cooled rocks, cooked potato and poached pork. A group of senior men took responsibility for the butchering of the cooked pork, cutting it into segments with slender bamboo knives that, upon becoming dull, could be resharpened merely by peeling off the edge and exposing the next sharp layer. The women settled into talkative clusters; the men set about allocating the food, which included a large, hot sweet potato each for George and myself. And while the Dani had their traditional feast, the Indonesians beneath the tarp had theirs—lunches of cold fried chicken and sweetened rice balls, boxed in pink and blue cardboard by a Jayapura caterer. I at first thought this the height of arrogance and insensitivity, this refusal of indigenous food at a festive event; then George reminded me that most Indonesians are Moslems and cannot eat pork in any case.

Just when I thought the event had entered the picnic stage, I heard the yodels and whoops of Dani warriors. What's this, I thought—a raid from an enemy alliance? From across the compound came as bizarrely dressed an army as any victim ever beheld, a gaggle of twenty young men in modern ceremonial garb: bright day-glo war paint with shimmering blue sprinkles on their cheekbones, pink-rimmed shades or oversized aviator glasses, funny hats and T-shirts with lurid messages from rock bands. They swept down on a cluster of women and demanded payment: the women happily handed each of them a sweet potato, and off they went, with more hoots and hollers. Then they repeated the raid on the next group of women, and the next, until this cheery Halloween mob had extricated their due dinner and just desserts.

I was elated by this display, uplifted from the depression the bastard pig feast had sunk me into. This series of mock raids, a hip and cynical parody of the traditional way of life, somehow managed to straddle more than two intersecting cultures—Dani and Indonesian, old and young, yesterday's and tomorrow's. It was like an open door into the hearts of the people. They might be growing rice and spraying their crops, wearing T-shirts and dark glasses, but the mock raids seemed an affirmation—beneath the modern face paint the Dani are still warriors.

The rice festival at Pugima is only one example of a historical trend in Irian Jaya that has many observers concerned. The issue is one of cultural integrity and identity. On the one hand are those who say that Irian Jaya should be absorbed into its mother nation, Indonesia, and direct its resources toward the well-being of the whole. On the other hand are the separatists, who hold that Irian—New Guinea, the land of the Papuans—has no natural place in what they see as the "Javanese Empire."

The western half of the island of New Guinea, Irian Jaya was politically separated from the eastern half of the island only in 1884, in a "gentlemen's agreement" treaty between Germany, Holland and England arranged at Berlin. The western half was allocated to Holland. After World War I Germany lost its claim, and England's interest fell to Australia, which controlled the two eastern quarters until they were united as Papua New Guinea, which, in 1975, became an independent country.

The demarcation between the eastern and western halves of the island is as artificial as any on earth—the border closely follows the 141-degree-east longitude meridian, except for a jog around a bend in the Fly River. In so doing, the frontier splits apart the island's biological and cultural communities. Only the relative obscurity of the island's resources and ecologies until this century, and its marginal role in international politics, made this arrangement acceptable.

In 1949, when the Indonesians gained their independence from Holland, the Dutch held on to their New Guinea possessions as the last prize in their rapidly disappearing East Indian empire. Their rationale was that the native population of the island was culturally and racially quite distinct from the Malays of Indonesia. In itself, this view is fairly accurate—the dark-skinned Papuans of the highlands are more closely related to the Melanesians of the South Pacific, and certainly the coastal people of the eastern half of the island are Melanesian. But the Indonesians have long held that their country extends more than 4800 kilometers from the Aceh region of Sumatra to Irian; and within this broad area, even apart from Irian Jaya, there is a wide range of different cultural and genetic types. "Unity in diversity" is, in fact, a national motto.

In 1961, the Indonesian government of President Soekarno began in earnest to demand Dutch New Guinea as part of a glorified plan for a unified Indonesia contiguous with the farthest extension of the precolonial empires. The sultans of Tidore and Ternate in the Moluccas (today's Maluku) had claimed sovereignty over the island (which they called Irian) in the century before the Dutch came, though their interest was primarily in slaves and colorful feathers from the birds of paradise. Their "convenient fiction" (as one historian termed it) was originally the basis for the Dutch claim on western New Guinea once they took over sovereignty of the sultanates. For Soekarno, it was a matter of national if not personal pride to wrest control of the region from the Dutch (much like his almost simultaneous confrontation with Malaysia over the provinces of Sarawak and Sabah on the north coast of Borneo). After much saber rattling, the Dutch finally acceded to changing times and the wishes of the United Nations and permitted the Indonesian flag to be raised over the capital, Hollandia, on the first day of 1963. The capital was quickly renamed Soekarnopura; the country became Irian Barat, meaning "West Irian."

Perhaps having to do with the absurdity of Indonesia's easternmost territory being called "West" anything, in the mid-1970s the province became known as Irian Jaya. Similarly, with the fall of Soekarno, the capital was renamed Jayapura and the Carstenz Pyramid became Puncak Jaya. *Jaya* means great—hence Great Irian, Great City, Great Summit.

Names alone do not annex a territory, and the Jakarta government has expended more than hyperbole. Indonesia has used money from the World Bank to finance the deforestation of primary rainforest and the relocation of people into these denuded regions of Irian Jaya. Its control of western New Guinea is not uncontested—witness the indigenous OPM, which came into existence in the early 1960s to promote an independent nation of West New Guinea. Indonesia has used army forces, paracommandos, air force, police and state security units to enforce submission of resident populations in Irian Jaya, according to the American journal *Cultural Survival*. And the number of refugees from Irian Jaya crowded into refugee camps in Papua New Guinea numbered fifteen thousand by the end of 1985.

The tenuous but aggressive nature of Indonesia's claim to half of the island of New Guinea, the effort to solidify this claim and the fate of the native people of the highlands, including the Dani, all come together in the national policy known as *transmigrasi*, or transmigration. *Transmigrasi* attempts to deal with the overcrowding of Java by offering land and housing to families who wish to live in the so-called outer islands—a revealing phrase in itself, meaning every one of the islands of Indonesia other than Java. On the surface this seems a reasonable way of dealing with the tremendous population pressures of Indonesia: there are almost a thousand people per square kilometer on Java, and more than half of the country's population of 170 million is less than eighteen years of age.

But the practical effect of *transmigrasi* is the implanting of the Javanese lifestyle—which increasingly includes materialistic priorities such as television and taxis as well as white rice—onto islands where it is a foreign order. The influence of the Javanese is profound, spreading as the population of the transmigrants grows, squeezing out the traditions and beliefs of the indigenes. Conflicts have arisen on Sumatra, where the tradition-minded Acehnese resent their new Javanese neighbors. Other locations chosen for *transmigrasi* settlements include those islands that have in the past most resisted Java's government: Sulawesi, the southern islands of Maluku, East Timor (a Portuguese colony until its military takeover in 1975) and Irian Jaya. Wamena itself, in the Grand Valley, is clearly a Javanese town transplanted from the heart of the empire, with the tacky houses, broadcast television and reliance on Bahasa Indonesia as the language of daily life that is assiduously supported by Jakarta.

These visible signs of change—in housing, recreation and language—may be just the tip of the iceberg. The entire social fabric of life is likely to be sacrificed eventually, as the Javanese influence suffuses places such as the Grand Valley and discourages the potatoes and pork economy. It's more than just a plate of food, for along with the dietary change is the overthrow of a traditional economy, labor, social order and belief system. It is the spreading of a monoculture, a social equivalent of American reforestation projects that cut down cypress, pine, fir, hemlock, alder and cottonwood and replace them all with a single species. Eventually, the pig feasts and marriage celebrations, the sacred places and traditions, the very man-as-bird mythology that makes the Dani unique will wane. They are waning now. And what is there to replace it all?

There may be no ready prognosis for what is certain to be a difficult future. But the visitor to the Grand Valley is witness to the inevitability of change, and the anthropologist realizes the realm of his study has shifted—to entropology, the study of a world winding down.

The Baliem River begins its three-hundred-kilometer course in the snow fields of Puncak Trikora. It flows first northward and then eastward, dives into the limestone underground for two kilometers and then slows in the majestic and fertile Grand Valley. But it enters another stage when it leaves the valley. Below Hetagima, a small mission settlement at the end of the road ten kilometers from Wamena, the gradient of the terrain steepens and the pace of the river increases: between here and the broad expanse of Irian's southern swamp, the river drops a hundred fifty meters in fifty kilometers over a series of cataracts and waterfalls. This is the Baliem Gorge, a narrow and virtually impenetrable region that remains as unknown as any in the world.

The story of missionary attempts in and near the Baliem Gorge reads like a chronicle of conflict rather than conversion. In 1961, a Christianized village near Kurima that had laid down its spears and arrows was attacked by traditional mountain tribes; the chief was killed along with many others, women were reportedly raped and some seven hundred huts burned to the ground.

In 1968, two Australian missionaries, Stan Dale and Phil Masters, were killed and eaten by tribespeople farther down the Baliem Gorge angry at the intervention in traditional ways. Six years later, a Dutch Protestant mission station at Anguruk was attacked and its native preacher and twelve assistants killed and eaten. Other attacks on missionaries and outsiders have occurred with such regularity that the regional mission head resisted pressure from Holland to return to the region because, it was suggested, he thought, "It sounds as though Holland wants a martyr."

Holland may have wanted a martyr, but like the missionary neither George nor I wanted the job. We just wanted to go for a hike in the area: from Hetagima down the Baliem for ten kilometers to Kurima, a town on the very lip of the gorge. It would give us the chance to see for ourselves the torrent the Baliem was said to become, for we both had an interest in river running and the Baliem had long been suggested as a likely whitewater adventure. In addition, it would allow us to meet some of the Dani people of this more difficult landscape, to see how their lifestyle differs from that of their valley-bound cousins.

After stocking up on bananas and bottled water at the Wamena market one morning, we walked out of town to the bridge over the Wamena River, a tributary of the Baliem that spreads over a broad gravel bed. Here families washed clothes and children swam in the shallow pools, while trucks rumbled over the long covered bridge on the way to the Grand Valley's southern end. We caught a ride on one of these trucks that was being used as a *taksi*, or bus, and bounced over the rough road to Hetagima past fields of potato, taro and sweet peas.

Once we began walking, beyond Hetagima, our path seemed a continuation of the road, or as though it had been at one time; it was no longer fit for most vehicles. It climbed a short but steep hill of sand and then rose and fell in an undulating course over a path alternately rutted and rocky. On our right, the wall of the Sudirman Range pressed close, at one point cut by a deep oxidized canyon that spilled a broad alluvial fan of rounded pebbles and powdery dust. Down the narrowing canyon, at the end of the valley, the clouds floated around the high, regular pyramid shape of a peak. Toward this dark bulk we walked, following the trail as it passed between occasional gardens and fallow land.

The only map we had on hand was a sketch in the third edition of Bill Dalton's *Indonesia Handbook*, a guide that had proved of mixed value. If it was in Dalton, we used to say, it's wrong: something like it may have once been true, but the version in the book has been invariably skewed by rumor, supposition and the passage of time, no matter how recent the edition. Nonetheless, our goal was a pair of suspension bridges Dalton's map shows in Kurima, making possible a short loop hike over the river below the village. Though we had no way of knowing whether these more distant bridges would be any more primitive than the bridge over the Baliem between Wamena and Pugima, we certainly hoped so, for the traditional rattan bridges are photographically as well as architecturally more interesting than cable constructions. To tread them would be more literally to walk in the footsteps of the Dani.

After almost two hours' walk we came to a vast white gully of gravel reaching far back into the hills, with a cloudy, cold creek meandering in its depths. At this confluence with the Baliem the creek's channel was at least two hundred fifty meters across, a natural funnel for the winds that whip between the steep Sudirman Range and the deep Baliem Gorge. Heinrich Harrar, the German explorer who was the first to climb the north face of the Eiger in the Alps (and later spent seven years in Tibet, when a Himalayan climbing expedition was disrupted by the outbreak of World War II), had come this way in 1962. He called this tributary the Yetni and noted that up its canyon is the other of the two major Dani salt springs.

As we surveyed this chasm, three men from the direction of Hetagima stopped to rewrap and tighten their loads, and we followed them down a trail of steep stairs cut in the cliff to the gravel beds. We all picked our way along the creek, looking for a place to cross. The barefoot Dani casually waded; I looked further and found a place to leap from rock to rock without getting my hiking shoes wet. George, with his burden of cameras, chose to walk carefully across; better to wear wet socks and shoes than to accidentally drop his equipment.

The Yetni is the border between the regions of Hetagima and Kurima, in the neighborhood of the 1961 attack by traditional Dani on their unarmed Christian brethren. More than a quarter century later it all seemed peaceable enough: in the middle of the trail we came upon a group of people having a ruminative smoke and stopped to take pictures of them with the black pyramid in the background. They ignored us but soon rose to continue on their way. The women trudged down the trail, bent beneath their net bags. The men let them get ahead, then greeted us with a quiet "*Nayak*" and traveled with us at our pace. I noticed the word had shifted from *narak*, indicating we were in the domain of another dialect.

The pathway by this point was too narrow for jeeps or trucks, since the Yetni had been an impassible barrier for such vehicles. We hiked on deeper into the stately terrain of the lower valley. On the far side of the river we could see terraced fields clinging to the mountainside at an impossible angle. They looked vertical but could not have been; neither could they have been fewer than seventy degrees from the horizontal. Small hamlets lined the Baliem, whose brown waters were now laced with white and whose roar reverberated between close canyon walls. Everywhere we looked there was the contrast between habitation and wildness, the civilized gardens of a peaceful people and the impossible landscapes of a primitive world.

Finally, three and a half hours after leaving Hetagima, we reached Kurima. At first I thought word of our trek had preceded us, for there was a festive crowd lining the trail through town. The spread displays of vegetables suggested a more likely reason, however—it was market day. We walked through the gauntlet of near-naked women selling carrots, cucumbers and sweet potatoes, smiling and saying "*La'uk*." On the edge of town, I stopped to take a photo of a crowd of kids playing volleyball; they posed eagerly and seemed disappointed that I took only one shot. In retrospect, so am I.

In our passage we had accumulated a small crowd of boys between five and ten years of age.

They were fairly well dressed by Dani standards; the missionary influence in Kurima is apparently strong enough to drape cast-off T-shirts and Levis on many of its inhabitants. Still, they shared with most children in the Grand Valley a minor but persistent respiratory infection, which is evidenced by a thick runnel of mucous pouring over the upper lip. Perhaps it is impolite to snort it back, for they rarely did; in any case, we had learned to overlook this cultural decoration.

Just at the southern end of town I spied a narrow trail veering off toward the river. Mustering my rudimentary Bahasa Indonesia along with broad gestures, I asked if it led to a bridge: "*Jembatan?*" I said, waving down the trail.

"*Ya, ya, jembatan,*" one of the older boys answered.

Encouraged by my linguistic success, I tried to enquire if this was the first of two bridges. "*Jembatan satu?*"

"*Tidak, jembatan dua.*" He pointed downstream. "*Jembatan satu disana.*"

"Ah," I replied knowingly. I turned to George to translate. "I think this is the second bridge, and the first is downstream. They're numbered for some reason."

"Great, a bridge," he replied. "Let's go."

Jembatan dua proved to be somewhat more traditional than the ones in the Grand Valley itself—it had rattan binding—but it too had steel cables, which we were a bit disappointed to see. Still, we happily joined a merry crowd of market goers in crossing it. People seemed inordinately friendly, as if white visitors were rare indeed; they laughed and nodded encouragement as we carefully walked across, holding onto the fiber handrails and keeping our knees bent to ride with the bridge's sway. I stopped in midspan to raise my camera and take a picture of the Baliem, racing mud red out of sight around the bend. This act caused great applause and comment from all sides, and I wondered if I had appeared foolishly brave or just foolish.

On the far side of the river we followed the boys down footpaths that led temporarily away from the river, through compounds, gardens and fields. In the valley the fences of the villages and gardens were built of wood, but here large limestone rocks formed the walls, rocks taken from the soil when the gardens were cleared. More than once we clambered over these fences and crossed through traditional village compounds —the round men's hut at the end, three or four women's houses and a long rectangular cookhouse, with small, shady gardens of banana and gourds just outside the walls. In the middle of the pathway in one compound, a bent old man sat, dark scarred flesh draping his bones, pounding a piece of bark with a stone adze. One of the boys went straight up to him, bent toward his ear and yelled something in a demanding but gentle voice. The man looked up with a dim smile and slowly crawled out of the way, looking at us bashfully as we passed.

When the trail broke into the open fields, we were across from the village pools. Families bathed and played in the river's quieter waters (apparently the Dani do bathe—at least some of them, at least some of the time) and spread their clothes on the smooth white boulders in the afternoon sun. When they saw us hiking downriver, on the east side of the bank, they hooted, cheered and waved their arms wildly. Was this some sort of greeting, I asked myself? Was there a local joke that we didn't know, but of which we were, apparently, the punch line? I waved back, then wriggled my arms; they cheered uproariously. Vaguely within me stirred a doubt: just how long ago had cannibalism been known in this valley? Were there few witnesses to cannibalism because they had all been victims of it?

After about twenty minutes, the trail deteriorated. It swerved around buttresses, dragged itself up muddy hillsides, ducked under leaf-heavy branches and spilled into puddles. At one point it dipped into a fern-fringed pool, where two young women bathed gracefully. The kids forged ahead without breaking stride, hopping and jumping as if it were all a game. George and I paused to take in the idyllic scene, then regretfully left it as our children's escort continued on without us.

Alongside the trail the Baliem gained in force as its gradient increased. Rapids were nearly continuous now, Class III and above, with churning holes and cresting waves in midcurrent and sharp calcite boulders along the banks. But it looked runnable, from a rafter's perspective, and I kept stumbling as my mind wandered to the proffered pleasures of whitewater. There was the little matter of logistics, of course: although the Baliem was clearly an enjoyably sporting river from Hetagima down this far, it could only grow more challenging as the gorge narrowed and steepened, and finding a place to take out—to get off the river and transport gear back—might prove impossible. The maps showed no airstrips or settlements from here on down; only gorge, jungle and swampland until the lands of the Asmat. To run the Baliem Gorge began to look like another glamorous impossibility.

Finally, we saw *jembatan satu* spanning the narrowest part of the gorge. Now I understood the numbering system: this was bridge number one because it was the first, the oldest, the original. From a distance, it looked like a moss-encrusted web across the river; up close, its ancient construction was a thing to behold, thick lianas wound into cables, twisting handrails, frayed supports. Many of the rough wood planks that served as the walkway were broken, especially at the draping center of the span where the bridge leaned at a sharp angle down toward the churning river. My first reaction was swift and sure: no way; I'm turning back.

Among George's earlier travels had been several in Papua New Guinea, and unlike me he had seen and crossed traditional bridges before. I glanced at him for his judgment. He clutched his expensive new camera system and stared through his thick glasses at the scene. Then he muttered, "Now this is a bridge," and laughed. "Sure like

A boy from Kurima village tests the strength of an old suspension bridge that spans the rushing waters of the Baliem River. (Christian Kallen)

to see someone else go over it first, though," he added.

We looked at the crowd of boys, which had been gaily leading us to this crossing. They stood silent, expectantly watching us, half-smiles of anticipation on their faces. I groped for my dictionary: "*Takut?*" I asked.

"*Ya, takut*," one of them replied. Then he added what sounded like "I know."

"*Berbahaya?*" I persisted.

"*Berbahaya*! I know!"

"He says he's afraid, and it's dangerous. I'm not sure what he means by 'I know'—unless it's 'I no,' he won't go across. So, George, that's good enough for me, let's head back."

But George climbed down to the bridge's steps and began to take photographs. Soon he was joined by one of the young boys, who boldly climbed the steps, stepped gingerly onto the bridge and swiftly moved halfway across it. He turned, waved and continued on to the other side. My heart sank; all George had needed was someone to show him it was possible, and he would do it himself.

"Well, I'll go," said George, "if you promise to recover the body." We both smiled stiffly and let the subject drop. He mounted the steps and purposefully, if carefully, stepped onto the bridge. I watched his progress across, focusing on his white hat as it moved steadily onto the steepest part of the span. The boy had weighed perhaps half of what George or I did and was lighter by at least twenty years and a thousand dollars worth of camera equipment. The bridge swayed under the weight, but it held.

Too soon, he turned and beckoned me across from the other side. No choice was left now: I fumbled with my camera, finally putting it into my backpack and slinging the weight over my shoulders. Then I mounted the bridge's crude steps, my dry hands gripping the old dead lianas of its rails.

Pausing for a moment with one foot on the bridge, my nerve failed: I just could not envision myself crossing this ragged, savage causeway. I've challenged rivers and crossed glaciers, but everyone has a weakness: I get nervous looking out a second-story window. I know the name for it, and usually I take pains to avoid invoking its oc-currence, but sometimes the wheel of fortune comes up "acrophobia." I tried to distract myself, looking upstream at the brown waters roiling in the sunlight and thinking how much I'd rather be in a raft punching a wave or being thrashed in a hole than on this high, narrow, broken bridge.

"Just don't think about it," George called from across the bridge. Right: like the old mind exercise, don't think about that white elephant. I glanced at him and shook my head angrily. His camera was pointed my way—the one with the 300-millimeter lens to pick up the doubt in my eyes. I looked back upstream into the sun, took a couple of deep breaths and at the last moment remembered I knew how to swim. Then I walked across.

Halfway to the other side I realized that these broken planks were broken by people, burdened women on their trail of labor, some of whom must have fallen through the shattered platform into the swift, heavy, brown waters. The boys who stayed on the banks behind us must have known some of these women; we who knew nothing could afford this adventure, this challenge to our pride. The brown water surged toward the Asmat; I stepped across the broken planks and the empty spaces, placing my boots on the twisted vine in the center of the bridge, swaying in the wind.

When I reached the other side, George still had his camera trained on me, and I flashed a smile. "Piece of cake," I said, stepping onto dry land. Then I checked my watch: it was nearly three o'clock, and we needed almost four hours to reach Hetagima and the wide road leading back to Wamena. We would have no more time to continue our survey of the Baliem Gorge and barely time enough to race back up-canyon to reach our hotel in Wamena before the dead of night. With barely a word, we turned our backs on the still-swaying suspension bridge and headed up the rough trail along the Baliem's western banks.

We made good time, trudging without stop back to the Grand Valley. We paused only for a few moments in Kurima to watch a late-afternoon gathering of the village in a square, where the khaki uniforms of rifle-bearing soldiers contrasted with the chocolate skin of the natives. We couldn't guess the point of the gathering and doubted that anyone would tell us. Then it was back up the trail between the villages and gardens, our footsteps steady against the roar of the Baliem in its channel. We paused again at the Yetni, to take off our boots and soak our swollen feet in the cold water, but the sinking sun cut short our rest.

It was just past six, on the far side of sunset, when we reached Hetagima; there were no trucks on the road, no minibuses running in the darkness. It was another ten kilometers back to Wamena, and we strode on down the pale path, between the quiet fields, through the dark groves and over the stick bridges spanning the creeks. In contrast to its daylight traffic, the road was all but abandoned: once or twice I spied the glow of a cigarette tip and smelled the smoke, but no greetings were extended from the darkness. I remembered the Dani fear of ghosts, who come out at night to trip the unprotected unless the moon is full. The moon was a week off full; we stumbled on toward Wamena.

At eight o'clock, more than an hour into full darkness, we reached Wamena—after ten hours on the trail, thirty kilometers of walking. My quadriceps were rigid with indignation, and the reward that often tantalizes the tired traveler—a cold beer at the end of the trail—was not to be found in temperate Wamena. Instead we made our way to the Cinta Prima Restaurant and dined on sweet tea and Baliem River crayfish.

When we finally collapsed into our beds at the Hotel Nayak I was sure we'd sleep through the night and dawn, right up to seven o'clock, when we had to be at the airport for the flight back to Jayapura. Instead I awakened at one in the morning, fully energetic and alert, ready to be on the move again. There was much of the Grand Valley and the Baliem Gorge yet to explore and the greatest discoveries yet to be made about the Dani. I was eager to engage this race with time, for I knew that outside it was a starry night, and the Stone Age was turning to dust even as I lay musing.

But finally sleep overtook me again, and the next morning my last glimpse of the Grand Valley was the same as the first—the round, thatch roofs of the simple houses, the narrow ditches and irregular gardens stretching across the flat green valley, the razor-straight line of the new road to the inevitable outside world.

Two weeks after we returned to the United States, I found out that the Indonesian authorities had temporarily stopped issuing permits to visit the Grand Valley. Warfare had broken out between two tribes, and outsiders were not encouraged to visit. I telexed a contact in Jayapura for more details and a week later received a reply: the warring alliances were those of Kurima and Hetagima, between whom tensions had long been building. I need not have worried: clearly the Stone Age had not disappeared overnight, and was not likely to do so.

INDEX